The Role of Concurrent Planning

Making permanent placements for young children

Notes About the authors

Dr Elizabeth Monck has worked as a social science researcher on psychological problems affecting children and adolescents. She has published several papers on depression among teenage girls, and the evaluation of treatment provided for sexually abused children. She worked for 15 years at the Institute of Child Health, and now holds a post as senior research officer at the Thomas Coram Research Unit, co-directing a project on post-adoption support.

Jill Reynolds trained as a medical social worker. She worked first in the community and in special schools and was later based in hospitals in London and Manchester. While her early work was largely delivering services to sick children and their families, her more recent work has been with research projects. She is an Assessor for the Family Trust Fund.

Dr Valerie Wigfall has more than 25 years experience in social research, before which she worked as an adoption social worker for the London Borough of Lewisham. Her research has focused largely on studies of the family, children and young people. It includes an evaluation of a multi-agency childcare network (the Coram Community Campus), a study of service provision for families with disabled children, and a comparative study of residential childcare in the UK and three European countries.

The Role of Concurrent Planning

Making permanent placements for young children

Elizabeth Monck, Jill Reynolds
and Valerie Wigfall

British Association for Adoption & Fostering
(BAAF)
Skyline House
200 Union Street
London SE1 0LX
www.baaf.org.uk

Charity registration 275689

British Library Cataloguing in Publication Data
A catalogue record for this book is available
from the British Library

ISBN 1 903699 23 1

Cover photographs posed by models
Designed by Andrew Haig & Associates
Typeset by Avon DataSet, Bidford on Avon
Printed by Russell Press Ltd (TU), Nottingham

BAAF Adoption & Fostering is the leading
UK-wide membership organisation for all those
concerned with adoption, fostering and child
care issues.

Contents

Acknowledgements

This research was supported with a grant from The Nuffield Foundation; we are particularly grateful to Sharon Witherspoon (Deputy Director) for her support throughout this work. Permission from the Secretary of State for Health for access to the children's records and from the Research Committee of the Association of Directors of Social Services is gratefully acknowledged.

We are also grateful for the support of the Advisory Group, chaired by Dr Alan Rushton. The members of the Advisory Group are listed below.

The research lasted for four years and involved five local authorities; we are grateful to the Directors of Social Services and the several social workers who helped with the study. We received particular support in collecting the statistics on looked after children from these local authorities: Dameshk Wijesinha (LB Camden); Louise Lawrence (Brighton & Hove); Arthur Taylor (Trafford); David Jump (LB Islington); and Diana Powell (Bury). Our thanks are also due to a small number of children's guardians for providing time to discuss with us some key issues in concurrent planning.

The workers in the three concurrent planning projects provided much help and support in collecting the data on the children and their families, and their new carers. It is not easy to be "evaluated" and we were aware of how much tolerance they had for our pursuit of information.

Brian Clatworthy, Director of the Manchester Adoption Society, initiated the introduction of concurrent planning into England. He was then involved in setting up the evaluation with the researchers and planning the integration of the research with the practitioners' work. Our particular thanks go to him for continuing interest and support over four years. His comments on drafts have been exceptionally useful. When they joined the evaluation, Jeanne Kaniuk (Head of Coram Family Adoption Service) and the Coram Family Concurrency Team, and Sharon Donnelly (Service Manager, Permanence Team) and the concurrency team in Brighton & Hove also provided considerable help to the researchers.

We were also given special help by Arthur Taylor, Team Manager, Adoption and Permanence Team, Trafford MBC, who acted as the link person for the researchers in relation to the Trafford cases and guided the development of the spreadsheet for recording the progress of the children through the various stages towards adoption and permanence.

Judy Stone and Sarah Borthwick from BAAF's Publications Advisory Group provided useful feedback on an earlier draft. Our particular thanks must go to our editor, Shaila Shah, Director of Publications at BAAF, for her skill and support in preparing this book.

Finally, and most importantly, we want to thank all the birth parents, the concurrency carers and the mainstream adopters who gave up quite considerable amounts of time to talk to us, often two or three times. They shared many personal details with us, were frank about their hopes and fears as the children joined them or left them. This report shows that their time and their efforts to make better lives for the children has borne fruit. We wish them all well in their future family plans.

Advisory Group

Dr Alan Rushton (Chairman), Health Services Research Department, Institute of Psychiatry
Sharon Witherspoon, Deputy Director, The Nuffield Foundation
Margaret Adcock, Consultant Social Worker
Dr Marian Brandon, School of Social Work, University of East Anglia
Brian Clatworthy, Director, Manchester Adoption Society
Peter Clark, Head of Legal Services, Oxford
Cherilyn Dance, Health Services Research Department, Institute of Psychiatry
Dr Elaine Farmer, School of Policy Studies, University of Bristol
Gill Gray, Coram Family, Concurrency Team Leader
Dr Jill Hodges, Hospitals for Sick Children, London
Jeanne Kaniuk, Head of Adoption Services, Coram Family
Julia Ridgway, Social Services Inspectorate, Department of Health
Dr Marjorie Smith, Executive Head of Unit, Thomas Coram Research Unit
Brian Minty, Department of Psychiatry, University of Manchester

Introduction

I suppose it is true that as long as a child has some rock of strength it does not matter who it is.

Mary Warnock: A Memoir

When concurrent planning was introduced into Britain by the Director of the Manchester Adoption Society (MAS), supported with funds from the Department of Health and a variety of charitable bodies,[1] it was seen as important to the overall success of the enterprise that it should be independently evaluated. The evaluation was funded by The Nuffield Foundation and based in the Thomas Coram Research Unit, Institute of Education, London. As Lewis (2001) and Utting (2001) have pointed out, central government support for new practice has, in recent years, rightly made evaluation a necessary element in developing new programmes (e.g. Sure Start), as part of the drive to establish an evidence-based childcare service. Too often there had been expensive changes in childcare practices which were not evaluated and yet judgments were made about efficacy. Maluccio (2001) has observed that outcome research seldom produces clear-cut evidence, but practitioners frequently behave as though it has.

Since 1987, the Department of Health has funded extensive research on outcomes for looked after children (Davies, 2001). The main drivers in the early years of this work were to find cost-effective services that promoted the successful development of children away from home. Assessing the services to adopted children, to their birth parents and to their adoptive parents was not an early priority in this programme. In 1999/2000 the Department of Health introduced several new performance indicators for local authority social services (Department of Health, 1999).

Evaluation, on the other hand, is concerned with whether the aims of a plan have been fulfilled. Patton (1981) offers a definition, which helps to describe the activities involved:

---

[1] The details are given in Chapter 3.

> *The practice of evaluation involves the systematic collection of information about activites, characteristics and outcomes of programs, personnel and products for use by specific people to reduce uncertainties, improve effectiveness and make decisions with regard to what those programs, personnel or products are doing and affecting* (p 15).

The importance of practitioners' positive involvement with any evaluation cannot be under-estimated. Monck (1997) outlined the difficulties and misunderstandings that can arise in service evaluations. Where senior staff see the advantages of monitoring and evaluation as identifying the strengths and weaknesses of practice, providing them with opportunities for improving a service, those closer to the coal-face may only worry that judgments will be made about their efficiency, and that their jobs or a whole initiative are on the line. Since data are almost always collected by, or with the help of, front-line practitioners, their understanding and commitment to evaluation is essential; we were fortunate to meet with such understanding almost all the time.

This book describes the results of the evaluation of the Goodman Project, as the MAS concurrency project came to be known, together with that of two other specialist concurrent planning projects started soon afterwards by Coram Family (London)[2] and Brighton & Hove Social Services, both of which were incorporated into the evaluation study at later dates. Both these latter teams were supported in their early stages by the experienced MAS concurrency team, and all three teams shared the services of a senior social work consultant.[3]

It is important to understand that the evaluation study started with no preconceptions about the likely outcomes. Obviously, the Goodman Project was hopeful that their work would ensure permanent placements for the children in shorter than average timescales. But this was an innovative project, with no absolute certainty about how concurrent planning – developed in the USA – might "translate" into UK practice. The study suggests the advantages of using this approach, but only because the research evidence supports this view. Any concern that the

---

[2] Funded in part by the Department of Health, and in part by LB Camden and LB Islington.

[3] Margaret Adcock

study "promotes" concurrent planning mistakes the purposes of evaluation. At each stage of reporting the evaluation, we have not hesitated to identify the difficulties faced by the project workers and their clients.

Evaluation must also include some assessment of the context and process of the programmes. In Chapter 1 we look at the national context of the introduction of concurrent planning into England, and discuss some of the underlying concerns about out-of-family child care. Chapter 2 outlines the method of data collection in the study (the measures are given in Appendices). The measures and procedures for evaluating the Goodman Project cases were planned with the MAS practitioners; because the other two projects joined the existing evaluation scheme, their concurrency workers inherited the established procedures.

Chapter 3 describes the three concurrent planning projects and the methods they used to set concurrent planning in place with the local authorities. The philosophy underlying the work of the Trafford MBC Adoption and Permanency Team that provided one of the comparison groups of parents and children is also briefly described.

Chapter 4 gives details of the referrals to the three concurrent planning projects from the local authorities that were collaborating in the specialist service. Some details are also given of the concurrency carers who joined the three projects. Chapter 5 presents the outcomes for the children, comparing the experiences of the concurrent planning cases with the mainstream adoption cases on a number of measures: the time taken to achieve a permanent placement, the number of moves between households, and the simple measures of attachment, development and behaviour completed by the parents and carers. Chapters 6 and 7 give the qualitative material drawn from interviews with the mainstream adoptive parents, the birth parents and the concurrency carers on a range of issues including the child's progress and their own satisfaction with the procedures and outcomes. Chapter 8 picks out the single, but vitally important role of the contact sessions that are organised by concurrent planning teams to maintain and promote attachment between birth families and their child, and presents the views of the adult participants. In Chapter 9 we return to the issue of the context in which the projects operated, and report the results of interviews with selected social workers in three local authorities and with a small number of children's guardians. These interviews explored the practitioners' understanding of the aims of concurrent planning and their perceptions of how useful such an approach could be to the looked after children's services.

Chapter 10 provides an overview of the practice issues that were raised, and largely resolved, by the three concurrency teams. Although we recognise that new concurrent planning projects will wish to draw directly on the experiences of the existing teams, we were able to see that they had faced some difficulties when they sought to introduce a completely new way of working towards permanence for young children. There had been occasions when the "learning curve" had been uncomfortably steep, even when their work was clearly indicating successful outcomes.

One of the problems with evaluating new practice is that policy initiatives frequently cannot wait for the outcome of pilot schemes to become clear. That has been our experience in this study. The concerns that led to introducing the first concurrent planning scheme in the UK, and the Government agreement to provide financial support, also led – inevitably one might guess – to some major improvements in the care of looked after children, and eventually to a high profile review of adoption[4] and a new Act.[5] This meant that the concurrent planning projects carried out their work in the context of children's services that were year-on-year improving the outcomes for children for whom adoption was the care plan.

Our conclusions in Chapter 11 note these changes, but also suggest that despite, or indeed because of, the Government's continuing interest in speeding up the placement of looked after children in permanent families, the concurrent planning approach has a role to play that becomes more, rather than less, important. We emphasise that concurrent planning is a complete programme, not a series of add-on changes to current childcare practice. It is based in best practice, but may require a considerable shift in the attitudes of all the professionals with responsibility, within any setting, for optimising the life chances of looked after children.

---

[4] *Prime Minister's Review of Adoption*, Performance & Innovation Unit, Cabinet Office, 2000

[5] Adoption and Children Act, 2002; the main provisions will come into force in 2004, although some parts will apply sooner.

1 The background to concurrent planning

Introduction

Concurrent planning was first developed to address two serious inadequacies in the care of looked after children in the USA. In 1981 Linda Katz and her colleagues in the Lutheran Social Services (LSS), Seattle, started to organise their childcare practice to achieve earlier decision-making and speedy resolution of legal procedures for children at risk of drifting in the care system.[1] The aim was to speed up the placement of children into permanent families, specifically to prevent drift and delay, where permanence would include birth as well as substitute families. In the first seven years of the project, their method of working had reduced the average time for their cases spent in impermanent care to 13 months. Over the next ten years, this figure had dropped to nine months. It is important to recognise that the LSS team was not working with "easy" cases, but with families in which there were grave problems of inadequate care and parenting. A detailed description of the selection of cases and the procedures they developed is given in Chapter 3.

In essence the work involved placing an at-risk child with a foster family, while the LSS social work team worked concurrently with the birth family to address the causes of the child's removal, and also sustained contact with a view to eventual rehabilitation. At the same time, social workers attempted to find and assess other members of the extended family who might take the child or support the birth family if they were reunited. If all efforts failed within the tight timescales set, the child remained with the foster family as an adoptive placement. An important component was thus the recruitment, preparation and support of the foster-adoptive parents. As Weinberg and Katz (1998) have said:

The concurrent planning strategy uses traditional good social work

[1] A similar scheme developed in parallel in San Mateo County, California (see also Chapter 11).

> *practice. The one notable addition is the idea of pursuing the contingency plan at the same time as efforts are made to achieve the primary plan of reunification.* (p 5)

Concurrent planning was not seen as a perfect solution to the problems surrounding placement of children in care, but it was a solution that put the child's needs at the centre of the social work decision-making.

Several earlier US projects had provided evidence that drift and delay in decision-making could be effectively tackled. The Oregon project set out to reduce the numbers of children in foster placements, partly with the aim of reducing the cost of child care (Pike, 1976). Birth parents were expected to co-operate with professionals in changing their behaviour enough for their children to be safely returned to them; if they did not do so, their parental rights were terminated. More than half the children were subsequently adopted, but a high proportion (27 per cent) was returned to their parents. These and similar projects challenged the accepted practice and decision-making that the child's place was necessarily always with his or her birth parents.

Katz (1996) has pointed out that the typical concurrency case involves children who might have waited four or five years in impermanent care if they had not been in the LSS concurrent planning programme. When the children are placed in permanent families using concurrent planning, although 'certainly harmed by parental drug or alcohol misuse, neglect and abuse, they have not been harmed by the foster care system'. Moving the children to an adoptive family is one of three positive outcomes in concurrent planning. Alternatively, the children may return to their birth parents, when the parents have shown that the original concerns about their lifestyle or their parenting have been fully addressed: they have become at least "good enough" parents.[2] Less frequently, the child may be found a permanent placement within the wider birth family.

This way of working and these achievements should be set in the context of what had been happening to children coming into care in the previous decades. The permanency movement in the US developed in

[2] See Adcock, M and White, R (1994) *Good Enough Parenting: A framework for assessment*, for definition.

the 1970s in response to the perceived failures of the previous drive to rehabilitate children into their birth families. By the early 1970s, children's services were increasingly being criticised for placing children in foster care with wholly inadequate care plans. In the UK these criticisms were famously summarised by Rowe and Lambert (1973), arising from their detailed study of the circumstances of a large sample of children in local authority care. They found that social workers were planning permanent care for only 22 per cent of these children, and adoption was being considered for only a tiny proportion of the sample. As Rowe and Lambert observed, social workers

> *. . . were seeking for the children not substitute parents, but professional foster care workers who, without usurping the role of the natural parents, would see the children through a temporary difficulty and then return them to their own homes*. (quoted in Morgan, 1998, p 47)

Unfortunately, "temporary difficulty" for these children often turned into years during which there was in effect no plan at all that addressed the child's best interests or that moved them into a placement that was truly permanent. Behind this institutionalised neglect lay assumptions about the birth family always being the optimal environment for children, a principle only to be over-ruled if extreme neglect, disadvantage or abuse was present, persistent and proven. Bowlby's comment that: 'I regard any substitute home as an exceedingly poor substitute for a child's real home' (cited by van Djiken, 1988, p 73) seems to have had unintended consequences for children in care. Often, a wait of years was thought justified on the off-chance that the birth parents would one day show that they could care effectively for their child. Adoption was nearly always seen as the second best solution, and only to be tried if all else had failed, not once, but several times. At the same time, neither the damage to the children inherent in moving them to and fro, nor the poor quality care in many children's homes and foster families was properly acknowledged. More specifically, there was a failure to understand which aspects of the substitute care were failing to support the children's optimal development; they were mostly safe, and well cared for in a material sense, but there was less understanding of their profound need for permanence, for the growth of warm attachments, and for certainty.

Looking back on this period it has been acknowledged that the parents' "rights" were given too much weight in postponing decisions about the permanent placement of their children. It follows that the children's interests were *not* at the heart of child-care decisions, although it was possible that, at times, the parents' and children's interests might coincide. The effect of giving such prominence to parents' interests was that large numbers of children in care spent years without permanency plans. They "drifted" in and out of the parental home, and in and out of multiple foster placements or they stayed for years in institutional care, while decisions about their future were postponed (Bullock, Little and Millham, 1993). The child's need for stability and permanence within a family was frequently sacrificed to the (then) stronger arguments about the importance of preserving birth family links and avoiding an adoption placement that would automatically terminate such links. Courts and social workers appeared reluctant to challenge the arguments from parents that their children should not be taken from them. In the UK the most notorious of these cases involved returning a child from the acknowledged security of her aunt's home to her mother, and her subsequent death (Howells, 1974).

Family preservation

One outcome of the strong contemporary criticisms of these patterns of inadequate care was the development and expansion of family-based services, both in the USA and the UK (reviewed by Pecora *et al*, 2000). The intention was to prevent the child entering the care system in the first place or at least to prevent repeated failures when he or she returned home by providing intensive support to parents.

In the UK, some local authorities were committing funds to intensive family preservation. Aldgate and her colleagues (1989) described a scheme in Oxfordshire that aimed to keep at-risk children out of long-term care. The scheme was not expected to apply to all families whose children were at risk of going into care: 'The skill lies in looking at a family's needs in detail, assessing their strengths as well as their weaknesses . . .' The scheme was designed to 'last over a long but finite period, to allow for . . . work to be accomplished at the family's pace'.

The interventions aimed to 'preserve and enhance the relationship between parents and children; enhance the competence of parents'. The social workers and short-term carers were expected to engage in a "working partnership", with parents also active at every stage. These families were '. . . often young, alone, inexperienced in parenting, poor, unsupported by extended family and feeling stressed' (*ibid*, p 33). They were the families in which social workers had identified strong enough chances of success for the professional support and the short-term care arrangements to be effective. The scheme was found to be most successful with children aged 4–12 years, and in families with a commitment to staying together, which was the strength on which the scheme could build. Typically, this scheme was expensive in the short term; resources were seldom available to local authorities on a scale to support a widespread application of this approach.

The research evidence on the success of these intensive family support systems was, however, very varied. As early as 1984, a House of Commons Social Services Select Committee had identified that services to families intended to prevent family breakdown were worthwhile, but that it was hard to tell wherein lay the exact benefits. The problem of establishing the effectiveness was partly due to the fact that the programmes involved widely varying family types and widely varying family problems. Cohn (1987) reviewed ten years of evaluation studies covering 89 treatment programmes and found that more than a third of parents continued to abuse their child while they themselves were in treatment. More than half of the children were judged still to be at risk of maltreatment by their parents at the end of the programmes. Of course, that also implies that nearly one half were judged not to be at risk; nevertheless it could be read as a disappointing outcome. Wald *et al* (1988) compared the outcomes for abused children kept at home with social work support for the birth parents, with abused children placed in foster homes with support for the foster carers. Both groups of children continued to show considerable distress and behavioural problems. Among many of the birth parents, the high levels of hostility and neglect shown to their children persisted, while at the same time few improvements were discerned in their parenting skills.

Through the 1990s the value of the Family Preservation Services (FPS) was increasingly called into question, although few reliable evaluations were commissioned to test them conclusively. In a review of 46 evaluations of intensive family preservation projects, Heneghan, Horwitz and Leventhal (1996) considered that only ten were worthy of inclusion, while the rest produced only blind ratings of outcome and minimal indications of the adequacy of programme content. The risk of eventual out-of-home placement was reduced in only two of the ten projects. The authors thus concluded that family preservation services showed no benefit in reducing rates of parental failure. One of the more rigorous studies suggested that while fewer children were placed outside the family from the FPS than from the control group, the differences dissipated over time (Feldman, 1991). Gough (1993), reviewing interventions with abused children, also found little evidence of effective practice.

In addition to increasing concern over the apparent lack of child protection or real improvement in life chances resulting from intensive family preservation programmes, there was a growing realisation that many children were continuing to experience a succession of placements, alternating between foster care and birth family because parents were being given too many "chances" to prove they could manage without risk of damaging their children. Despite frequent failure, permanency rarely became the childcare plan. The lack of any long-term studies of these families meant that there was no way of assessing accurately the damage subsequently suffered by the children.

In the 1980s a number of UK studies revealed the extent of the delays in care proceedings and suggested that, if anything, they had worsened in the previous decade. Murch and Mills (1987) compared the length of care proceedings in 14 courts in 1986–1989, with similar material collected in 1983–86; the mean number of weeks from first to final hearing nearly trebled from 5.9 to 14.2. These data were, of course, collected before the Children Act 1989 in which the need to avoid delay was made explicit. The Act stated:

> *In any proceedings in which any question with respect to the upbringing of a child arises, the courts shall have regard to the general principle that any delay in determining the question is likely to prejudice the welfare of the child.* (section 1(2))

The Children Act 1989 included a section enabling local authorities to work in voluntary partnership with parents to provide short periods of accommodation for the children, with the express aim of preventing family breakdown. The difference was the emphasis on keeping the child's need at the forefront of decision-making. The Children Act 1989 stated that the child's welfare should be paramount, but this was subsequently undermined by the emphasis placed on the rights of the birth parents, particularly mothers, often to the detriment of the child (Hunt, 1997). As Wall (1999) stated, the whole emphasis of the Act was still that children were 'better off being brought up by their natural families' (p 100). Morgan (1998) noted that the Children Act 1989 was widely interpreted as insisting on childcare plans being developed "in partnership with parents", and pointed out that this was a misconception which had grave effects for children. Wall (*ibid*) has noted the paradox at the centre of the Children Act 1989: that delay in achieving a permanent placement was likely to be damaging to children in care, but that a duty on local authorities remained – confirmed by the courts – to keep children within their families at almost any cost. Inevitably such confusion had the effect of limiting early intervention. Reviewing the advantages of concurrent planning, Wall emphasised that 'comprehensive planning for children from the moment of their entry into the care system is essential. Such comprehensive planning must include contingency planning for the child' (*ibid*, p 106).

Hunt (*ibid*) also found that, despite this intention to put children at the heart of decision-making, the Children Act 1989 was followed by 'damaging delays in bringing cases to court . . . and limited success in tackling delay within the court process'. This had been one of the key objectives of the Act. Hunt concluded that the Act had done much to reduce drift, but little to reduce delay (here making a distinction between delay as a lack of planning and drift as slow implementation of an existing plan). She did, however, suggest that the Act had succeeded in encouraging the courts to see delay as a problem to be tackled, not something to be tolerated. The Children Act Advisory Committee reported that court proceedings were taking on average 43 per cent longer in 1996 than in 1993 (Children Act Advisory Committee, 1994 and 1997). While it is true to say that not all these care proceedings would have involved seeking permanence for the child, a substantial proportion may have done so.

Beckett (2000) discusses the reasons why care proceedings have become steadily longer since the Children Act 1989, and firmly concludes that in the context of children's timescales these delays are a form of "system abuse". Triseliotis (1998/99) suggested that the way the Act was being implemented might even have made adoption more difficult.

The inspection report of ten voluntary adoption agencies (VAAs) prepared by the Department of Health Social Services Inspectorate (1999a) noted that 'delay was a major concern in the inspections of local authorities', as a result of which 'children were being referred to voluntary adoption agencies for placement later than they should have been, sometimes too late for successful adoptive placements to be made' (p 53). The role of the voluntary agencies in reducing delay was emphasised by the SSI: 'Sustained partnership between SSDs and VAAs is needed if delay and drift are to be avoided and children placed at the point most likely to lead to a stable and successful placement' (*ibid*, p 53).

Although the jurisdictions and court management were different, it is worth noting that over the same period court proceedings for children in the USA were also found to be associated not only with extraordinary delays, but also with drift, for children in the care of the state. Bishop *et al* (1992) reported that children experienced an average of more than two foster placements in the (average of) 18 months they waited for a placement decision in the Boston juvenile courts. The Adoption and Safe Families Act 1997 in the USA set up mandatory systems for States to achieve safety, permanency and family improvement. Targets were set nationally to double the rates of adoption over the subsequent five years; the concept of "planning concurrently" was specifically endorsed; and tighter timescales were set for the courts to reach the final decision on permanent placement.[3]

Why be concerned about delay or drift?

Despite the underlying intentions of the Children Act 1989, the results for children in care over the subsequent decade seemed to repeat the delay

[3] Under the Adoption and Safe Families Act 1997 States are required to initiate termination of parental rights proceedings for children who have been in foster care for 15 of the most recent 22 months. Under this Act also it is expected that States legislate for earlier and more decisive permanency plans, and time-limited family re-unification services.

and drift identified by Rowe and Lambert (1973) 20 years before. But now there was more tangible evidence of the adverse effects on the children themselves.

By the 1970s it was becoming increasingly clear that, on the way to achieving a permanent family, the frequent movement of children between households or children's homes could itself be a damaging experience. There was a growing recognition that impermanence carried risks, even when associated with individual placements of a high quality. Bowlby (1953) had shown that being parted from the main caregivers for any length of time severely damaged a child's attachment capability in the short term, but had also insisted that some children are damaged for life (Bowlby, 1965). At this date many children were in institutional care, with its uniquely damaging effects on attachment capabilities with adults (Tizard and Tizard, 1971). Further evidence that multiple changes of caregiver could have lifelong effects for some children was also accumulating, but most importantly there was a greater understanding of the mechanisms underlying the apparent effects on children's ability to form new attachments. Genetic factors affecting both the capacity of the child to respond to attachment-enhancing behaviour by others and the sensitivity of the caregivers are obviously influential in the emerging patterns of behaviour.

It was also recognised that children from "broken homes" and living in impermanent care frequently exhibited significant behaviour problems, but research established that such behaviour was often present before, though it might be exacerbated in the short term by the separation from parents (Lambert, Essen and Head, 1977). Reviewing the field, Rutter (1972, 1979) pointed out that it was the parental discord preceding so many family breakdowns that led to many children's distress or conduct disorders. However, in an important contribution to the study of the effects of impermanence, Rutter, Quinton and Hill (1990) showed that even when there is good substitute parental care, being placed with non-permanent parents over a long period of time had cumulative adverse effects on the child's development. Such children suffered not only from the circumstances that brought them into care but also from the effects of the impermanent care. However, later work has suggested that the quality of the experience in the new family may also be influential. Rushton,

Treseder and Quinton (1995) studied a small sample of late-placed boys over eight years. They observed that disruption and poor outcomes were associated both with more severe early adversity and with less positive parenting in the new family.

The longer-term damage to the growing child associated with extensive periods in the care system is now widely recognised. Most of the evidence comes from studies of children in care homes and of disadvantaged groups such as prisoners, the homeless and the unemployed, among whom a high percentage have histories of public care. For example, nearly 40 per cent of young prisoners have been in care during their childhood, which is 50 times the rate for 16–24 year olds (Prison Reform Trust, 1991); and 30 per cent of the young single homeless have been in the care system (60 times the rate for 16–24 year olds). It has also been known for years that the educational achievement of children and young people in care is far below that of their peers for reasons that have been clearly linked to institutional neglect of their educational needs (Jackson, 1989).[4] Even if they moved infrequently, children and young people in care who in childhood lacked permanent placements within a family have been found at grave risk of educational underachievement, and of failing to adjust successfully to adult life (Jackson, 1994). Morgan (1998) reported that three-quarters of those in care at age 18 leave with no qualifications – a figure that is 12 times the national rate for 18-year-olds. This, in turn, is probably causally linked to the very high rates of unemployment among young people who have been in care: between half and four-fifths of 16–24-year-olds who have been in care are unemployed, compared with between 10 and 20 per cent nationally for this age group (Garnett, 1992; Stein and Carey, 1986; quoted in Morgan, 1998).

Children joining their adoptive home when they are older appear to be at increased risk of poor outcomes, such as placement breakdown or behavioural disturbance (Triseliotis, 2002). While not all these children will have suffered from drift and delay in the care system, a significant number experience delay before adoption (Ivaldi, 2000). Conversely, there

---

[4] See also the Department of Health figures for the educational achievement of looked after children in England in the 12 months to September 2001 compared with all children: on www.doh.gov.uk/public/oi2001.htm

is mounting evidence that very early permanent placements are particularly likely to lead to low risks of later problems. For example, among the severely deprived Romanian children and babies adopted by UK families, those placed before six months showed substantial improvement in physical and cognitive condition, although placement at slightly older ages also carried a good prognosis (Rutter and ERA Team, 1998). Howe (1997) has also found that the parents of children adopted before six months reported fewer childhood or adolescent problems up to age 18 compared with late-adopted children. However, within the latter group, those who had experienced satisfactory care in their first year of life before being adopted were also less likely to show later problems.

Thus there are several strong reasons why delays need to be cut and drift avoided for children in the care of the state. Firstly, there is the risk that disrupted and/or poor care in the early years can lead to a failure to develop warm mutual attachments with peers and adults. Two points are worth emphasising. First, it appears that this is only true for a minority. Poor attachments with both parents were observed by Quinton *et al* (1998) in 27 per cent of late-placed children. Second, Rutter (1995) has noted that Bowlby's original notion of a short "critical period" in the first two years of life, during which the quality of attachment to the primary carer will determine later relationship behaviour, needs modification. Rutter (*ibid*) argued that, though desirable, the time frame may be longer than the first two years, and the harm of adverse experiences not irreversible. However, there is some evidence that achieving a placement in a responsive, permanent family when the child is under six months may be particularly advantageous. Late-placed children, interviewed as adults, have reported feelings of alienation and not being loved by their adoptive families (Howe, 2001). Howe pointed out that these results support the notion that the late-placed children from disturbed childhoods carry into later life the internal working models of relationships that may be profoundly distorted by their pre-adoption experiences. In addition to the evidence of problems of attachment in the new family, there is strong evidence that the poor quality of early care carries a higher risk of subsequent behaviour problems. Both outcomes have emerged from studies of late-adopted children (Quinton *et al*, 1998) and of children with multiple placements (Thorpe, 1987).

For many looked after children, the causes of their removal from home include experiences potentially damaging to their normal development, in turn leading to difficulties that may be carried into adult life. Early abuse and/or neglect in childhood, together with the additional damage caused by exposure to domestic violence are all strongly associated with subsequent behaviour problems, for example, becoming a victim or perpetrator of sexual abuse, being bullied, or lacking the ability to form close friendships (e.g. Jaffe, Wolfe and Wilson, 1990; Fergusson and Horwood, 2000). The delay in finding permanent families for neglected or abused babies and children is associated with more behaviour disturbances (Deutsch *et al*, 1982) and poorer outcomes:

> *Coming from chaotic backgrounds, too many enter a system which inflicts yet further damage on their social, emotional and cognitive development by its failure to provide a place where they can be confident of staying for any length of time, and which then labels them as disturbed and disruptive.* (Jackson and Thomas, 2000, p 4)

However, in this field, *causal links* are particularly hard to find. Delays in finding permanent families are frequently associated with multiple moves. In turn, multiple moves appear to be associated with disturbed behaviour. Yet it is not clear whether the moves are producing disturbed behaviour, as opposed to the child's disturbed behaviour, preceding placement, leading to breakdown of placements and moves to new settings. One Australian study (Barber, Delfabbro and Cooper, 2001) has shown that age (more than 10 years) and previously recorded conduct disorder were the significant predictors of foster placement breakdown. As they comment:

> *. . . older children and children with mental health problems or conduct disorder are the least likely to survive in foster family care, presumably because of their disruptive behaviour.* (pp 787–788)

These authors looked also at a measure of the positive qualities of the placements: children's prior mental health problems were associated with only a two per cent chance of a satisfactory outcome, compared with a 64 per cent chance for children with no mental health problems. Clearer evidence emerges from a study of foster placements in California: Newton, Litrownik and Landsverk (2000) found that, when children who initially had Child Behaviour Checklist scores in the "normal" range subsequently experienced multiple moves, externalising, internalising and total problems increased in the following 18 months. Few would argue that multiple moves alone have created these particular difficulties: there is almost complete agreement that the poor parenting from which many have suffered is directly related to the problems the child subsequently exhibits. A high proportion of primary school-age children come into care already showing moderate or severe behaviour or conduct problems (Quinton *et al*, 1998). Often it is the problem behaviour that has led to the local authority intervention in the first place. These are very disturbed children by the time their removal from their birth parents is considered. Being "on the move" between families may also be associated with failure to deliver appropriate support to either the child or his/her carers to deal with such difficulties. Bailey, Thoburn and Wakeham (2002) also noted a highly significant link between the number of placement changes experienced by looked after children and the presence of emotional and behavioural problems, but also warn against assuming causality in any one direction (p 196).

It is commonly argued that, even if the moves out of foster homes are at least in part the result of prior disturbed behaviour, the moves themselves may independently contribute to an increase in behavioural or mood disturbance. For example, moves between foster or parental households or residential homes may be associated with other adverse events or circumstances, like moving school or nursery. Most importantly, such moves are likely to disrupt or prevent the establishment of long-term relationships. Such disruptive events appear to place the child or adolescent at risk of developing depressed or anxious mood (Goodyer *et al*, 1987; Monck *et al*, 1994). However, at present the data on moves do not include reliable information about the child's behaviour problems at the beginning and end of each placement. Until those data are available it will not be possible to determine with any certainty the question of whether more moves lead to more behaviour difficulties.

Attachment and the care of looked after children

The continuation or development of disturbed emotional behaviour and/or conduct problems after children are taken into care are not the only major concerns of those who care for or adopt looked after children. For a decade or more, concern has also been expressed about the damage caused to children's capacity to develop secure attachments to their caregivers when they have experienced multiple moves. Adcock (1991) noted that local authorities might unwittingly cause harm to children in care 'by ignoring the importance of attachments and attachment theory' (p 13), and moving them from placement to placement. Each placement and each move proposed for a child in care needed specifically to be considered in relation to the child's attachment needs.

Attachment to a primary carer or a small and stable number of carers is an essential ingredient in the normal development of children and infants (Bentovim, 1991). It seems likely that, before the age of six months, changes of carer disturb infants relatively little, but that from 6–18 months they become increasingly selective (Jones *et al*, 1991):

> *The loss of the prime attachment figure between ages six months and three years can be followed by profound distress . . . Multiple breaks can lead to the child being virtually unable to make true relationships.* (p 118)

Goldberg (2000) in a major review of the research on attachment, noted that many children have several attachment figures and that what determines the quality of the attachment is in large part the sensitivity and responsiveness of the attachment figure. She also notes that the effects of early attachment on later development are reliable but small to moderate, quoting Thompson (1999): 'The outcomes of attachment security appear more contingent and provisional than earlier expected.' Attachment takes its place as one of several powerful influences on the child's future.

Without the experience of close attachment to the caregivers, it appears that the growing infant or child will be at risk of developing problems in later life (see Campbell, 1995). In particular, a warm affective bond between child and caregiver or caregivers has been associated with successful socialisation and pro-social behaviour in young children

(Hartup, 1989). Bowlby (1969) suggested that responsiveness and warmth in the caregiver provided the growing infant with a sense of the availability of significant others, in turn allowing the growing child to become securely attached. The work of Ainsworth and her colleagues subsequently supplied experimental validation of this argument (Ainsworth *et al*, 1978; Main, Kaplan and Cassidy, 1985). Attachment is not a quality within the child, but a capacity to initiate and respond to others in relationships. The early development of secure attachments with the primary carers is the foundation of the child's ability to optimise what he or she can subsequently gain from new experiences and relationships. In contrast, the infant experiencing the opposite (persistent inconsistency or rejection by the primary carers) is more likely to develop disturbed behaviour patterns, including counter rejection of the caregiver and others. Some evidence of the longer-term effects emerges from studies of older children. Among other home variables, research has shown that poor early mother–child interactions are associated with deviant adolescent interactions with the peer group (Fergusson and Horwood, 1999). Studies of young children suggest that interpersonal relationships in adult life may be affected by the quality of attachment in the first three years of life (Rutter, 1995).

Children who enter the care system have nearly all experienced serious neglect and/or abuse from their parents or close family, and all will have suffered at least one (and often repeated) separation from their primary carer. A high proportion of the children who have been maltreated have been reported as showing attachment disorders (Howe *et al*, 1999), although there is an absence of studies with valid psychiatric diagnoses of the children. They have also been described as cognitively less competent and less likely to make new friendships (Cicchetti *et al*, 1989); less good at pretend play, and exhibiting smaller vocabularies with which to describe their feelings (Lyons-Ruth, 1996). These latter deficits in turn inhibit the development of childhood friendships or warm relationships within the family, either birth or adoptive, and thus contribute to further attachment difficulties. Children with severe attachment problems have been described as feeling highly vulnerable (George, 1996), with poorly developed abilities to discriminate between anger, fear and sadness. A recent study by Fergusson and Horwood (2000) using data on a birth cohort collected over a 21-year period found that suicidal thoughts and behaviour between 15 and 21 years were associated with family environments in which, among other adverse factors, poor child–parent attachment had been observed in the child's early years. The childhood factors were mediated by exposure to stressful life events in adolescence, but it appears that at least some part of the vulnerability to later depressive mood originates in the early attachment patterns.

However, Zeanah *et al* (1997) pointed out that there is considerable evidence for the lack of specificity in risk factors and outcomes, citing insecure attachment in early childhood as predictive of a multiplicity of poor outcomes (e.g. poor peer relations and/or behaviour problems). The same authors also emphasised that multiple risk factors may predict the same outcome, for example, poverty, poor maternal attachment and family adversity may all be highly predictive of insecure infant attachment. In addition, Rutter (1995) pointed out that many of these associations are tenuous, and studies do not always support a causal inference; frequently other factors are highly associated both with poor infant–parent attachment and with later problems in the child. 'Attachment concepts are clearly useful in thinking about relationship disturbance, but it is important that we should not be unduly constrained by thinking only in attachment terms' (*ibid*, p 565). Campbell (1995) has questioned the evidence for the direction of causality: to what extent does the growing infant's behaviour determine the nature of the affective bond with the mother? Rutter (*ibid*) pointed to evidence that the child's temperament almost certainly plays a part in the development of the dyadic bond between caregiver and infant. Despite these important studies, many public policy documents still assert or assume that poor attachment between parent and child is the *cause* of later problems in that child's life (see, for example, Objective 1 in the aims of the Sure Start programme).[5]

Attachment in permanent placements

For a long time the most usual identification of "success" in adoption and other forms of permanent placement was the relatively crude outcome measure of absence of breakdown, that is, where the

---

[5] see www.surestart.gov.uk

relationships were so unsuccessful in the new family, or the child's behaviour so difficult to manage, that the child was eventually taken away, often at the instigation of the adoptive parents. In a study of adopted boys, parents cited the child's disruptive behaviour and aggression as the most frequent reasons for the placement breakdown (Rushton *et al*, 1995). Absence of breakdown remains an important indicator of success and stability for the child.

In more recent studies of the success of adoptive placements, measures of the quality of the family relationships, and the integration of the child in school and peer group have been used. In looking at "success" in this way, attachment is increasingly seen as one of the most important ingredients in those families in which the adoption has been stable and rewarding for children and parents. But its absence is certainly not the only factor leading to unsuccessful adoptions. It is important also to recognise that poor attachment is reported as arising in adoptive families that show the same parenting deficits or dysfunction that produce poor attachment in birth families: lack of warmth, inconsistency in defining acceptable behaviour, and parental conflict (Wachs, 1992; Bagley, 1993). Although some children arrive in adoptive placements already lacking the capacity to form warm attachments, others may meet with poor parenting in the new family, which either confirms the avoidant behaviour they learnt in their birth family, or actively discourages the development of closer attachment behaviour.

In looking for the causes of poor attachment, some studies also identify poor bonding.[6] Adopters sometimes report their own difficulty in getting close to the child, apparently associated more often with adoption after infancy (Holloway, 1997a and b). For example, Raynor (1980) noted the critical attitudes of adoptive parents when they themselves had defined the adoption as "unsatisfactory". As has been noted above, the causal direction of this particular failure is not clear; all that can be said is that there appears to be an association between unsuccessful adoption and cool, "un-bonded", critical and inconsistent parenting. Since these

[6] Using the differentiation identified by Fahlberg (1994) and others who describe the child's emotional connection to caregivers as "attachment" and the caregivers' emotional links to the child as "bonding".

characteristics are associated with poor outcomes for children in nearly any family, it is difficult to tie them specifically to success in adoptive placements – a point made by others (Raynor, 1980; Howe, 1998, p 60). Some young children who returned to their birth families after an infancy spent in institutions also showed attachment deficits (Tizard, 1977) indicating again that adoption *per se* is not the issue. More recently, Dance *et al* (2002) have found that children who were singled out from siblings for rejection by the birth parents and had moved to families with low levels of parental sensitivity were at particular risk of poor outcomes in the first year of placement.

The evidence for and the effects of poor attachment developing or continuing in the adopted child's new family is mixed. For children taken into care and placed at older ages, the effects of the failed relationships with the original caregivers may linger even after joining a family that is functioning well. On the other hand, traits such as poor peer relationships among school-age children may have no effect on poor attachment in the new family (Hodges and Tizard, 1989). While they may co-exist, such traits may originate from a third group of factors: the child's earlier experiences. Parents' reports suggest that certain children adopted post infancy resist intimacy and emotional reciprocity; there are some indications that this particular deficit translates into difficulties with relationships in young adulthood, particularly for young men (Maughan and Pickles, 1990). More recently, however, Howe (1996) found that 93 per cent of adopters reported good parent–child relationships by the time the children reached their 20s. However, the group who coped best were those who had adequate parenting in the first year of life, even if that was followed by adversity over a period of years before adoption. It is also important to note that the numbers of adopted children showing disorders of attachment (not the same as the ICD or DSM-V clinically significant attachment disorders) are not known with any degree of accuracy (Howe and Fearnley, 1999). Since the backgrounds and personal characteristics of UK adopted children have changed considerably over the last 20 years, it may well be that the prevalence of such damaged relationships has also shifted; this may mean that earlier studies are not a reliable guide to present day prevalence.

Howe and Fearnley (*ibid*) describe a state of resistance that an infant or child may develop if intimacy is perceived to be the source of distress or loss. They also point out that the birth parents defined as 'low on warmth and high on criticism' may be responding to a child with attachment disorders – even if they are of the parents' own making; there is a strong possibility of circularity in these definitions.

Attachment as a theme in recent UK childcare policies

The Children Act 1989 in England and Wales and the Children (Scotland) Act 1995 were constructed to support the concept that the child's needs should be placed at the centre of decision-making in cases involving children in care. The central precepts were that children need certainty, that decisions should be taken that enhance their chance of a permanent and safe family, and that timescales should reflect those needs. Although not explicitly recognised, the underlying intention of the Act was to promote timely and permanent placement. White (1991) has stated that,

> *Care is not defined in the Act [the Children Act 1989], but it must be more than the mere physical care that would be provided if the parent were to resume care of the child. It should connote love and attention, without which it could be argued that the child will suffer harm even though not returned home.* (p 8)

In the same publication, Bentovim (1991) stressed that 'knowledge of the course of attachment emphasises the crucial nature of the timescale in legal disputes' (p 40) – delays undermine the child's chances of forming new attachments in a permanent setting that will optimise his/her development. Early strong attachment to a significant adult can help to protect a child from the traumatic events or long-term abuse and neglect that led to the removal from the birth family. Finding a new family that can reproduce such positive attachment assists the child's recovery. The fact that a child may have developed some strong attachments within the (wider) birth family is predictive of a greater capacity for developing strong relationships with other carers or peers. When all the other family circumstances dictate a child's removal, this single factor may yet predict a positive long-term outcome.

Several recent developments in childcare practice have emphasised the importance of secure attachment in providing the optimal environment for a child's development. In the late 1980s Parker, Ward and others (1991) developed Assessment and Action Records for use by social workers responsible for looked after children. These were intended not to assess final outcomes for children, but to track the intermediate outcomes that measure the quality of care, including 'a supportive environment, a caring and attentive parent, and a secure and stable family' (pp 57–58). They point out that these intermediate outcomes have no particular value in themselves, but are relevant because of their known or presumed effect on final outcomes.

Providing substantial financial backing to local authorities, the Quality Protects programme, introduced in 1998 by the Department of Health, was intended to secure better outcomes through greater placement stability for looked after children. Its first objective is 'to ensure that children are securely attached to carers capable of providing safe and effective care for the duration of childhood'. This strongly endorses the idea that stability must go hand-in-hand with finding a placement that provides for the child's secure attachment. From such a base the child will be in a position to gain maximum life chances. Local Authority Circular LAC (98)20 (Department of Health) emphasised the role of adoption in securing permanent placements for looked after children. Delays in making a permanent placement 'deprive children of the opportunity to form long-term relationships and many, especially those who have spent some years in care, find it difficult to do so as they become older, often an underlying cause of subsequent disruptions' (LAC 98(20), p 5). More recently the Sure Start programme, which is intended to enhance the early years' experiences of disadvantaged children still living with their birth families, also aims to 'improve social development by supporting bonding between parents and children'.[7]

Thus we can see a developing theme: the number of moves and the length of impermanent care should be cut to the minimum to increase the chances of looked after children growing up in families with a high level of mutual attachment and positive parenting, which brings in turn the

---

[7] see www.surestart.gov.uk

advantages that flow from such a placement. Without neglecting the opportunities of birth parents to improve their parenting skills, decisions about the future of children in care should be made in timescales that best serve *the child's* needs.

Introducing concurrent planning into the UK

As noted above, concurrent planning aims to place children in permanent families, without drift and delay in care. At the heart of a concurrent planning programme lies the recognition of the importance of the child's attachment to the concurrency carers,[8] and the carers' capacity in turn to bond with the child (Fahlberg, 1994). In its early work, outlined in training manuals, the Lutheran Social Services team stressed the importance of securing good attachment and bonding. With the one exception of the child separated at birth (and some would argue, for these children as well), there is an explicit acknowledgement that the birth parents are 'the child's primary attachment figures' (Katz *et al*, 1994a, p 23). Again, with the same caveat, emphasis is placed on the fact that 'children's identity originates from the birth parents' (*ibid*, p 23). All the preparation of the concurrency carers is predicated on their ability to sustain a high level of contact with the birth parents[9] until the final hearing settles the child's future placement. The contact sessions have the specific aim of keeping alive, and improving if necessary, the attachment between child and birth parents. Frequently, other members of the birth family are included in contact meetings so that the child's understanding of the wider birth family is maintained.[10]

As early as 1996 the Director of the Manchester Adoption Society (MAS), his key professional advisers and the MAS Adoption Team were

---

[8] Throughout this study we have chosen to refer to the people who act as the children's carers within the concurrent planning procedures as "concurrency carers". In other reports, e.g. in the US literature, they are usually referred to as "foster-adopters" or "fost/adopters".

[9] The point has been made to the researchers that "high" in the USA context is once a week, whereas in the UK some social workers would argue that three times a week – the pattern common to the three concurrent planning projects – is not high enough.

[10] See also Chapter 8.

considering the introduction of concurrent planning into their practice. As a "traditional" voluntary adoption agency, MAS was frequently asked to place children who had experienced years of uncertainty about their future. MAS staff were only too aware of the potential damage to the children's normal development associated with such delays. Concurrent planning fitted the Society's aim to work with children at an earlier life stage in order to avoid the risk of subsequent drift and delay. In 1997 staff from MAS visited the originators of the concurrent planning system in Lutheran Social Services, Seattle, and concluded that such a programme could contribute effectively to this aim. No legal barriers existed to prevent the introduction of concurrent planning; the procedures and aims lay within the framework of the Children Act 1989, and locally the scheme received strong judicial support from the judiciary. Subsequently, concurrent planning was introduced into the work of the Coram Family in London, and the children's services within Brighton & Hove local authority.

The cases from all three concurrent planning projects, together with two comparison groups, formed the sample of the evaluation study that is reported here.

Summary

- Concurrent planning was developed in the USA in response to the damage arising from delay and drift in the effective planning for children in care.
- This concern was apparent in the UK, but even after the improvements introduced by the Children Act 1989 and the Children (Scotland) Act 1995, delays were still to be found; the absence of effective tracking of the children's placements was clear.
- Impermanence introduces additional and cumulative adverse effects on children's development, particularly for older children.
- In the last two decades the critical importance of attachment to a primary carer or carers in the normal development of young children and therefore in the optimal care of looked after children has been more widely recognised.
- Government policies increasingly emphasise placement stability, and

setting targets and timescales in achieving permanent placements for looked after children.

- The mid-1990s saw the introduction of the first concurrent planning projects in England.

2 The aims and design of the evaluation

Introduction

In 1997 the Director of the Manchester Adoption Society (MAS) started to plan the introduction of a concurrent planning team within the independent adoption agency. The Goodman Project[1] concurrency team was "launched" in March 1998, as a pilot project with special funding largely from the Department of Health. It was a requirement of this funding that the Project should be evaluated independently (Lewis, 2001; Utting, 2001).[2] The present authors based at the Thomas Coram Research Unit were selected to do this work, with funding from the Nuffield Foundation. The research took place over a four-year period, commencing in June 1998.

The aims of the study

The aims of the evaluation study were to test the effectiveness of concurrent planning compared with the traditional adoption plans for looked after children. In this context, "traditional" is being used to describe the approach to finding a permanent placement that conventionally follows a sequential pattern, with different options for placement being investigated in turn. Specific hypotheses the project set out to test were:

1. That concurrent planning cases would achieve permanent placement for the children more rapidly and with fewer moves between carers compared with the care careers that led to traditional adoption.
2. That the children placed through concurrent planning would show, at the time of follow-up, fewer difficulties on standardised measures of

---

[1] The Goodman Project was named after the medical advisor to the MAS.

[2] See *Children & Society*, vol. 15 (2001) for a series of papers on the problems of evaluating non-experimental projects.

development and behaviour than children placed by the traditional method.

3. That birth parents in a concurrency project would have a particularly positive view of the procedures leading to their child's final placement.

The study design

The initial study was set up to evaluate the specialist concurrent planning service provided by the Goodman Project, taking referrals only from the social services departments at Bury and Salford local authorities. The initial aim for the Goodman team was to place 30 children over the three years of Department of Health funding: eight children in Year 1; ten children in Year 2, and twelve children in Year 3. Since the expectation was that concurrent planning would provide a "better" outcome than the traditional adoption system, it was necessary to include some comparison cases. Two comparison groups were included, drawn from placements by MAS Adoption Team, and by the Trafford Social Services Adoption and Permanency Team. Trafford Social Services was not involved in referring children to the Goodman Project.

As the work progressed, the research evaluation expanded to include cases from the concurrency team based at Coram Family (an independent adoption agency in London) taking referrals from the London Boroughs of Camden and Islington, and the concurrency team located within Brighton & Hove Social Services Department. Coram Family planned to target children under two years, on the grounds that such children often become the children who experience multiple placements and frequent, unsuccessful trial periods with their own parents, and so turn into the hard-to-place children of 5–8 years. The Brighton & Hove concurrency team planned to place children under five years, but very quickly changed this to under-twos in response to local needs. Chapter 3 describes the setting up and organisation of the three concurrency teams.

The sample

The final sample of children and families thus falls into five placement groups: the three concurrent planning populations from the Goodman Project (Manchester), Coram Family (London) and Brighton & Hove

Social Services, and the two non-concurrent planning samples from Trafford Social Services and the MAS mainstream adoption service. In some parts of the analyses in later chapters the data from the three concurrency teams have been combined to form a single concurrent planning group.

In the present evaluation, the sample comprises 23 children placed by the MAS Adoption Team and 21 referred to the Trafford Adoption and Permanency Team over the period from February 1998 to December 2001. In this same period there were 11 children accepted into the Goodman Project, among whom three were included as pilot cases, and eight were included in the evaluation study. To these were added seven children placed by Coram Family concurrency team and nine placed by the Brighton & Hove in-house concurrency team in the period from January 2000 to December 2001. In all there were 24 concurrent planning placements, not including the three pilot cases from the Goodman Project. The final study includes 68 children.

Method and procedure

Since numbers were small, a mixed method approach was adopted, incorporating both qualitative and quantitative data. Documentary material was collected from case notes for all the children, including dates of key events such as matching, placement, final hearings, freeing orders and adoption orders. Home interviews were conducted by the researchers with the concurrency carers, the (Trafford) foster carers, and adoptive parents. Semi-structured interviews with birth parents were planned across the five placement groups. In the family interviews, researchers combined the use of standardised measures with a semi-structured narrative approach. With the concurrency carers, interviews took place after they had been approved by panel, but before the placement of a child; a second interview was held six weeks after the child had been placed with them.[3] The same pattern was followed for the adoptive parents in the MAS Adoption Team sample – interviews were held before the placement and

[3] In the Brighton & Hove sample it was not always possible to see concurrency carers before placement, but the qualitative material in Interview I was incorporated into Interview II.

six weeks after placement. In the case of the fostered Trafford children, a brief interview was held with the foster carers during which material was collected using the standard questionnaires and checklists (see Appendix B).[4] Where possible, follow-up interviews were held with the carers approximately 12–15 months after the first interview (Trafford) or placement (all other children). Interviews were sought with birth parents following the placement of their child. Birth parents were each paid a small sum in recognition of their help.

With the permission of the interviewees, all the interviews were tape-recorded from which either detailed notes or full transcriptions were made for later analysis (using NUDIST) to illustrate particular issues that had been identified in earlier discussions with practitioners. For example, the concurrency carers and adoptive parents were asked to describe their reasons for choosing a particular route to adoption; birth parents were asked in detail for their understanding of what concurrent planning meant for them. (A more detailed account of the interview content and procedures is included in Appendix A.)

Both after placement and at the follow-up, questionnaires were completed by teachers or nursery staff when parental (or local authority) permission had been given (see Appendix B).

Social work records were consulted for dates of relevant decisions, key events and court hearings. At the time of the final hearing, the concurrency teams were asked to rate the quality of relationships existing between the concurrency carers and the birth parents during contact sessions.

Towards the end of the evaluation period, interviews were held with a number of local authority social workers and children's guardians who had been involved in working with two of the specialist concurrency teams (Chapter 9).

---

[4] Permission was granted by Trafford Social Services to interview foster carers with responsibility for the children who were subject to care proceedings and where adoption was the recommended care plan.

Measures

Dates of Key Events (see Chapters 3 and 5 for details) were collected to enable the researchers to track the progress of the children from the start of the last episode of care to a permanent placement. The number of months between last care episode and the various legal steps towards permanence were obtained from case notes, and checked with concurrency carers and adoptive parents. The number of moves between families that each child experienced before a permanent placement was also recorded from case notes.

Breakdown of a placement was not expected to occur in the 12–15-month follow-up of each concurrency placement, nor of the adoptive placements by the MAS or Trafford Adoption Teams. The young age of the very large majority of the cases increased the likelihood of stability. A recent review of stability of placement in adoption (Triseliotis, 2002) has confirmed the view that breakdowns are extremely rare in adoption (or long-term fostering) for very young children in the period up to six years after placement.

In the current study, therefore, a range of measures was used to assess both children and adults. These were chosen to reflect aspects of the child's behaviour and development that would provide a more sensitive picture of "success" within the foster-adopt or adoptive placements. Foster carers, concurrency carers[5] and adoptive parents were asked to complete the questionnaires detailed below. Where the children returned to their birth family on a permanent basis, family members completed the questionnaires. In addition, the views of birth parents, adoptive parents and concurrency carers were obtained on how satisfied they were with the procedures and outcomes of mainstream adoption or concurrent planning (as appropriate). This approach theoretically provided the opportunity for more than one type of "success" (e.g. at home or in school) to be studied.

[5] Concurrency carers are, in legal terms, foster carers and only become adoptive parents when and if the placement is confirmed at final hearing. We have chosen, however, to distinguish the carers in the concurrent planning projects, from traditional foster carers, by the use of the term "concurrency carers".

1. The children

The choice of instruments to measure the progress of the children was dictated, in part, by the aims of the study, and in part by the need to impose as little as possible on the participating parents and carers. This was in response to early advice about the high levels of stress these adults were already experiencing. A group of measures was derived from the Looking After Children Assessment and Action Records (Department of Health, 1995)[6] that give checklists for the social worker to complete, covering seven developmental dimensions: health, self-care skills, social presentation, education, identity, family and social relationships, and emotional and behavioural development. Questionnaires covering three of these dimensions were used in the present study:

i) Emotional and behavioural development: aged under 12 months; 1 and 2 years;
ii) Social relationship/attachment: aged under 12 months; 1 and 2 years; 3 and 4 years;
iii) Self-care skills: ages 1and 2 years; 3 and 4 years.

The Assessment and Action Records (AARs) provide a description of a child's progress and were intended originally to be used both at the individual level and at the level of service provision across a local authority, giving outcome data for groups of children and teenagers. Recent work suggests that the checklists for older children require revision to be useful as a practice tool for social workers and others (Quinton and Murray, 2002). Revisions have not yet been suggested for the younger age groups. For a full description of the content of the measures, see Appendix B.

In the present research, the items in the AAR checklists completed by parents and carers were allocated values and summed to produce a total score.

On the **Self-Care Skills checklists** ratings were given of 2 – Fully mastered; 1 – learning skill; 0 – no skill at present.

---

[6] These were developed and designed by the Dartington Social Research Unit in association with colleagues from the Universities of Bath, Bristol and Swansea, the National Children's Bureau and other agencies in the childcare field.

On the **Emotional and Behavioural Development checklists**, scores were given as follows on the positive items (e.g. smiles at carer): 3 – Definitely like the child; 2 – Quite like the child; 1 – A bit like the child; and 0 – Not at all like the child. The negative items (e.g. has difficulty sleeping) were scored in the opposite direction.

For each checklist these scores were totalled. A high score indicated a more positive rating. There are no normative data for these checklists; a decision was taken to describe as "positive" the following levels of scores supplied by the parents and carers.

Table 2.1

Age group		***Emotional and behavioural checklists***	
	Number of questions	*Possible total score*	*"Very positive score"*
Children under 1 year	10	30	26+
Children aged 1 and 2 years	15	45	38+
Children aged 3 and 4 years	15	45	38+
Age group		***Self-care skills***	
	Number of questions	*Possible total score*	*"Very positive score"*
Children aged 1 and 2 years	6	12	10+
Children aged 3 and 4 years	7	14	11+

For the children over four years at placement, we asked parents and carers to complete the Strengths and Difficulties Questionnaire (SDQ) (Goodman, 1997). With the permission of parents and social workers (as appropriate) teachers and nursery staff were asked to complete the SDQ on the children. The SDQ incorporates items that tap into five dimensions of child behaviour for which it is possible to generate separate scores: conduct problems, hyperactivity, peer problems and emotional symptoms. These four sub-scores are added together to give a score of Total Difficulties. The SDQ also provides a Pro-social score. The expectation is that in a community (i.e. non-clinic) population, roughly 80 per cent of the children would have "normal" scores, 10 per cent borderline and 10 per cent "abnormal". As the children in the present sample would generally be regarded as "at risk" of behavioural difficulties, it was planned to combine the high and borderline scores to identify children with problems. Unlike the LAC checklists, the SDQ has established cut-off points determining the range of "normal", borderline or "abnormal" scores.

The attachment ratings taken from the LAC checklist were applied to all the age groups. Parents and carers were asked to rate the children as "closely attached", "quite closely attached", "not closely attached" or having a "poor relationship". These received a rating of 3, 2, 1 and 0 respectively.

2. The adults

The General Health Questionnaire (GHQ) is a self-administered screening test, designed to identify short-term changes in mental health (Goldberg, 1978; Goldberg *et al*, 1997). This instrument was used in the research to test the mental health of both the birth parents and the concurrency carers, although it is not generally intended to identify diagnostic categories. In the present study the 28-item scaled version was used, designed to test for anxiety, somatic distress, social dysfunction and depression in the general population.[7] A recent paper on the stability of the factor structure of the GHQ suggested that the original social dysfunction and depression factors were particularly robust; the anxiety and somatic symptom scales were more highly inter-correlated (Weneke *et al*, 2000).

3. Data from local authority social workers and concurrency teams

Social workers were asked to complete two sets of material for the researchers. The first was the information on the two checklists developed by the Lutheran Social Services team in Seattle that together form the differential diagnosis used to identify the likelihood of success in treatment (Katz and Robinson, 1991). Known as the "Poor Prognostic Indicators" (PPI) and the "Strengths in Families", these checklists give details of the strengths and problems of the referred family. Five items from the

[7] Using a 0011 scoring system, the suggested threshold for "caseness" in the total score is 4/5; there are no thresholds for the four subscales.

PPI are described as 'in and of themselves (showing) extreme conditions making family reunification a very low probability' (*ibid*, p 27).

The Strengths in Families checklist has 30 items that break down into six categories and the Poor Prognostic Indicators checklist has 20 items in four categories (see Table 2.2; for the full checklists, see Appendix C). For example, in the Parent–child relationship group of items, the sub-headings include 'Parent shows empathy for the child', and 'Parent accepts some responsibility for the problem that brought the child into care or to the attention of the authorities'.

Table 2.2

Main categories in the Strengths in Families and Poor Prognostic Indicators checklists

Strengths in Families	*Poor Prognostic Indicators*
Parent–child relationship	Catastrophic earlier abuse
Current support systems surrounding parent(s)	Dangerous lifestyle
Past support systems available to parent(s)	Significant child protection system history
Family history of own childhood care	Parents have inherent deficits
Parent's self-care and maturity	
Child's current development	

These checklists were used to rate the strengths and difficulties in the birth families at the point that the children were referred to the three concurrent planning teams. Trafford family social workers were asked to rate the children referred to the Trafford Adoption and Permanency Team. For each child referred to the MAS Adoption Team, the family social worker in the referring local authority was asked to complete the checklists.

The second issue on which concurrency teams were asked to contribute was the quality and quantity of contact there had been between the birth parents (or other family members) and the concurrent carers. This information was collected at the time of the follow-up interviews with the families, in order to reflect the full extent of the contact period. For a small number of cases, the follow-up period was truncated by the end of the research, but the material was collected up to that date. This information was not collected for the two traditional adoption samples, as the nature of the contact between the birth parents and the adoptive parents was both in legal and quantitative terms completely different to the contact arrangements that are integral to the concurrency procedures.

In the next chapter we outline the work of the Concurrent Planning programme developed by Lutheran Social Services in Seattle, and thereafter of the three UK concurrency programmes that modelled their practice on the LSS work. A brief description is also included of the work of the Trafford Adoption and Permanency Team and the Manchester Adoption Society Adoption Team.

3 The work of the three concurrent planning projects and the two traditional adoption teams

Introduction

In Chapter 1, the developing pattern of temporary child care during the last three decades in England and Wales was briefly outlined. After a substantial drop in the numbers of children in care from the late 1960s to 1995, the totals have started again to rise. During the same period the numbers of adoptions dropped dramatically from a high point of 25,000 to less than 6,000 in 1995. Over half of the latter group were step-parent adoptions, and under 2,000 were adoptions from care. The numbers of adoptions from care continued below 2,000 for the next two or three years. In addition, the statistics for England were showing that significant numbers of children were still experiencing drift and delay within the care system (Ivaldi, 1998). It was against this background that the first concurrent planning project in England was launched by the Manchester Adoption Society (MAS) in 1997. The Government's own initiative, Quality Protects,[1] which aimed to improve the use of adoption by local authorities and reduce delays for looked after children, still lay in the future.

The description of the first of the three concurrent planning projects in England, planned in 1997 and launched in 1998, and from which the next two projects derived their models of working, should thus be seen in the context of an acknowledgement of widespread drift and delay for children in the care system.

The MAS team developed their work from the concurrent planning programme initiated and designed by Lutheran Social Services (LSS)

[1] The Quality Protects initiative, backed by Department of Health funding to local authorities social services from 1999 to 2002, required the setting of clear outcomes for children in need, with measurable performance indicators and targets. The extra funding has been assured until 2004.

in Seattle. It is valuable, therefore, to start with an outline of the original programme developed in Seattle, before describing in turn the programmes developed by Manchester Adoption Society (the Goodman Project), Coram Family and by Brighton & Hove Social Services. We have chosen to describe the LSS programme and the Goodman Project in some detail: the former because it was the pattern for UK projects, the latter because this was the first attempt to bed concurrent planning into the childcare systems of England and Wales. When describing the subsequent projects in Coram Family and Brighton & Hove, we have largely limited ourselves to highlighting features in each project that might distinguish their way of working from the Goodman Project.

The Seattle Lutheran Social Services Programme

In the early 1980s, LSS had already shifted their approach from sequential to simultaneous planning, and this change in philosophy led to a change in case management methods of their adoption cases. The new approach combined established methods of working with families with some new systems of support and intervention. The aim was the early resolution of legal cases for young foster children – a group already identified as at highest risk of drift in the childcare system (Fanshel, 1982). The birth families included in the project were typically selected from among those families where the adverse circumstances were likely to be remedied in the time allotted, and with markedly few strengths or resources especially when there are no relatives or support systems surrounding the parents.

Katz (1990) has detailed the methods used by this team: reduced caseloads, early case planning, intensive services to parents, highly specific written contracts of the expectations of parents, and frequent supervised contacts between parents and children. The term "concurrent planning" came from the approach that both the possible return home and adoption should be considered and worked on *concurrently*, not sequentially. The most innovative part of the programme was the intention to place the children with foster families who would be committed to adopting them if the plan to return home did not materialise. This was directly linked to the intention to reduce the emotional harm to children arising from multiple placements and to foster the development of attachment to safe parents.

In the early 1990s, the LSS team developed a risk-assessment matrix that was designed to help workers identify the children most at risk of drift in foster care (Katz and Robinson, 1991). At that time, in the USA, the children most at risk of such drift were those under eight years who had remained in care longer than a few weeks. The matrix developed into the Poor Prognostic Indicators used in the "differential diagnosis" at the start of any concurrent planning case. Five indicators on the matrix and in the PPI checklist indicate almost no hope of family reunification; the remaining indicators suggest reunification is likely to be extremely difficult. The authors state clearly that 'the more factors present, the more guarded the prognosis' (*ibid*, p 349). Some of the distinctive features of concurrent planning that were later codified by Katz and her colleagues are already explicit in the case plan laid out in the matrix. The case plan for these families 'must be intensive, proactive and well-monitored' (*ibid*, p 349), with the following elements:

- 'sustained, persistent outreach to involve parents in services that address problems identified by the agency, as well as by the parents themselves;
- an accurate assessment of all aspects of parental pathology or inadequacy;
- access to all records pertinent to the parents' criminal, psychiatric and substance abuse history; written contracts with parents to identify parent and agency responsibilities and short-term goals, and to back court reports;
- an explicit plan for frequent and observed parental visits with the child;
- careful documentation of parental compliance with services and visits, and agency efforts to involve parents;
- time lines for parental compliance set and enforced;
- education of parents in child's developmental need for early permanence;
- outreach and documentation of all efforts to involve relatives in planning for the child;
- concurrent planning for parental rehabilitation and/or removal of parental rights (i.e. foster-adoptive placement, proceeding with legal

steps, legal consultation) so that the agency is prepared to implement in a timely manner whatever permanent plan is appropriate for the child while causing the least damage to the child by the process;
- permission for parents to relinquish the child by initiating discussion of this option when appropriate.'

(Katz and Robinson, 1991, pp 349, 356)

Within a few years, Katz and her colleagues had produced detailed manuals codifying the procedures and philosophy underlying concurrent planning as it was developing within LSS (Katz, Spoonemore and Robinson, 1994a; ditto, 1994b; and Katz, Colacurcio and Cordes, 1994). The original timelines developed for concurrency cases are now incorporated in Federal law[2] and in the laws of several individual states. Court orders in concurrency cases have replaced written service agreements and now specify the actions parents must take and what the agency is expected to do.

More recently, Weinberg and Katz (1998) have described the essential elements of concurrent planning as:
- an early prognostic assessment;
- placement with a family that potentially can adopt;
- open communication with all parties;
- the protection of the child's attachments;
- establishing parent–child contact;
- legally valid timeframes for decisions on permanency.

Concurrent planning was developed against the background of US Federal law [PL 96-272; 1980], which required "reasonable efforts" to be made to reunite parents with children taken into care because of parental difficulties. As Katz *et al* (1994a, p 93) have stated, although there was some variation in practice between courts in the USA, some basic guidelines existed on the definition of "reasonable efforts". These included:
- The problems which necessitated removal of the child must be identified and well documented.

---

[2] Adoption and Safe Families Act 1997.

- The agency must develop a written service plan to correct the deficiencies, with long-term and short-term goals with specific timeframes.
- The agency must describe specifically how the parent will profit from the service plan.
- The agency must refer parents to the necessary services and support them in attending.
- The agency must make a record of participation in service plan.
- The service plan and parental compliance must be reviewed every six months.
- A permanent plan must be determined at the 18 months review.

It is clear from such a list that the reasonable efforts are largely those of the agency, but require parents to show their reasonable efforts to comply with the service plan. To quote Katz *et al* (*ibid*, p 97) again: 'If the social worker has developed a process that fully meets the requirements of reasonable efforts, the case outcome becomes the responsibility of the parents within their abilities.' In the US courts the principle of "reasonable efforts" emphasises the provision of services, and the parents' efforts to take advantage of those services.

In the LSS programme, concurrent planning continues to have other features that clearly distinguish it from *parallel planning* or *twin tracking*. It may be helpful to outline here the differences between concurrent planning and some other methods of developing care plans that have – at times – been confused with it.

- *Parallel planning/twin tracking*: it is now a legal requirement that the three following possibilities are considered in parallel – assessing the parents, the extended family and the development of a care plan for placement outside the family. The child is meanwhile in foster care or residential accommodation; there is no built-in expectation or plan that foster carers will adopt the child if the rehabilitation with her birth family proves impossible;
- *Concurrent planning*: the capacity of the birth parents or wider birth family to parent the child are investigated. At the same time the child is placed with foster carers who, if the birth family cannot parent, become the adopters.

First, the birth parents (the Plan A family) are explicitly informed about the targets that they must achieve to have their child back. Second, all the participants, including lawyers, are to be made aware of the damage that delay and drift in impermanence can inflict on children. Third, although the level of support birth parents receive is high, and focused on those aspects of their parenting which the courts have recognised puts their child at risk, it is also time-limited. From the start of concurrent planning proceedings all the participants know when key decisions will be made: courts set final hearing dates usually no more than six months ahead. The final distinguishing feature is that, throughout the period up to the final hearing, the child lives with the Plan B family – the foster carers who will adopt if rehabilitation is judged not to be in the child's best interests.

Clearly, in concurrent planning, the professionals had to be persuaded that there was some hope of achieving a permanent placement with the child's own parent(s) or the case was not suitable for the programme. Predominantly the project worked with severely dysfunctional families, so the emphasis was on careful assessment of strengths and deficits in the birth parents and their families. As Katz *et al* have pointed out, the case record will be one of failure, but '*reunification decisions are based not on the original abuse and neglect, but on the parents' response to the services provided*' (Katz *et al*, 1994a, p 61, their italics). The professionals' skills and responsibilities lie in identifying the parents' needs, identifying the programmes of work that are needed to enhance their parenting or deal with their deficiencies, and monitoring the parents' progress towards defined and agreed targets. The published guidelines on concurrency emphasise the need for workers to be briefed on the key issues of child welfare: particularly attachment and loss.

This assessment (termed the Differential Diagnosis) is, therefore, an extremely important ingredient of the concurrent planning process. The Differential Diagnosis is applied within an overall service philosophy that is distinct from traditional social programmes. In common with many family-based services and intensive family preservation services coming to the fore in the United States in the same period, concurrent planning is built on the following principles:

- avoiding the use of labels and previous diagnoses;

- assessing the family's present situation;
- building on family strengths.

The Differential Diagnosis is composed of two checklists: the Strengths in Families and the Poor Prognostic Indicators. The authors recommend that the Strengths in Families are investigated before the Poor Prognostic Indicators. There are guidelines on the need for cultural sensitivity in the assessments, and in the choice of whom to assess in the wider family where that is necessary. The parents who show some ability to nurture their children must be distinguished from those who cannot. (The details of the two checklists are given in Appendix C.)

On the basis of this Differential Diagnosis, the case will be judged as suited or not suited to concurrent planning. Reading the guidance manuals it is difficult to establish exactly what weight is attached to the various components of the differential diagnosis, apart from the five PPI items carrying very low chances of success with the birth parents. In the end, the experience of the worker will probably differentiate the most suitable cases. In essence there has to be some gleam of hope – hence Katz's emphasis on first using the Strengths in Families section – some aspect of the birth parent's current or previous experiences and behaviour that suggests the possibility of sufficient change within the tight timescale to become a "good enough" parent. The prognosis may be poor, but there will be counter-balancing strengths that, however rudimentary, could be developed to support the child's early return to the birth family.

Concurrent planning was never expected to apply to all children and their birth parents. Katz and Robinson (1991) made this plain: it is used most appropriately for children under eight years, who have been in care for some time, and who are known to have no parent or relative to whom they can safely be discharged. The parents will need intensive services to correct parental deficiencies. The authors note that the rise in drug abuse added to the numbers of parents to whom children cannot safely return (*ibid*). In the early years of the LSS programme, 7 per cent of children returned to their birth parents; in later years the rehabilitation rate rose to 15 per cent.

The Goodman Project[3]

Drawing on the well-established work of the LSS team, the Manchester Adoption Society built up its own programme.[4] The intention from the start was to prevent young children from becoming "stuck" in the care system, and becoming the older, hard-to-place children. The Goodman team also aimed to become more closely involved with birth parents, at an earlier stage in the development of a care plan for their child. From the outset it was planned that the Goodman Project would accept cases only from Bury MBC and the City of Salford. This gave the Project team the chance of building up effective working relationships with a limited number of social services workers. It was also initially envisaged that referrals would come from two selected teams within each social services department (SSD). Liaison meetings were held regularly with each local authority by the concurrency Team Manager and the Director of MAS. The selected teams were also regularly visited and supported. In the early months, the concurrency team's Social Work Practice Adviser, Margaret Adcock, provided a seminar on assessment for the two local authorities. Later it became apparent that referrals should be considered from all the teams in each authority and liaison meetings were extended accordingly. Salford and Bury SSDs each seconded one social worker to work half-time in the Goodman team. This was important not only in terms of the commitment of resources but increased an understanding of the project's aims and way of working among the local authority teams.

The Goodman Project concurrency team was "launched" in March 1998, although it was preceded by a lengthy planning period. At first based in the same building as the MAS Adoption Team, the later move to separate premises supplied by Salford took up a significant amount of the team's time. These were centrally located and well suited to the contact

---

3 We are grateful for permission to quote from the Report prepared by the Director of Manchester Adoption Society on the first three years' work of the Goodman Project: Goodman Project Evaluation Report 2001. See also the article in *Community Care* Magazine 29 August 2001: 'Ideas in Practice: Concurrent affairs' by Nina Gardner.

4 This innovative work was supported by the Department of Health, the Hayward Foundation, Pilgrim Trust and Lloyds/TSB Foundation.

arrangements for birth parents and their children, and for professional meetings.

Essential components of concurrent planning

The components of the Goodman Project work were established in discussion with two local authorities:

- selection of cases having "poor prognosis" on the basis of severity or chronicity of family history;
- full disclosure to all parties, including birth parents, of the concurrent plan, and its acceptance by the court;
- time limits for parental rehabilitation that prioritise the child's urgent need for a decision;
- regular contact between child, birth parents and carers to maintain attachment and build a non-adversarial relationship for the child's sake;
- foster families that are simultaneously trained and prepared to be adoptive families;
- assertive advocacy for timely permanence by social workers backed by regular legal consultation and representation;
- redefining success as early permanency (without multiple placements) rather than viewing the family reunification as the sole measure of success.

The Goodman team, with the Director of the Manchester Adoption Society, spent a considerable amount of time in the early months of the Project talking to professionals locally about the components of concurrent planning. This preparatory work, which was also undertaken in the other concurrency projects, was described by the Goodman team as extremely important. The Director of MAS has noted that there is usually considerable scepticism about whether concurrent planning can be successful in this country. Doubts centre on whether adoption applicants would opt to become concurrency carers, whether they would "sabotage" the rehabilitation work, whether sufficient numbers of children would be referred, and whether lawyers would see the project as offering 'adoption by the backdoor'. In the 2001 MAS Annual Report on the project it is clearly stated that: 'The importance of communication in all aspects of this method of working cannot be sufficiently emphasised.'[5] The support of the local judiciary was highly valued by the team.

One extra point is worth recording. It was noted that at first some of the adoption workers on the mainstream adoption team were uncomfortable with the philosophy behind concurrent planning, and this issue had to be addressed within the adoption agency.

Selection of the carers

When prospective adopters approached MAS, they were sent an information pack that included an introduction to the idea of becoming concurrent planning carers. Attending the first open evening, applicants would again be given information about MAS adoption and also about the concurrent planning Goodman Project. If, after these introductory sessions, families decided to go further with their application to adopt, they would be asked to attend three days of preparation groups. With the passage of time it became usual for one of the experienced concurrent planning carers (often by then an adoptive parent) to contribute to a preparation group, and provide advice. Prospective adopters were given ten days to think about whether they wished to put their names forward for the concurrent planning scheme, but could take longer if they wished. At this stage, the carers were told that they were more likely to have a young child placed with them if they followed the concurrent planning route compared with the traditional adoption route, and this undoubtedly influenced several carers (see also Chapter 6).

At this point those who had opted for concurrent planning were given specific training by the Goodman Project workers. The responsibilities of being a concurrent planning carer (for example, the high level of contact with the birth parents and the need to work positively for rehabilitation with the birth parents), and the risks associated with the work (the possible return of the child to the birth family) were fully explained. We later report on how often the carers mention the importance to them of serving the child's best interest (Chapter 6), a point they undoubtedly considered in these sessions.

---

[5] Goodman Project Evaluation Report 1998–2001, Manchester Adoption Society.

Opting for concurrency led to the family being allocated a Goodman team worker[6] and being assessed for this demanding role, in addition to the home study work that would have formed part of their assessment as traditional MAS adopters. These prospective adopters had themselves to decide whether they were emotionally strong enough to withstand the risks associated with concurrent planning, and in particular, the possibility that the child might return to the birth family. During the first two years (of the four years that formed the period of this evaluation research), the Goodman carers' applications were submitted to separate adoption and fostering panels. From February 2001, carers were able to submit a single application to a joint fostering and adoption panel.

Selecting the children/families

The first enquiry by Bury or Salford SSD was frequently in the form of a telephone call, during which a quick decision could often be taken as to whether the case was appropriate for the concurrent planning project at that particular moment. For example, a case might be rejected if the referral was of a sibling group and there were no concurrency carers registered to take more than one child. If, on the other hand, the Goodman Project had suitable carers who might take the referred child, a form would be sent to the local authority to check the referring criteria, and to obtain a preliminary assessment of the birth parents' capabilities. Goodman Project workers also made themselves available to read the case files and to discuss the suitability of potential cases. This exchange of information was followed by a formal referral meeting between the local authority and the Goodman workers.[7]

Referral criteria

- Child is under eight years,[8] and subject to proceedings which will last for several months, and potentially add to delay in achieving permanence.

---

[6] Birth families in the concurrency programme had their own concurrency team worker who was not the carers' worker.

[7] The detail of these meetings can be gained from the Goodman Project Evaluation Report 1998–2001, available from 47 Bury New Road, Manchester M25 9JY.

[8] Although initially the intention had been to take possible placement for children up to age eight years, it became clear that the age group preferred by the concurrency carers was younger. Referrals were not, in the event, considered over the age of four years.

- The family history or background would indicate adoption is one strong option but there are issues to be resolved and work to be done with the immediate or extended family which might lead to rehabilitation.

It is interesting to note that, at this stage, the referring local authorities were not being asked to use the two "differential diagnosis" checklists (Strengths in Families and Poor Prognostic Indicators), although the Goodman workers routinely used these at an early stage to decide on the suitability of the cases.

After acceptance of a case, the Goodman Project workers met as soon as possible with the birth parents to explain the concurrent planning option. In this meeting they took the birth parents through the processes, explaining in full the possibility of adoption; the birth family were told of the three-pronged approach – that their child might return to them, live permanently with another member of the family, or be adopted. They would be given a copy of the leaflet that had been especially prepared for birth parents. No child was accepted by the Goodman team without the agreement of the birth parents.

After these meetings with birth parents a formal contract was signed with the local authority, outlining the services offered by the Goodman team, and the responsibilities of each party. The legal departments in the two local authorities drew up a model letter of instruction, that was issued jointly by the parties at the first directions hearing, at which the judge would note if the placement was a concurrent planning placement. During the first three years of the Goodman Project, the cases were heard before only two judges. At this first hearing the need for expert witnesses would also be considered, and contact arrangements were established. The Project offered three sessions a week, up to three hours long, or longer if appropriate. The timescales and timetabling were agreed by all parties and in most cases the date for the final hearing was also set at this time. However, while the concurrency team regarded this as ideal practice, it could not always be achieved.

After individual preparation, the concurrency team arranged meetings to take place between the birth parents and the carers on the project premises. The Goodman worker was always present throughout these meetings. Some of the children were placed direct from hospital, but more usually they were moved from an interim foster family (see Chapters 4 and 5).

The Goodman workers met regularly with the birth parents in order to identify with them the central problems in their parenting capacity and the support required for them to reach the target of "good enough" parenting. After this, the concurrency team worker and the birth parents jointly signed an Assessment Agreement (see Appendix G) that summarised the current concerns, what needed to change, and who would be responsible for each task. The Assessment Agreement also covered the dates of future assessment sessions and arrangements for contact with their child. The concurrency team undertook to set up the appropriate services for the birth parent, and monitored attendance and progress, but there was no written contract between the Goodman team and the birth parents. This was considered to be implicit in signing the Assessment Agreement.

Contact arrangements were supervised and always took place at the Goodman Project premises, with the exception of one case, when contact was moved to a family centre to facilitate the return to the birth family. The concurrency carer was expected to bring the child to the contact session and hand him/her over to the birth parents. At the end of the session, the carers would receive the child back from the birth parents. This procedure was regarded as essential to building up the relationship between the carers and birth family (see also Chapter 8). After the first few months of the project, an experienced family aide was appointed specifically to undertake this work, a move that was strongly recommended by this concurrency team. She contributed to work undertaken by the team with birth parents, and was responsible for the assessments of each contact session.

Family members who might take the child were identified early on, and interviewed at the same time as the birth parents. This early work identified potential family carers, and established whether comprehensive assessments of their parenting capacities were needed. These assessments were presented at the final hearing.

The pattern of work continued thereafter along lines agreed with the local authorities within normal expectations surrounding the care of looked after children. The Goodman workers attended the Statutory Reviews and local authority planning meetings over the period up to the final hearing.

When the care plan was rehabilitation, Goodman workers liaised with local authority workers on the transitional arrangements, e.g. for increased contact times or frequencies. When the care plan was adoption, the Goodman workers arranged the "farewell" meetings (when the birth family wanted these). Post-adoption contact arrangements were set up in discussion with the concurrency carers and local authority, and the birth parents. Goodman workers attended the adoption panel that decided whether to recommend approval of the linking of child and carers. For children placed with concurrency carers, statutory reviews continued until the adoption order was granted: Goodman workers continued to attend these. With the local authority social workers, the Goodman workers prepared the Schedule 2 reports, that were sent to the local authority for scrutiny and signing.

The Goodman team provided post-adoption services to birth parents and their families when they wanted it, and to the concurrency carers' families when they had adopted the children. When rehabilitation was the eventual plan, support services to the concurrency planning family were especially important, both during the transitional period while the rehabilitation took place and after the child had actually moved. The work with birth families built on the established practice of the agency, providing post-adoption services subsequently for birth parents and their families for several years.

The Coram Family Concurrent Planning Project

The Coram Family Adoption Service is a voluntary adoption agency based in central London. The concurrent planning service was launched in late 1999, supported by Department of Health funding plus grants from the two local authorities (Camden and Islington) from which the project takes referrals. Planning meetings held in early 1999 led to agreement that the families would broadly be those identified by the criteria suggested by Katz *et al* (1994a), with the addition of the criterion identified by Jones (1987, 1998) of a family's inability to work with professionals.[9] By the time the

---

[9] It is interesting to note that, although the research evidence would support the expectation of very poor outcomes for the children of such families, Lutheran Social Services started, as we have noted above, with the notion of including "untreatable" families (Katz, 1990).

concurrency project was ready to launch, these had been refined to acknowledge that several factors may indicate poor ability to parent a child. The concurrency team suggested that a case would be suitable for referral if there were concerns on one or more of the following clusters of problems:

- chronic substance abuse/long-term mental health problems;
- birth parents have a poor attachment history which appears to have resulted in difficulty in sustaining close and constructive (e.g. non-violent) relationships;
- absence of support networks.

Setting up the scheme

The information about the new concurrent planning service was given to the professional bodies that would be involved in the cases: members of the judiciary, children's panel solicitors, barristers, social services, children's guardians, and local authority legal advisors and solicitors (Appendix E). The benefits for birth parents, children and the interim concurrency carers were clearly laid out. It was, for example, made clear that:

> *Birth parents will be assured of a service which offers them considerable personal support as well as access to a range of specialist resources. There will be clear expectations, set out in a written agreement as to arrangements regarding any assessment and treatment services and for regular contact with their child.*

Information about concurrent planning was incorporated into the literature that went to everyone who enquired about adoption. It was described as 'speeding the achievement of permanent placements for children under three (later two) years – whether by reuniting them with their birth parents/birth relatives, or by adoption. We will be using concurrent planning as one way of achieving early decisions about placements.' A similar pamphlet was prepared for (birth) parents (see Appendix D).

The Coram Project was modelled on the Goodman Project in Manchester, but developed in slightly different ways. The following paragraphs summarise the main differences and some distinctive features of the Coram Project work:

- The Project was set up to serve only children aged less than two years at referral.

- Effective communication with social workers from the two local authorities was slow to get established, and more than one year into the Project, many social workers apparently still did not have a clear understanding of concurrent planning.
- The Project experienced some delay in getting placements straight from hospital. In certain cases, babies born to drug-addicted mothers were kept in hospital for their drug withdrawal treatment, but for others there were health concerns (e.g. Hepatitis C) that led to carers being reluctant to take babies without assurance on these issues. A Steering Group minute of January 2001 noted that the team was not able to function in the way that the Brighton & Hove concurrency team worked (see below), with involvement in every pre-birth assessment, even where the case did not finally progress to concurrent planning. This remained a point of concern a year later.[10]
- Concurrency carers needed to be confident that the extended family's capacity to care for the child on a permanent basis had been fully explored. The local authorities preferred not to delegate this work to the concurrency team. Due to pressure of work and time constraints, local authority staff were often unable to provide this information at the outset to the concurrency carers. In the early days this resulted in carers

[10] This was an area in which several concurrency carers, not just at the London Project, felt that they were not given sufficient or timely information. Sometimes the information was slightly inaccurate, and only clarified by carers using their own medical information systems (including the internet). Inevitably, the information was in the form of probabilities, especially on HIV and Hepatitis C infection from addicted birth mothers. At other times, the information was provided only just ahead of the court hearing at which it would be confirmed that this particular carer would take this particular child. This made decision-making very hard for the carers. It is clearly a difficult area, but one in which insufficient information can sometimes have serious long-term repercussions. It should be noted that it is particularly difficult to provide full or accurate information and predictions with babies who are only a few days or weeks old. There may always be a tension between the need for speedy and early placement and the acquisition of accurate medical predictions. We noted that, at the stage of placing children with the carers, the medical forms (Form A) were barely ever fully completed. It should be noted that other researchers have found the same gaps in medical information supplied to adoptive parents (Quinton *et al*, 1998).

refusing certain placements or in long delays in placements while additional information was acquired.

- The referrals to the Project were all dealt with in the Central London Family Proceedings Court. When a referral to court was planned, the borough legal departments undertook to alert the Justices' Clerk. Considerable preparatory work by the Inner London and City Family Proceedings Court and Islington legal department went into developing a protocol for these referrals (see Appendix H). The Justices' Clerk established that she or her deputy should be notified as early as possible by the local authority legal departments so that they could ensure judicial continuity and the avoidance of delay.
- Although not a necessary requirement for referral to the concurrency team, the birth parents' consent was sought. For one non-UK family it later became clear that, although they had agreed to participate, they had not fully understood the concurrent planning principles, nor even the concept of adoption. Cultural differences needed to be understood from the start of a case.
- In the early months, the local authorities were reluctant for the concurrency workers to attend court for the initial hearing. After resolving this difficulty, concurrency workers were able to attend court to offer advice to all parties, although only at the court's invitation, in order to maintain the concurrency team's independence.
- The concurrency team recruited carers directly into the Project, and did not rely on recruitment from the mainstream Coram Adoption Service. Information coming from the two local authorities about the characteristics of their looked after children suggested the need for carers from black and other minority ethnic communities. For some months the team advertised in the minority ethnic press with notable success. Later, it became apparent that the referrals were more often of white than of black or mixed race children. The team changed their recruiting policy to increase the number of white carers, particularly those from the Roman Catholic community. The team made it plain that single adopters were welcome to apply.

Looking back on the early stages of the concurrency work, the Project team leader has commented that, at that time, local authority staff generally approached the prospect of a placement with the concurrency team in much the same way as they would if preparing to place a child with a temporary foster carer. In contrast, the concurrency team approached the placement more from the point of view of a prospective adopter, and therefore required much more detailed information regarding the immediate and long-term health and developmental issues for the child.

Since the early "bedding down" problems, the concurrency team has become involved alongside the local authority social workers in information gathering and early assessments, before placement. The team leader confirmed that the concurrency team's role in this area of work was recognised in the new service agreements in place from 2002 with the two boroughs.

Although not a legal requirement, the absolute necessity of birth parents being committed to rehabilitative programmes was agreed with other agencies. The concurrency team leader expressed this in one case as follows:

> *In order to achieve this aim [rehabilitation], it is expected that P's parents will engage with Camden Social Services and participate in a residential rehabilitation programme, or a community detoxification project in conjunction with the substance misuse team. As they both have a long history of drug misuse it will be essential for them to demonstrate a commitment to their abstinence from street drugs within the community . . . The timescale for achieving this aim will be within the remit of the concurrent planning timetable. [They] will need to display motivation in seeking support for their drug dependency as well as commitment to engaging with the local authority and other relevant agencies for the purpose of assessment . . . a realistic timescale that promotes P's well-being.*

This matches the point raised later with the researchers by the Brighton & Hove Service Manager, Permanence Team, who also managed the concurrency team, that birth parents need to demonstrate by their actions, not just by their promises, that they are sincere in their desire to change.

Coram Family introduced one interesting variation on the training and support programme used elsewhere. One of their single concurrency carers, in the absence of a partner, had relied heavily on her own parent for support and substitute care. In response to a request from this carer, the concurrency team started a dedicated support group for the relatives of the carers. Only a few such meetings were held, but the carers reported to the researchers that their relatives found these interesting and helpful. One carer commented that it was important to reassure relatives that informed decisions had been made.

The Brighton & Hove programme[11]

The concurrent planning team in Brighton & Hove was set up in August 1999 within the local authority SSD using Quality Protects monies. This followed a multi-agency conference arranged by the SSD the year before, addressed by Linda Katz. The aim of the new team was to place selected children up to the age of five years in a programme that would speed up the achievement of permanence. Local figures on adoption and permanency placements were compiled that confirmed delays in issuing care proceedings because of a lack of clarity and confidence in meeting threshold criteria. There was also evidence that alternative placements within the kinship network were not being pursued in a vigorous and timely way. In this, Brighton & Hove mirrored the practices common in the rest of England.

As with the other two concurrency projects, the Brighton & Hove team undertook development work, setting up the operational guidelines and contacting the professionals who might become involved with concurrency cases. The team consisted, throughout the research evaluation period, of two full-time and one part-time experienced social work practitioners, with the later addition of two half-time Community Family Workers, who supervised the contact sessions. The concurrency team worked as part of the local authority's accommodation service, and was led by the Service Manager of the Permanence Team. Members of the concurrency team attended, at intervals, the meetings of fieldwork and accommodation teams to update colleagues.

---

[11] We have been able to draw extensively on the two annual reports prepared for this project, for which we thank the Service Manager.

Like the Coram concurrency team, the work was modelled on the Goodman Team's experience, but because it was located within the SSD, some distinctive working methods emerged:

- The permanency team ran the duty office for all adopters and took the initial enquiries from all prospective adopters (see Appendix F). The authority also advertised concurrent planning from the time that the project began, and some adopters contacted the concurrent planning enquiry line direct. A regular article was inserted into the local free magazine (for parents) that could be picked up in shops, libraries and medical clinics. Leaflets explaining concurrent planning were also produced for birth parents (see Appendix D).
- All those who expressed an interest in adopting a baby or toddler under two years were visited by one of the concurrency team workers. The permanency team gave priority to those families who opted for concurrent planning, because the authority had a waiting list of baby adopters who preferred to use the traditional route to adoption.
- A session was held on medical issues by the medical advisor to the Panel, who was a local consultant paediatrician. She focused particularly on issues relevant to the placement of very young babies where it is likely that little is known about the birth parents' medical histories, and where the birth mother may have had very little ante-natal care. These discussions tended to be largely about the *probability* of something happening or some disability emerging, rather than accurate prognoses. The local authority's policy was that full information should be given to concurrency carers (known locally as foster-adopters), before the match was considered at Panel.
- The assessment of the families was exclusively the responsibility of the concurrency team, work that increasingly was found to include pre-birth assessments of the birth parents. The team took key work responsibility for both the child and the assessment work with the birth family once concurrent planning had been agreed in Court (p 6, Annual Report 2; para 4.2). The team provided an extra component in the assessment to cover the ability of applicants to cope with the challenges and risks inherent in being concurrency carers.
- In view of these responsibilities, it was seen as essential that the support and assessment of the concurrency carer was held by a

different worker in the team than the key worker for the child, to avoid any possible conflict of interest. In the other two projects, of course, the responsibility for the concurrency children remained with the local authorities, so this specific issue did not arise (*ibid*, p 6, para. 4.2).
- The Permanence Panel recommended the approval of the concurrency carers as both prospective foster carers and prospective adopters. The Brighton & Hove concurrent planning programme differed from the other two concurrency programmes in that the care plan and the match were endorsed at Panel before placement. However, to avoid delays, the concurrency team had the opportunity to place cases on the Panel agenda at every fortnightly meeting. If necessary, an emergency Panel could be convened to avoid delay in agreeing plans for a potential concurrency placement.
- The Poor Prognosis Indicators and the Strengths in Families checklists were frequently completed *with* the birth parents.

The team leader has argued that it is essential to have a dedicated concurrency team within the authority. She stresses the specific needs of concurrency: to provide very focused work with the birth parents, to keep supervised contact at a high level throughout the period leading up to the final hearing, to organise and monitor specific educational programmes for the birth parents, and to provide knowledgeable support to the carers. She has expressed the fear that, if the principles of concurrent planning were incorporated into fieldwork services generally, they would rapidly become diluted and filter away.

Post-adoption work

All three concurrency teams continued working with prospective adoptive families up to the adoption hearing. They were responsible for setting up the post-adoption contact systems, and completing the life story work with the birth family. Adoptive parents were frequently invited to attend the monthly support group meetings and appropriate training events.

Trafford Social Services

Alongside the three concurrent planning teams, we drew one of the comparison samples from the children looked after by Trafford social services, who had adoption as their care plan, and had therefore been referred to the authority's Adoption and Permanency Team. The team manager described the team:

'The Trafford team has existed for 10 or 11 years, though at times under different names. It has been called the Alternative Families Team, the Care Management Team and currently the Adoption and Permanency Team. In all its formats, however, it has been a team dedicated to finding permanent families for children and helping and preparing the children for the move. It is difficult to do justice to finding families if, at the same time, you are part of a team that has a lot of child protection work. That must take priority when social workers are a scarce resource. Similarly, a team is not as focused if it is part of a Family Placement Team because again there are other matters calling on your attention – supporting carers, recruiting and training and so forth.

'A team dedicated to the permanency needs of children is clearly more focused. It can work quicker, so children are placed quicker and it develops specialist expertise. There is also, however, a bonus from the authority as a whole having a philosophy that is ever mindful of permanency needs. Even before the new Adoption Standards requiring that permanency decisions should be taken at the four-month review and before LAC (98)20 spoke of parallel-planning, Trafford had developed a system of "Early Warning Meetings" to make the Adoption and Permanency Team aware of possible need at an early stage. Work could be started even then, in parallel to the main work. Form Es were prepared far quicker, and with some level of expertise from regular familiarity with the issues, and there were timely presentations to Panel.

'Some areas would feel that having such a team is a luxury that they can ill afford when they are already short of staff. Trafford has been short of staff, too, but hopefully will not have to re-deploy the team in general duties just yet. It is better for the children to have a dedicated team and [this team] can still act so as to take some of the burden from the area teams. It can do this by doing [some of their] very time-consuming work.

Also work that is not within the usual practice experience of all social workers can be undertaken with a high level of good practice knowledge.'

Recent changes in the context in which concurrent planning programmes are working

The reader should be reminded that, during the lifetime of the three concurrent planning projects and of the research evaluation, the circumstances of looked after children have changed quite substantially. A larger number of children are in care than in the early years of the Goodman Project planning, but many more children are now moving from care to adoption. The Government has supported a new approach to adoption through the Quality Protects initiative, that provided extra monies to local authorities to cut the numbers of moves experienced by looked after children, and to advance the proportion of children in permanent placements.

That particular initiative included the specific target of reducing the number of moves experienced by children either before adoption or before they return home. Each move except the first (taking the child away from abuse or neglect) and the last (placing them in adoptive households) might be taken to represent a failure to achieve stability, although it is clear that some moves are carefully planned and can be judged to have improved a child's life chances. Protracted court proceedings are commonly experienced in child protection cases, and were identified in all their convolutions in the *Prime Minister's Review of Adoption* (Performance & Innovation Unit, 2000). Each delay is also associated, obviously, with the passage of time, and research has consistently shown that the rates of adoption breakdown rise with age at placement (Department of Health, 1999b).

Tracking the adoption cases: timescales and the National Standards

Reducing delay and drift is central to concurrent planning. In August 2001, new National Standards[12] were introduced to increase the numbers of children in care who can be placed for adoption and ensure a high standard of practice for all parties. A key part of setting high standards

[12] National Adoption Standards for England (Department of Health, 2001a and 2001b).

was the intention to cut the delay and drift that had been reported in the Prime Minister's Review of Adoption (PIU, 2000), and acknowledged by many practitioners over previous years. In response to the setting of National Standards, tools have been developed that enable local authorities to track the progress of all cases of adoption from care. The tracking tools identify the time taken for a child to progress through the various critical stages (Key Events) towards adoption or permanence.[13] Dates of Key Events are recorded at which particular decisions are taken in traditional adoption cases. These include, in sequence: the Permanence Plan, Adoption Plan agreed by the Court, Best Interests decision, Linking Decision, Placement and Adoption Order.

Aware of the possibility that concurrent planning cases might not "fit" with these, and that, in particular, the sequence of the Key Events is substantially different, the team leaders were consulted for their views. The Coram Family team leader pointed out that the stages within concurrent planning do not accurately follow those in mainstream adoption situations. While the 'Date of "best interests" recommendation' and the 'Date of Linking plan recommended by Adoption and Permanency Panel', should be retained as separate stages, in concurrency cases these decisions are usually considered on the same day. In terms of the recommended timescales, the National Standards suggest that 'a match with a suitable adoptive parent should be made . . . within six months of the agency agreeing that adoption is in the child's best interests'; this does not apply in concurrent planning cases. Nor does the timescale for identifying and approving adoptive parents 'up to six months' from the date the court agrees the care plan. These differences highlight the way in which concurrent planning speeds up the achievement of permanent placements.

Consequently there was a need to identify whether a different model is needed specifically to help with tracking the concurrent planning cases. Below are some suggestions that emerged from consultation with two team leaders.[14]

---

[13] The tool was developed by three local authority social services departments and the Catholic Children's Society, Nottingham, funded by the Department of Health. The "Tracking Children" tool was developed by the London Borough of Richmond upon Thames.

[14] We are grateful for permission to draw on these discussions in the following paragraphs.

The date of the Permanency Planning meeting, which is identified as a "Key Event" in the national case tracking model, for example, tends to happen in concurrent planning at the same time as the official referral to the concurrency team. At this meeting the concurrency team agrees in principle to a case being taken forward as a concurrency case. Team leaders considered that the most useful heading for this stage would identify both aspects: 'Date of permanency planning meeting/agreement for concurrent planning.' The date of the first Interim Care Order is seen as important by all the teams, since no child can be placed with concurrency carers before the local authority has been granted this order in respect of the child. The teams have recommended that the next key event occurs at the granting of the Freeing Order. To clarify this, Coram Family has suggested the wording should be amended to read 'Date the Freeing Order is granted'.

The Brighton & Hove team has also developed its own tracking tools, after finding that the Key Events identified in the National Standards were not wholly appropriate when following the progress of concurrent planning cases. They have defined the overall target for their cases as nine months; locally the courts have endorsed this approach.

Summary

- A detailed description is given of the work of the specialist team at Lutheran Social Services, Seattle, responsible in the early 1980s for the development of concurrent planning. The essential components of this way of working with children in care and their parents are outlined, drawing attention to the unique features: selection of cases; contracts with parents about the work they are expected to do on the problems that prevent them providing a secure environment for their child; interim placement of the child with carers who are able to adopt him/her if rehabilitation is not possible; the concurrent work on rehabilitation to the family, *and* support for the foster placement; limitation on the time before final hearing.
- Attention is drawn to the difference – not always fully understood – between parallel planning or twin tracking and concurrent planning. It is now a legal requirement in England and Wales that the three

following possibilities are considered in parallel – assessing the parents and the extended family, and the development of a care plan for placement outside the family. The child is meanwhile in foster care or residential accommodation; but there is no built-in expectation or plan that foster carers will adopt the child if the rehabilitation with his or her birth family proves impossible. In concurrent planning cases, on the other hand, while a return to the birth parents or wider birth family are investigated, the child is placed with foster carers who, if the birth family cannot parent, become the adopters. The timescales are rigorous; final hearings are frequently within 6–9 months of the concurrency placement.

- The work of the three concurrent planning teams in the research study is described drawing attention to the different ways of working within the two voluntary agencies and the Brighton & Hove SSD specialist team.
- A description is given of the philosophy underlying the work of the Trafford Adoption and Permanency Team.
- A brief discussion is included of the need for systems to be developed that would enable local authorities and voluntary agencies to track the progress of their concurrent planning cases through to the permanent placement of the child. Attention is drawn to the fact that the current Department of Health proposals for tracking adoption cases cannot be transposed without amendment to concurrent planning.

4 The children and families referred to the projects

It is important to recognise that the data on outcomes (largely in Chapter 5) are derived from selected samples. In this chapter the information is given for each concurrency project on the numbers of families/parents who applied to become concurrency carers and how they were recruited. This is followed by data on the reasons why, in each project, referrals could not be accepted into the concurrency programmes. For each concurrency team it has also been possible to indicate the larger populations of looked after children in the appropriate age groups within the referring local authorities. The numbers are also given of looked after children who were referred within Trafford Social Services to their own Trafford Adoption and Permanency Team during the research evaluation period. In Chapter 5 the data are presented on the number of moves and the care careers of the children accepted into each project.

Referrals to the MAS Adoption Team and the Goodman Project

Figure 4.1 shows the numbers of people applying to the Manchester Adoption Society who, in the course of their preparation groups, opted to become Goodman Project concurrency carers. It is worth mentioning at this point that very many of the adopters (in the MAS sample) and concurrency carers (in all three projects) had experienced what they saw as a poor service from local authorities in their areas of England. It was not unusual to hear that when families had telephoned local authorities to enquire about adoption they had to leave answer-phone messages, or they were put through to departments where no one could be found who dealt with adoption applications, or forms were promised and not sent, and sometimes they were told the adoption lists for younger children or babies were closed. Almost all the concurrency carers reported that the Voluntary Adoption Agencies in the current project provided a superior service in terms of promptness, friendliness, politeness and responsiveness compared with their own local authority.[1] These experiences confirm the point subsequently raised in the *Prime Minister's Review of Adoption* (Performance & Innovation Unit, 2000). Judging by the descriptions given by the carers in the present study, we believe this is an area in which local authorities appear still to need guidance on best practice.

Between February 1998, when the Goodman Project started to recruit their concurrency carers, and December 2000,[2] 45 prospective adoptive families joined the Manchester Adoption Society (MAS) preparation programmes to become mainstream adopters. All these families were recommended as adoptive parents by Panel, and all were invited to take part in the research by the Director of MAS.

Concurrency carers joining the Goodman Project

Figure 4.1 shows how the 12 families that agreed to become part of the evaluation project were recruited by the Goodman Project. All the families recruited to the Goodman Project were living as married couples, and all were white, with one carer from a European background. In the eight families that were eventually included in the research evaluation sample, one couple had previously adopted a child, and three had birth children living in the family. The mean age of the women was 34.5 (range 28–42) and that of the men was 36 (range 30–42).

Mainstream adopters joining the MAS Adoption Team

The 32 families in the MAS Adoption Team group were asked to take part in the research, but one couple had to decline as the local authority with responsibility for their adoptive child refused permission to include the child. Ten further couples decided not to take part. During the period of the research evaluation, 23 children were placed for adoption with 15 families. Among these families recruited to the MAS Adoption Team sample, two were mixed ethnicity couples, the rest were white European; all the mainstream MAS adoptive parents except one applied to adopt as

---

[1] Paragraph 9.5–9.7: *Meeting the Challenges of Changes in Adoption: Inspection of Voluntary Adoption Agencies*, Department of Health/Social Services Inspectorate, 1999 (p 37).

[2] The years during which the research evaluation by TCRU was taking place.

married couples. Six families had previously adopted children, and two different families had birth children in the household. The mean age of the adoptive mothers was 37.5 (range 32–43) and of the fathers was 39 (range 32–52).

Figure 4.1

Recruitment of potential adoptive parents to the MAS Adoption Team and concurrency carers to the Goodman Project concurrent planning team

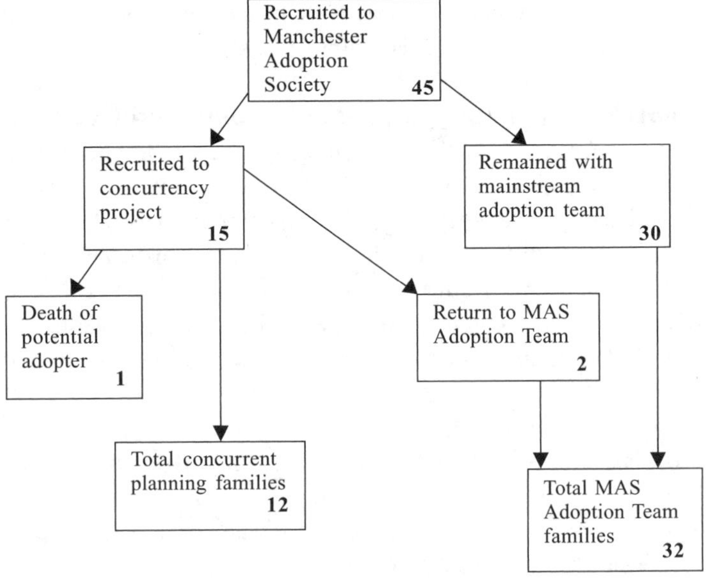

Referrals of the children

All the concurrency carers in the Goodman Project had got approval from Panel to foster/adopt children from birth; but the research interviews suggested that all the carers had expressed a preference for younger babies and toddlers, and that they had often opted for concurrency because of this (see also Chapter 6). A high proportion of rejections by the Goodman Project of referrals from the two local authorities in the early months of the project were of children over *c*. 18 months, because there were no

Table 4.1
Predominant reasons for cases from Bury and Salford not being accepted into the Goodman Project

Referring borough	*Predominant reason for "rejection" by Goodman Project*		*Numbers of children (sib groups)*
Bury	No suitable carers	i) Sibling group	12 (6×2)
		ii) No match for ethnicity	1
		iii) Medical problems	0
		iv) No specific reason	4
	Sub-total		**17**
	Rehabilitation extremely unlikely		3
	No care proceedings		3
	Did not meet project criteria		0
	Reasons unknown, case "open" or in discussion		4
	Placed by Goodman (including three Pilot cases)		5
	Total referrals		**32**
Salford	No suitable carers	i) Sibling group	18 (6×2; 2×3)
		ii) No match for ethnicity	1
		iii) Medical problems	2
		iv) No specific reason	5
	Sub-total		**26**
	Rehabilitation extremely unlikely		4
	No care proceedings		0
	Did not meet project criteria		5
	Reasons unknown, case "open" or in discussion		10
	Placed by Goodman		6
	Total referrals		**51**

carers willing to take the older children while the possibility of younger placements existed. However, it is apparent also that the Salford childcare teams soon understood that this was the case and, over the three-year life of this evaluation study of the Goodman Project, more than half of the referrals were of children under 12 months from this authority. The age groups of children coming into the care of Salford was also skewed to younger children and babies under 12 months, but it is also clear that, selectively, the childcare teams were referring a disproportionate number of babies to the Goodman team (Table 4.2).[3] The figures from Bury were not available at the time of writing, but it is probable that they showed a similar age distribution.

Table 4.2

Age distribution of Salford referrals to the Goodman Project, 1998–2000 (including the six cases accepted by the concurrency team)

Age groups	*Salford LAC at entry into care*		*At referral to Goodman*	
	N	*%*	*N*	*%*
0–12 months	71**	39	30*	55
1–2 years	41	23	4	13
2+ years	57	31	11	10
Age not recorded	12	7	26	31
Total Salford referrals	**181**	**100**	**83**	**100**

*18 of these referrals were of unborn children, including two eventually placed by the concurrency team.
**18 of these children were taken into care at birth.

In the event not only did Goodman receive a disproportionate number of referrals of very young children, but the Project also largely placed babies (Table 4.3). Of the 11 placements, only one child was over 15 months at referral; seven (64 per cent) were less than three months at referral. It is clear that the suggestion made to potential carers, when they were deciding whether or not to become involved with concurrent planning, that by doing so they stood a higher chance of getting a baby, became a reality.

[3] The figures from Bury were not available at the time of writing, but it is probable that they would have shown a similar age distribution.

Table 4.3
Age at referral to the Goodman Project of children placed with concurrency carers, 1998–2000

Age at referral to Goodman team	*Number*	*Percentage*
At or before birth	7	64
3–12 months	2	18
1 year or more	2	18
Total	**11**	**100**

The majority of the children referred by Bury and Salford were single children, or at least the placement was being sought for a single child. But over one-third were in sibling groups for which a placement together appears to have been the aim; as we have noted above, no concurrency carers were available when siblings were referred. In one way this is not surprising, since, as we have seen, most of the concurrency carers had decided to follow the concurrent planning route in return for having a baby placed with them. The risks attached to concurrency were seen by them as balancing the placement of a baby, but not an older child: *a fortiori*, they were unlikely to see the risk of losing two children after several months' placement as a "reasonable" option.

The referrals were evenly divided between boys (37–39 per cent) and girls (34–35 per cent), but for a substantial number of referrals (25–26 per cent) the gender was unknown. This was usually because the baby was still unborn, but sometimes because the information passed to the team at the time of referral identified immediately that there would be no suitable carers (e.g. because of the size of sibling group), and no further information was recorded by Goodman. Among the 11 placed children there were six girls, and five boys. Four were placed with the concurrency carers from hospital, and seven were placed with concurrency carers after an interim foster family placement.

Table 4.4
Sibling groups among the Bury and Salford referrals and among those placed by Goodman Project

Sibling status of children referred by Bury and Salford	*Bury and Salford referrals*		*Goodman Project cases*	
	No.	*%*	*No.*	*%*
No siblings – single child	53	64	11	100
Two children	24	29	–	–
Three children or more	6	7	–	–
Total	**83**	**100**	**11**	**100**

Referrals to Coram Family concurrent planning team

Concurrency carers joining the Coram Project

Coram Family started to provide the concurrent planning service to Islington and Camden from November 1999. The recruitment of concurrency carers took a slightly different form from that found in the Manchester Adoption Society for the Goodman Project. Figure 4.2 shows that in the first two years the majority of concurrency carers were recruited direct to the special project through advertising. Among these applicants, five were single women and six were couples. One couple were of mixed white Italian and English origin; three single parents (mothers) were black, the rest white. Among the seven families that were part of the evaluation, one was black and six were white. One family had a previously adopted child, but none had birth children. The mean age of the women was 41 (range 38–46) and of the men 42 (range 40–47).

Referrals of the children

The expectation was that the concurrency team would place children up to two years old (see Chapter 3). Between January 2000 and December 2001, 30 children in this age group were referred by Camden Social Services. Table 4.5 shows that the large majority of these cases were thought not suited to the concurrency programme, the commonest single reason being that the team did not have carers of appropriate ethnicity or

Figure 4.2

Applications to become concurrency carers made to Coram Family Concurrency Project, January 2000–December 2001

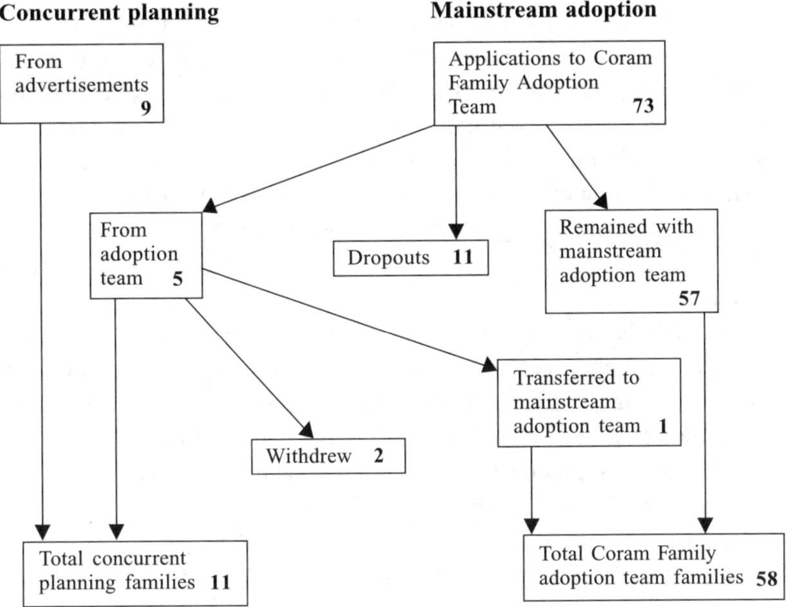

religious affiliation to match the children; a frequent problem was the absence of concurrency carers with a specifically Irish and/or (other white) Catholic background. Surprisingly, only three Camden children were placed in the two years of the evaluation. It appeared that less than half the looked after children (and babies) in the care of Camden were judged by their social workers to meet the concurrent planning criteria sufficiently closely to justify even a referral to the concurrent planning team. One Camden senior social worker made the point that the borough only sees about 8–15 babies a year for whom adoption becomes the care plan, and that most would be from ethnic minority families. She thought that the concurrency team expected there to be many more and thought that Camden must be "hiding" them. Her estimate on numbers was accurate: in the two years 2000 and 2001 a total of 26 babies had become looked after within three weeks of birth. But the estimate of "well over half" of these very young babies being from ethnic minorities was not borne out.[4]

In Islington, 35 (33 per cent) of the 106 children under the age of two years in care between January 2000 and December 2001 were referred to concurrency. As with the Camden referrals, the commonest reason why referred cases could not be accepted was the lack of carers from an appropriate religious or ethnic background. The issue of ethnicity and religion is important in the inner London area served by the Coram Family concurrency team. Taking the referrals from the two boroughs together, a third could not be matched with concurrency carers for religious or ethnic reasons.

Although the service was planned for children under two years, in the event the eight children who were placed by the concurrency team were all under nine months at placement; four were placed aged less than three months and four were placed aged from 3–9 months. Referrals for these placed children were, however, at even earlier ages: three-quarters at birth or from pre-birth conferences. It is difficult with such small numbers to deduce patterns, but it seems likely that the two referring boroughs were accepting the possibility that concurrency is well suited to very young children and new-born babies.

Referrals to the Concurrent Planning Team – Brighton & Hove Social Services

Recruiting the concurrency carers

The Brighton & Hove concurrency team established a rolling programme of preparation groups for both regular and concurrent routes to adoption for children under five years. In the first preparation groups about one-third of the prospective adopters opted for concurrency, but later

[4] During the period covered by the evaluation, the total number of looked after children in Camden, who were under the age of two years when coming into care, was 68. Of these, 40 were white (59 per cent); 28 (41 per cent) were mixed or black heritage. In Islington, 43 per cent were from white parentage, and 43 per cent from mixed parentage; nearly all the rest (14 per cent) were from black families.

Table 4.5

Predominant reason why children referred by Camden and Islington Social Services were not accepted into the Coram Family Concurrent Planning Project

Referring borough	*Predominant reason for "rejection" by Project*	*Numbers of children*	
Camden	No suitable prospective carers		
	i) Sibling group	2	
	ii) No ethnic/religious match	12	
	iii) Medical problems	0	
	iv) No specified reason	0	
	Sub-total	**14**	
	No prospect of rehabilitation	1	
	No care proceedings	1	
	Did not meet project criteria, including:	7	
	i) To mainstream adoption		1
	ii) To birth family (not parents)		3
	Reasons unknown, or case "open" or in discussion	3	
	Died before placement decision	1	
	Placed	**3**	
	Total referrals	**30**	
Islington	No suitable prospective carers		
	i) Sibling group	2 (twins)	
	ii) No ethnic/religious match	9	
	iii) Medical problems	0	
	iv) No specified reason	0	
	Sub-total	**11**	
	No prospect of rehabilitation	0	
	No care proceedings	0	
	Did not meet project criteria, including:	15	
	i) To mainstream adoption		1
	ii) To birth family (not parents)		4
	Reasons unknown, case "open" or in discussion	4	
	Died before placement decision	0	
	Placed	**5**	
	Total referrals	**35**	

this rose to two-thirds, and in a group meeting late in 2001 all the prospective adopters asked to be considered for concurrent planning. As the Team Manager stated:

> . . . *recruitment activity is high and the team have contributed significantly to the proportion of adoptive [concurrency] carers that are approved each year.*[5]

In the judgment of the concurrency team, it has not been difficult to recruit carers to take on this complicated role. Among the nine families of carers that formed the evaluation sample, all were white, all were married couples, three had birth children and three (different families) had previously adopted other children. The average age of the women was 37 (range 31–42) and of the men was 40 (range 31–46).

Referrals of the children

The first Brighton & Hove concurrency carers were approved by Panel in April 2000, and the first baby was placed in July 2000. By the time the evaluation researchers had ceased to collect new cases (February 2002) 69 children in 49 families had been referred to the team. Of these, 47 children (68 per cent) were unborn or under the age of two years at referral; the rest were older siblings for whom the concurrency team would not have been making placements. For 14 of the 47 children, assessments indicated that, despite initial professional concerns, birth parents or family members were judged capable of taking the child. For the majority of these 14, the assessments were pre-birth, and family members took the children at birth. One baby died at birth on whose family the pre-birth assessment indicated that concurrency would have been the right option. Table 4.6 indicates the predominant reasons why it was not possible or reasonable to pursue concurrency as an option.

The decision to work with children under two years led to an expansion of their pre-birth work. The flexible work pattern of this concurrency team has meant that they have been responsible for selecting concurrency cases, but also for supporting placements at home and with extended families. Four of the children were moved to concurrency placements

[5] Concurrency Team Annual Report 2, December 2001.

Table 4.6

Predominant reason why children were not accepted by the Brighton & Hove Concurrent Planning Team

Referring agency	*Predominant reason for "rejection" by Project*	*Numbers of children (sib groups)*	
Social Services Department	No suitable prospective carers		
	i) Sibling group*	21 (1×6; 1×4; 1×3; 4×2)	
	ii) No ethnic/religious match	1	
	iii) Medical problems	3	
	iv) No specified reason	2	
	Sub-total	**27**	
	No prospect of rehabilitation	0	
	No care proceedings	0	
	Did not meet project criteria, including:	26	
	i) To mainstream adoption		10
	ii) To birth family		14
	iii) Too old		2
	Reasons unknown, case "open" or in discussion	6	
	Died before placement decision	1	
	Placed	**9**	
	Total referrals	**69**	

*Only seven of these siblings were under the age of two or unborn, at the time of the referral, but at the time of referral the intention was to keep the families together.

directly from hospital and five went initially to a foster home. Among the latter, three were under three months old and one was six months old when the transfer to the concurrency carers took place (Table 4.7).

These figures for the referrals to the concurrency team should be set against the overall figures of looked after children under the age of two in Brighton & Hove in 2000 and 2001. In this period, there were 50 children in the care of the authority in the appropriate age group. Of these: 23 were boys, 27 were girls; 39 were being cared for under interim or full

Table 4.7

Age at referral to the Brighton & Hove Concurrency Team of cases accepted into the programme compared with ages of children under two years old coming into the care of Brighton & Hove, 2000/01

Age	*At referral to concurrency team*		*Age of children under 2 years coming into care of B&H 2000/01*	
	Number	*%*	*Number*	*%*
Pre-birth	6	66	None	–
At birth	1	11	10	20
Less than 6 months	2	33	14	28
6–12 months	–	–	10	20
12–24 months	–	–	16	32
Totals	**9**	**100**	**50**	**100**

care orders. Table 4.7 shows the age distribution at the time of first coming into care for the whole population of looked after children under two years, compared with the referrals to the concurrency team. This strikingly illustrates the importance of the very early referrals to concurrent planning in this authority.

Referrals to the Trafford Adoption and Permanency Team

Between May 1998, when the research team set up the interview systems with Trafford Social Services and the Adoption and Permanency Team, and December 2000 when the research team ceased to take further referrals, 34 children aged under eight years[6] were taken into care by Trafford Social Services, and then referred to the Adoption and Permanency Team. Table 4.8 shows the reasons why 13 of these children were not referred to the researchers.

[6] The original research evaluation had been expected to involve children up to eight years referred to the concurrent planning teams. The comparison groups were drawn from this age range.

Table 4.8
Referrals to the Trafford Adoption and Permanency Team and subsequently to the researchers

Referrals to Trafford Adoption and Permanency Team: May 1998–December 2001	*Numbers of children*	
Not referred to researchers:		
i) No care proceedings, relinquished at birth		4
ii) No plan for adoption (2 home care orders; one long-term fostering)		3
iii) "Wrong timing" for project: 3 too early/1 too late		4
iv) Reasons unclear		2
Total not referred		**13**
Referred to researchers	21	
Total	**34**	

Most of these children were in sibling groups (Table 4.9); there was a predominance of girls and of white children.

Table 4.9
Selected characteristics of looked after children in Trafford MBC referred to the Adoption and Permanency Team, 1998–2000

Children's demographic characteristics		*N*	*%*
Single children		14	42
Sibling groups of 2		10	29
of 3		10	29
Total		**34**	**100**
Sex	male	13	38
	female	21	62
Total		**34**	**100**
Ethnic groups	White	29	85
	Mixed heritage	5	15
Total		**34**	**100**

Like the MAS comparison sample, the Trafford comparison sample was significantly older than the concurrency cases at the time of their entry into care: seven children (33 per cent) were under one year, ten (48 per cent) were between one and three years, and four (19 per cent) were over four years (mean: 1 year 9 months). The profile of their family backgrounds showed some differences compared with the concurrency cases, but these were not significant. All the parents of these children were reported as having some child protection history, usually associated with other children in the family; for 57 per cent of the birth parents, more than three out of six items were checked on this particular category of the Poor Prognostic Indicators. All the birth parents were also reported as lacking effective social and family support systems. By contrast, none of the parents were reported to have drug or alcohol problems.

The adoptive families with whom the Trafford children were placed during the evaluation period were predominantly white, with only one family of mixed ethnicity. Three families had previously adopted other children and four already had biological children. Not all the new parents were interviewed at follow-up, but of the 14 that were, the mean age of the mothers was 42 (range 33–51) and of the fathers was 44 (range 32–54).

Comparison of referrals to the three concurrent planning projects with referrals to MAS Adoption Team and to the Trafford Adoption and Permanency Team

The total number of concurrent planning cases in each project was small, and the decision was taken to collate the figures for all three teams for the analyses. Considerable experience of the backgrounds to the cases suggested that there was no obvious bias in the selection procedures of any of the three concurrency groups that might make the cases they accepted distinctively different from the other teams. The projects were all running along very similar lines, even if there were some small organisational differences. Practice was very similar in the three projects, and, as we noted in Chapter 3, they had the advantage of sharing the professional guidance of the same consultant social worker.

Selecting the children and their birth families for inclusion in the concurrency programmes

Table 4.10 collates the figures from the three concurrency projects on the reasons why the majority of the children and babies referred to the teams could not be accepted.

Thus out of 219 children referred to the three projects, it can be seen that carers were not available for 95 (43 per cent) at the time of referral. Another 56 children (26 per cent) did not meet project admission criteria. It is interesting to note that, in an early report on the outcome of the

Table 4.10

Predominant reasons why the concurrency projects were unable to accept referrals

Referring local authorities	*Predominant reason for "rejection" by concurrency projects*	*Numbers of children*
Bury, Salford, Camden, Islington, Brighton & Hove	No suitable carers	
	i) Sibling group	55 (1×6; 1×4; 3×3; 10×2)
	ii) No match for ethnicity	24
	iii) Medical problems	5
	iv) No specific reason	11
	Sub-total	**95**
	Rehabilitation extremely unlikely	8
	No care proceedings at referral	4
	Did not meet project criteria, including:	56, including:
	i) To mainstream adoption	12
	ii) To birth family	21
	iii) Too old	2
	Reasons unknown, or case "open" or in discussion	27
	Died before placement decision	2
	Placed (including 3 pilot cases not included in the research evaluation)	27
	Total	**219**

Seattle project cases, Katz (1990) showed that, out of a total of 121 children referred to the project over the first four years who also met the intake criteria, 82 (68 per cent) could not be accepted because of the absence of suitable carers. As in the three UK projects, Katz also noted that many of the referrals came from large sibling groups, or from minority ethnic groups, or had medical problems.

Only one of the concurrency carers was black at the time of the evaluation project.[7] Five of the 24 families had previously adopted children, and six (different families) had biological children. The mean age of the women carers was 37 (range 28–46) and of the men was 39 (range 30–47). A comparison of these figures with the ages of the adoptive parents in the two mainstream samples (MAS and Trafford Adoption Team cases) showed that the Trafford mothers were significantly older on average than either the concurrency mother carers and father carers (respectively $F = 10.04$, 1df, $p<.004$, and $F = 6.48$, 1df, $p<.02$) or the MAS Adoption Team mothers and fathers (respectively $F = 11.38$, 1df, $p<.003$; and $F = 5.83$, 1df, $p<.03$). There is no obvious explanation as to why this is so.

Differential diagnosis: Strengths in Families and Poor Prognostic Indicators

Selecting the children and their birth families for whom concurrent planning is the appropriate model for assessment and support cannot be an exact science. Guidelines for estimating the chances that a family can be helped within a concurrency programme exist in the training materials published by Lutheran Social Services. The emphasis is on an early estimation of whether there are sufficient strengths in the birth family for rehabilitation to be feasible in the child's timescale.[8] The philosophy behind concurrent planning requires that the professionals clearly identify the possibility of change in the birth parents' lifestyle (for example, a new partner) or parenting skills or style. If such possibilities are absent, the chances are that

[7] It is known that four more black carers have since been recruited during early 2002.

[8] As we have noted in Chapter 2, the Framework for the Assessment of Children in Need and their Families (Department of Health, 2000) also includes the expectation that strengths within the family will be recorded along with their problems, and that 'parental and family strengths should be built on' (p 11).

the case would have been identified for traditional adoption and not been referred for the intensive concurrency work. However, it was clear that many of the local authority social workers who made referrals were not entirely clear about which families could benefit from the concurrent planning approach and asked the projects to take on inappropriate cases. Using the Differential Diagnosis can help to determine suitability, although professional judgment remains crucially important.

In the present study, concurrency workers assessed the Strengths in Families and the Poor Prognostic Indicators (PPI),[9] but tended to do this after the initial decision about whether or not to accept the case. The results of the checklist exercise might confirm or lead to a review of the decision. Neither of these checklists has established scores and cut-off points, but they provide the background to the overall judgment that concurrency teams will make about the suitability of a case.

At the request of the researchers, these checklists were completed for the concurrency cases and for children referred to the MAS Adoption Team and to the Trafford Adoption and Permanency Team. In these cases the ratings were not made by the adoption team workers, but by the field social workers with responsibility for early assessment of the family, who therefore knew them at the point when the children came into care.

Strengths in Families

Significant differences in the ratings made on the Strengths in Families (SiF) checklist were apparent between the concurrency cases and the cases referred to the two traditional adoption teams. In all except one dimension the concurrency team workers rated their cases more positively than the local authority social workers rated the cases referred to MAS or Trafford. The tables giving the full figures for the six dimensions of the SiF are given in Appendix I. What follows is a summary of these findings.

Within the "Parent–child relationship" dimension, the concurrent planning cases were judged to show aspects of a closely bonded relationship with their child significantly more frequently than in the comparison cases. Both present and past family support systems were also judged to be in

[9] These checklists are given in Appendix C.

place significantly more often for the concurrency cases. At first glance, this might appear surprising. However, it is likely that the better ratings on current and past family support systems and the family history for the concurrency cases may reflect the selection processes into the concurrent planning projects. We have seen that to be eligible, the concurrency birth parents needed to have some positive attributes in their family life or their own lifestyle that would enable them to work towards rehabilitation, and thus to "qualify" for inclusion in the concurrency work. It is likely, therefore, that these more positive scores among the concurrency cases are the result of the search for positive features of the birth family. One concurrency team leader emphasised exactly this point.

By contrast, the birth parents in the MAS and Trafford Adoption team samples had presumably moved beyond that stage: by definition, rehabilitation had been ruled out by the time the children were referred for adoptive placements. These latter samples were also highly selected groups of children, whose families did not show the strengths that professionals could build on to achieve rehabilitation. The differences were striking: for example, none of the Trafford children's families showed any evidence of the birth parents having supportive family systems, and two-thirds of the MAS children were also judged to lack family support systems. By contrast, just under half (45 per cent) of the birth parents whose children had been referred to the concurrency teams were judged to have families showing some evidence of current support systems (see Tables 2 and 3 in Appendix I).

The same pattern was evident in the next dimension in the SiF checklist. Significantly fewer of the birth parents in the Trafford and MAS Adoption Teams samples showed evidence of themselves having been brought up in families in which there was a strong tradition of mutual support and where their own childhood care had been of reasonable quality (Table 4, Appendix I).

The only aspect of the SiF in which there was no evidence of a difference between the placement groups was the Parents' Self-Care Abilities (Table 5, Appendix I). A surprisingly high proportion of the birth parents in all three placement groups had positive scores: over half the concurrency birth parents had ratings that indicated they had reasonable health, housing and work histories.

Finally, there were found to be differences in the age-appropriate level of the children's development between the placement groups (Table 6, Appendix I). However, half the children referred to the concurrency teams were not rated by the social workers on this set of items: for ten concurrency children who were referred at birth, several of the items were not applicable (see Appendix C for details of the questions in this section of the SiF checklist). Among the children who were rated it was clear that the concurrency children were, at the time of referral, less likely to show these aspects of age-related maturity. However, in the view of the researchers, this may be an artefact of the significantly younger age of the concurrency cases in which such judgments require considerable knowledge of child development.

Given the strong associations between the majority of the SiF sub-scores and the three placement groups, it is not surprising to find a significant association between the total SiF score and the placement groups (Table 4.11). However, at this point it becomes apparent that the distinctively disadvantaged group is of birth parents with children referred to MAS, where the large majority of cases had medium scores. It appears likely that the MAS Adoption Team are receiving referrals from adoption placement consortia and local authorities that have proved particularly hard to place; the lower (more negative) scores on the SiF suggesting how little chance of rehabilitation there has been in these families. The families referred to the concurrency projects are evenly spread across the "scores" for Family

Table 4.11
Total scores on the Strengths in Families checklist in the three placement groups

Total score on SiF checklist scores	*Placement by:* *MAS Adoption Team*		*Concurrency projects*		*Trafford A&P Team*	
	N	*%*	*N*	*%*	*N*	*%*
<7	1	6	7	30	8	38
7–13	16	89	7	30	9	43
14+	1	6	9	39	4	19
Totals	**18**	**100**	**23**	**100**	**21**	**100**

(N = 59; not known = 9) χ^2 =16.11, 4df, p = <.002 (Fisher's Exact test).

Strengths, but nearly 40 per cent were given high ratings, suggesting that there may be enough strengths to provide some chance of rehabilitation to the birth family.

Poor Prognostic Indicators

The Poor Prognostic Indicators (PPI) is also a checklist for professionals rather than, strictly speaking, a "diagnostic" tool. It provides guidelines for decisions about the suitability of referring a case to concurrent planning. The PPI breaks down into various sub-sections indicative of the following broad themes: catastrophic prior abuse by the parents (of the same or another child); parents' dangerous/criminal lifestyle; a parental history of serious child protection events; and inherent deficits in the birth parents. There were no significant relationships between any of the sub-sections of the Poor Prognostic Indicators, nor of any of the individual items with the three placement groups. This suggests that the items on the PPI tap into characteristics that are common in the lives of families from which children are taken into care. For example, all the children referred to the Trafford Adoption and Permanency Team, and all but two children (11 per cent) referred to the MAS Adoption Team, and all but three (15 per cent) referred to the concurrency teams came from families with a previous child protection history. A third of the parents in the concurrency projects and in the Trafford sample, and a fifth of those in the MAS Adoption Team sample were identified as drug or alcohol addicts. The incidence of recent domestic violence in the parents of the three samples was high: MAS – 22 per cent; Trafford – 29 per cent; the concurrency projects – 35 per cent. Total scores on the PPI checklist showed no significant differences between the three placement groups. In this aspect of family life the placement groups were similar, even if the SiF data differentiated between them.

Katz and Robinson (1991) identified five items on the PPI checklist that carried particularly poor prognoses: that a parent has killed or harmed another child; or tortured this child; that the parents' only visible means of support is drugs, prostitution or street life; that parental rights have been terminated to another child and no change has occurred in the interim; or that the parent is diagnosed with a severe mental illness that prevents effective or safe parenting. The presence of these five items would not, in their judgment, rule out the use of concurrent planning, but made rehabilitation to the birth parents themselves extremely unlikely. In the present sample of 59 children for whom information was available, the parents of 25 (42 per cent) were rated in one or more of these categories. However, there was no significant association between the total score on this group of high-risk items and the families within the three placement groups, emphasising again the similarity of the three groups in their adverse family characteristics.

Selecting the children into the concurrency projects

It is clear from the above that selecting children into concurrency projects was not systematic, but tended to be responsive to local needs. First, there were the constraints imposed by the recruitment of carers, who had their own expectations and hopes for the sort of child they wanted for their family. Some wanted siblings; some came from particular religious or ethnic backgrounds; some felt able to take children with disabilities; some wanted boys, some wanted girls. At all times the concurrency teams attempted to work with these hopes.

Second, the teams selected the cases where they could see that the parents might be able to make major changes to their lifestyle or parenting. An example may illustrate some of the difficulties inherent in these decisions. If a parent has a severe personality disorder and is judged to be unable to parent any children, this might argue for the child to be placed for adoption by the local authority. However, concurrent planning may be considered as a better model to answer the child's marked needs and one that puts the child's interests at the heart of the decision-making. In the first place the wider family can be speedily assessed. Second, the child can meanwhile move straight to the family of the concurrency carer, with which he or she stands a relatively high chance of spending the rest of his/her life. If the concurrent planning approach was not used, but the care plan was for adoption (which seemed very likely), the child would necessarily be placed with foster carers in the short term. How long this "short term" might be and how many moves might be involved before a permanent home was found can be judged from the statistics for this age group nationally. For children under one year at entry into care, legal status, ethnicity, and the presence of siblings have all been found to affect the length of time before a best interest decision in favour of adoption (Ivaldi, 2000). Age also affects the length of time between the best interest decision and the adoption placement. In both periods younger age was associated with less delay.

In our example, a white child aged 1–12 months at the time of starting to be looked after, with no siblings, might wait for an average period of up to 18 months before an agency decided to proceed with adoption and an average further six months to placement. Older children and black or mixed ethnicity children wait far longer than others both for best interest decisions and for adoptive placement. Children between 1 and 12 months old when starting to be looked after experience on average four placements in their first year in care (Ivaldi, 2000). Thus there were obvious advantages to the child in our example to be brought into the concurrent planning programme. The single most marked advantage for the child (too young to appreciate the legal milestones) is the opportunity for becoming securely attached to the concurrency carer, with a high probability that these parents will be hers or his for life. For the wider birth family there is the assurance that they had been fully assessed for their capacity to take the child in a timescale that served her or his needs.

The ages of the children at the time of referral to the three placement groups

Collating the figures from the three concurrent planning projects shows that a very high proportion of these children (96 per cent) were under one year at the time of placement with the carers (Table 4.12).

Placement of the concurrent planning cases was sometimes only weeks, and in a few cases, only a few months after the baby or child had been taken into local authority care. Children from the two comparison groups (MAS and Trafford Adoption Teams) were significantly older at placement than the concurrency team placements.[10]

Table 4.13 shows that there were significant differences in the ages of the children when they entered the care system in the three concurrency

[10] Comparing those placed in permanent care aged more or less than one year by the three placement groups: Fisher's Exact test $\chi^2 = 56.04$, 2df, $p<.001$.

Table 4.12

Ages of children at placement with concurrent planning carers: all concurrency projects (N = 24)

Age at referral to concurrency team	*Number*	*percentage*
Pre-birth or birth	13	54
Less than 6 months	10	42
1 year or more	1	4
Total	**24**	**100**

Table 4.13

Age at entry into care for children in the three placement groups

Age at entry into care	*Placement by:*					
	MAS Adoption Team		*Trafford A&P Team*		*Concurrency projects*	
	N	*%*	*N*	*%*	*N*	*%*
Less than 26 weeks	1	4	2	9	23	96
More than 26 weeks	22	96	19	91	1	4
Totals	**23**	**100**	**21**	**100**	**24**	**100**

$\chi^2 = 56.59$, 2df, p =<.001 (Fisher's Exact test).

projects compared with the MAS and Trafford Adoption Team cases. Two of the three concurrency projects were set up for very young children, and the third changed the pattern of placements to providing for children younger than the original expectation. In the research evaluation period, 96 per cent of the children referred to the three concurrency teams were under six months when they started being looked after. The reverse was true of the MAS and Trafford Adoption Teams: respectively 96 per cent and 91 per cent were over six months when they were taken into local authority care. The mean age at placement for the two comparison groups was very similar (MAS Adoption Team: 3 years 5 months; Trafford Adoption and Permanency Team: 3 years 3 months), but contrasted significantly with the mean age of the children in the three concurrency projects (6 months) [F = 26.75, 2df, p<.001].

This is a clear reflection of the recruitment criteria, particularly in Coram Family which recruited only under-twos from the start of the project. By contrast, there were no differences in the size of the families from which the children came, nor in the numbers of boys and girls in the three placement groups.

In the next two chapters we consider the experiences and views of the concurrency carers and the adoptive parents (Chapter 6) and the birth parents (Chapter 7) as they went through the processes associated with concurrent planning and with mainstream adoption.

Summary

- The characteristics of the children and their families at the time of being taken into care illustrate the important differences between the populations of the concurrency teams and the two comparison groups. The original intention of comparing samples matched for age was not possible as the three concurrency teams in reality only provided a service for very young children.
- The distinctive features of the children in the concurrent planning service in the present study can be gauged by comparing them with figures for children placed for adoption in England in 1998/9 (Ivaldi, 2000). In the country as a whole, only one-quarter of the children placed for adoption were under 12 months at the time of placement. In the present study, 82 per cent of the Goodman placements and all the Coram Family and Brighton & Hove concurrency placements were completed before the children were 12 months old.
- The concurrent planning cases were also untypical in that all the placements were of single children (although at later stages some concurrency carers took later-born sibs). In the comparison placement groups (MAS and Trafford Adoption Teams) a large number of siblings were placed together (Trafford – 14 children (66 per cent); MAS – 13 children (57 per cent)). In an analysis of adoption in England 1998/9, Ivaldi (*ibid*, p 37) recorded that just under 40 per cent of the adopted children had been placed with siblings.
- The children in the three placement groups[11] are not drawn from the same age groups, but – probably arising from that fact – also have

markedly different personal histories. The babies placed from birth with foster carers or concurrency carers will not have experienced directly the effects of inadequate, neglectful or abusive parenting. Decisions about not sending them home with birth parents were therefore largely based on the previous or current performance of the family, or the experience of older siblings, far less often on the child's own experiences. For the other two placement groups, the children were more likely to have been the subject of care proceedings initiated to rescue them from neglect or abuse; the high PPI scores for these two comparison groups will have tended to reflect the experiences of the children themselves. However, the lack of significant differences between the PPI scores for all three placement groups underlines how similar the families are, even when the concurrency children have not themselves experienced persistent or extensive abuse or neglect.

- The important difference between the concurrency cases and the comparison cases appeared to lie in the judgment by social workers that the birth parents might be able to change in the timescale set by the courts. The Strengths in Families checklist scores significantly distinguished the birth families of the concurrency cases from the birth families in the two comparison groups. The social workers completing this checklist clearly considered that there were at least some reasons why the concurrency birth parents might be able to look after their children again; but this was not true for the birth parents of the Trafford and MAS Adoption Teams' cases.
- Selecting children into concurrency projects was not systematic, but tended to be responsive to local needs and local circumstances. Out of 219 children referred to the concurrency projects, carers were not available for 95 (43 per cent); another 56 children (26 per cent) did not meet stringent project admission criteria that had been negotiated with the local authorities.

---

[11] Much of the analysis and comment from this chapter will use collated figures for the three concurrency projects. The "three placement groups" will refer to the MAS Adoption Team sample, the Trafford Adoption and Permanency Team sample and the collated sample from the combined concurrency project cases.

- In the judgment of the three concurrency teams, it has not been difficult to recruit carers to take on this complicated role, although the London project found difficulty in balancing the characteristics of the carers to the emerging needs of the two "feeder" boroughs.

5 Outcomes for the children

One of the most important aspects of the evaluation study was to assess whether the concurrent planning approach to finding permanent families for looked after children reduced the number of moves they experienced between families, and reduced the length of time that elapsed before their permanent family was found. The move to permanency could, as we have said, either be a return to their birth parents and/or another member of the birth family or to a new adoptive family. The experiences in terms of moves and timescales of the looked after children placed by the Trafford Adoption and Permanency Team and by the MAS Adoption Team were used as comparators. Bury and Salford also provided information on the outcomes for children who had been referred, but had not been accepted by the Goodman Project, but for whom care proceedings and possible adoption were being considered. The outcomes for these two latter groups were available only in terms of the dates of the Key Events, and the number of moves experienced by the children.

The number of moves children experienced before a permanent placement

National targets in England for reducing the numbers of moves experienced by looked after children were introduced for local authorities in 1999 (Department of Health, 1999b), but these targets were couched in terms of the whole looked after population, rather than for individual children. Clearly, there are some children for whom a move from one carer to another, even if not into a permanent placement, increases rather than decreases their life chances. At the time of writing, the target for local authorities is that no more than 16 per cent of children looked after should have had three or more placements in the previous year. This figure was based on the performance of the top quartile of local authorities over the previous three years (*ibid*, Annex A, p 3). By 1999/2000, roughly half-way through the present evaluation exercise, the six local authorities involved in the concurrency projects varied in the proportion of children with three or more placements in the previous year from 6 per cent (Trafford) to 20 per cent (Brighton & Hove).

For the large majority of the cases in the research evaluation, whether from the concurrent planning projects, from the MAS Adoption Team or from the Trafford Adoption and Permanency Team,[1] the children's last care episode was also their first care episode. The numbers of moves these children had experienced up to and including the move to a permanent family are given in Table 5.1. These figures refer to the total experience from the start of the last care episode to the end of the follow-up year for all except four children, who were, at follow-up, still living with the original foster carers. At the time of writing these children had not been placed for adoption. We have included each move: on this basis a child who moved from the hospital where she was born and where she had stayed for some weeks while being weaned from drug dependency, had one move. We have also included as "one move" the experience of a child who spent her first few days with her birth mother before going to a concurrency placement. These first few days with a parent are sometimes described as especially important in establishing the first phases of attachment. We have therefore included the move out of hospital and away from the mother as the first placement move. This is sometimes recorded as no moves *before* a permanency placement, but we would argue that each and every move away from the primary carer should be counted.

Using this definition of a move, Table 5.1 shows that ten concurrency cases (42 per cent) had experienced only one move, which reflects the large number of babies who were placed directly from hospital with concurrency carers. However, 58 per cent of concurrency cases had moved twice or more within the year since first coming into care. This group included children and babies who had spent some time with "traditional" foster carers before moving to concurrency carers. The overall figures in Table 5.1 apparently indicate significant differences between the three placement groups. However, further analysis showed that it was only the

---

[1] On occasion, and for the benefit of the reader, when these two sources of comparison data are referred to together we have used the combined term "MAS and Trafford Adoption Teams".

Table 5.1

The number of moves experienced by the children before permanence, or final research interview, by the three placement groups

Number of moves to permanence or final research interview	*MAS Adoption Team*		*Placement by: Trafford A&P Teams*		*Concurrency projects*	
	N	*%*	*N*	*%*	*N*	*%*
1 move only	–	–	4	19	10	42
2+ moves	23	100	17	81	14	58
Totals	**23**	**100**	**21**	**100**	**24**	**100**

Fisher's Exact Test: $\chi^2 = 13.33$, 2df, p =<.001.

experiences of the concurrency cases and the MAS Adoption Team cases that were statistically different. The number of moves experienced by the Trafford comparison group did not differ significantly from either the concurrency children or the MAS Adoption Team group.

The significant difference in the concurrency and the MAS Adoption Team children is not unexpected given the divergent circumstances of these two groups. One of the prime aims of the concurrency teams was to cut the number of moves the children experienced. Only two concurrency cases returned to birth family, leaving 22 out of 24 cases still in their concurrency placement, which became the potentially permanent adoptive placement after the final hearing. By comparison, in the MAS Adoption Team placements, the children will have moved from their birth parents to at least one foster placement before the adoption placement, so the *baseline* for these children is two moves. Several will have experienced more than two moves. The children referred for placement by the MAS Adoption Team are those for whom their own local authority has not been successful in finding a permanent family. This makes the Trafford Adoption and Permanency Team placements an interesting group in view of the apparent success in placing more of the children before they experience numerous moves.

One of the key differences between the groups that is essential to bear in mind when comparing these figures is that the concurrency children were significantly younger than the comparison cases when they first entered care (see Chapter 4, *Referrals*).

Tracking the children's progress to permanence

The time taken to resolve impermanence is regarded by professionals as of considerable importance for looked after children, because of the impact of impermanence and uncertainty on attachment, and – though with less evidence – on behaviour. The *Prime Minister's Review of Adoption* (Performance & Innovation Unit, 2000) cited figures on the care careers of looked after children in England and Wales, showing that a child who had stayed in care for more than six months had a 60 per cent chance of staying in care for four years or more (*ibid*, p 83). These data showed how urgent was the need for ensuring that children did not drift in the system.

In response to these concerns, the Department of Health funded the development of National Standards that could be used to track the progress of children's cases through the care proceedings to adoption (Department of Health, 2001a). This tool is intended to give managers the information they need to avoid delays in decision-making for every looked after child. Guidelines now exist for recording the length of time taken at each stage before a permanency plan is completed. Early work by the Catholic Children's Society, Nottingham (CCS) and the LB of Richmond upon Thames (LBRuT) with other organisations, tracked the progress of three groups of children from the start of the last care episode to adoption. The group most relevant to the concurrent planning cases are those under five years who are subject to care proceedings, as all concurrency cases are. The LBRuT research identified the Key Events in the care careers of these children for each of which a target could be set for completion of that stage. Thus, the stage from the start of the last care episode to permanence becoming the care plan lasted on average six months. From these data it appeared that the CCS under-fives who were subject to care proceedings waited on average 33 months before the Adoption Order was granted, and similar children in the LBRuT research group waited on average 31.5 months. The average time quoted in the *Review of Adoption* (*ibid*, p 85) from the 1998/9 BAAF survey was also 33 months to adoption order. The National Standards (Department of Health, 2001a and 2001b) for the children subject to care proceedings[2] proposed timescales for the early stages of adoption proceedings that are the clear responsibility of the local authority (i.e. up to the child's placement). The Government, however, judged that it was not appropriate to provide similar guidelines for the subsequent stages of the proceedings, because these are at least partly in the hands of the courts. It is known that the pressure on court time is considerable, but there is the prospect of improvement in the future as more emphasis is placed on monitoring the progress of cases involving children. It is worth noting that the experience of one programme in the USA suggested that the timescales inherent in a good concurrent planning project caused pressure on courts, processes and procedures.[3] The LBRuT research identified from their own figures on the post-placement stages that it would not be unreasonable to set an average of 30 months from the start of the last care episode to the granting of the Adoption Order, and an average of 16 months from adoption placement to Adoption Order.[4]

However, as we noted in Chapter 3, at least one concurrency team considered that the National Standards were not wholly appropriate when tracking the progress of concurrent planning cases. The key stages that we have preferred to use for concurrent planning cases are noted in Table 5.2 (below): the length of time from the start of the last care episode to placement with the concurrency carer, from placement to the Care Order, and finally from Care Order to Adoption Order.[5] The amendment of the national schema takes account of the fact that the Court agrees the concurrency placement that *might* become an adoptive placement before, not after, the final hearing Court Order. The schema proposed by the concurrency teams would appear to be an effective way of recording the timing of the Key Events in concurrent planning, and it will be used therefore in this report.[6]

---

[2] All the concurrent planning cases were subject to care proceedings.

[3] Personal communication.

[4] Personal communication: LBRuT.

[5] For any child returning to her family, permanence is agreed at the time of the Care Order, although there may be supervision or residence orders granted at the same time. These children's cases have been excluded from the tables assessing time taken to Adoption Orders.

[6] With acknowledgements to the Brighton and Hove concurrency team.

There are two ways in which the progress of the children in the evaluation study may be presented: in graphical format (e.g. Figure 5.1) or in tabular format (e.g. Table 5.2). Figure 5.1 shows the profiles for the three concurrent planning projects, and Table 5.2 shows the figures. Two projects had very similar profiles; in the other, there were delays in granting Adoption Orders for several children, and for one child it still had not been granted at the time of writing. For this analysis, the two concurrent planning cases that returned to their birth families have been included in the calculation about the time to the Care Order, as this was the point of decision about permanence.

Figure 5.1
Average months to achieve Key Events in three concurrent planning projects

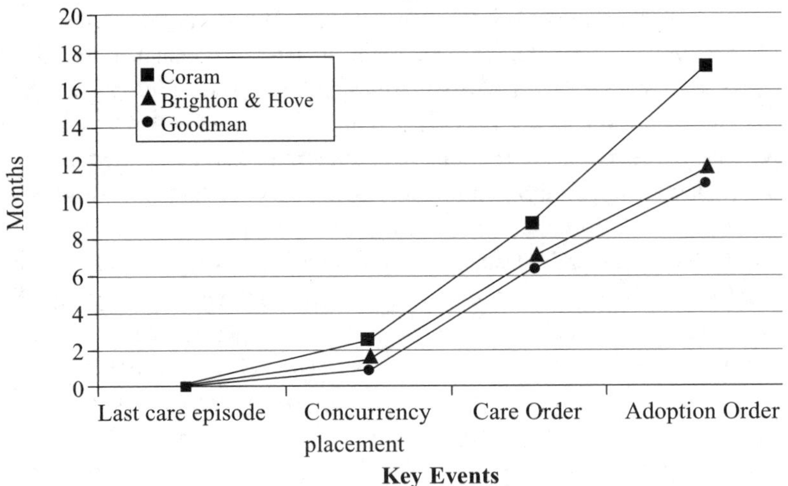

An exact comparison of each Key Event stage with the cases placed by the two traditional adoption teams is not possible, as the placement with the mainstream adoptive family only occurs *after* the Care Order confirms adoption as the care plan. In a strict sense this is also true for the concurrency cases. The granting of the Care Order changes the temporary "holding" placement with the concurrency carers into a permanent placement, or the child returns to his birth family as a permanent placement.

Table 5.2
Average length of time between Key Events for children in the three concurrent planning projects (months)

Three concurrent planning (CP) projects	*Last care episode to concurrency placement*	*Concurrency placement to Care Order*	*Care Order to Adoption Order*	*Last care episode to Adoption Order*
Goodman Project (N = 8)*	0.9	5.3	4.0**	10.9**
Coram Family Project (N = 7)	2.5	6.3	8.8***	17.2***
Brighton & Hove CP Team (N = 9)	1.4	5.4	4.9	11.7

* Only the eight children in the evaluation research are included here.
** Seven children; one returned to birth family.
*** Six children; one returned to birth family.

As we have seen, the purpose of the concurrency placement is to provide a permanent placement "in-waiting" that will only change if the birth family can offer sufficient security and stability for the courts to make an Order in their favour. Table 5.3 and Figure 5.2 both show the length of time between the start of the last care episode and the placement of the child in a potentially permanent family (concurrency placement or adoptive placement). Additionally, the table and the figure show the total time between the start of the last care episode and the granting of the Adoption Order.

The concurrent planning cases experienced roughly half the length of time between being taken into care and achieving full adoption status as the cases placed by Trafford A&P Team, and a third as long as the MAS Adoption Team placements. We have already drawn attention to the fact that the concurrency children were significantly younger than the children in the two comparison groups and that none of them were in sibling groups (Chapter 4); direct comparisons are therefore hard to make. The different timescales in the two comparison groups can probably be explained by the fact that the children referred to the MAS Adoption Team were largely

Table 5.3

Comparison of selected stages in the achievement of permanent placements in the three placement groups: average months

Three placement groups	*Start of last care episode to adoption placement or concurrency placement*	*Adoption placement or concurrency placement to Adoption Order*	*Total looked after status to Adoption Order*
MAS Adoption Team (N = 23)	23.2	13.5	36.7
Trafford A&P Team (N = 15)**	15.4	8.5	23.9
Concurrency Projects (N = 22)*	1.5	11.6*	13.1*

* In the concurrency projects, two children returned home to relatives.

** Adoption Orders had not been granted for six children at the time of writing.

Figure 5.2

Selected stages in achieving permanency in three placement groups

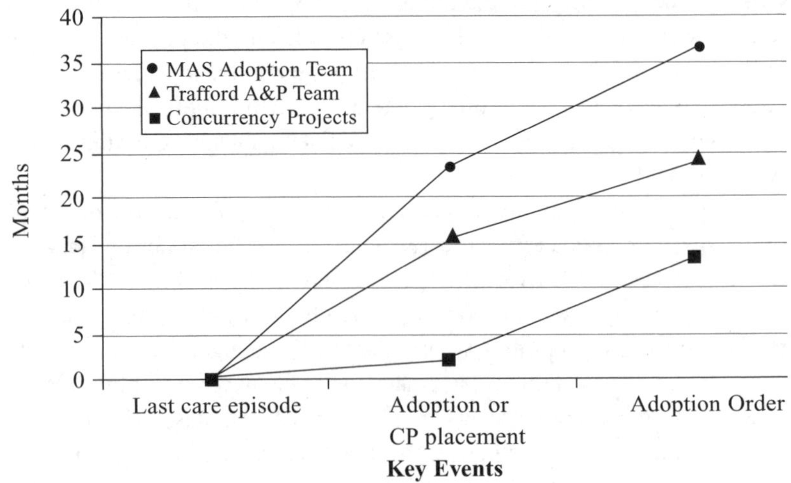

those for whom local authorities had not been successful in finding adoptive placements. The absence of earlier success in placing these children appears to add considerably to the total time before an adoptive placement is found.[7]

Since the comparison groups in the present study proved to be significantly different in important characteristics, a more useful comparison is with national figures for England of children under one year when taken into care. Table 5.4 compares the average number of months spent in selected stages before permanent placement for looked after children entering care aged under one year and adopted during the year ending March 2001 (extracted from Figure 1.6, p 17; Department of Health, 2002a), and the concurrent planning cases in the present study. As we have explained (Chapter 3), only some of the Key Events and stages are shared by the two procedures: these Key Events have been selected for presentation here. It is also important to recognise that, while none of the concurrent planning children were placed with siblings, this may not have been true for the children in the England sample. On the other hand, some of the concurrent planning children had special needs, in which respect they may have been comparable to the national cohort, although we do not have exact figures. Figure 5.3 gives the same data in graphic form. These data indicate very considerable differences between the two groups, with the children in the concurrent planning projects waiting on average less than half as long before the Adoption Order was granted compared with the national cohort.

One further recent UK comparison may be of interest. Harwin and Owen (2002), in a study funded by the Department of Health, followed up 100 children from 57 families to assess the outcomes of their care plans. For 33 children the placement plan at final hearing was adoption, and the majority of these were under two years old. However, for only 19 (58 per cent) was the adoption plan completed within the 21-month follow-up period. On average, it took these 19 children about 10 months to join their adoptive families: 13 of the 19 children took less than a year.

---

[7] The Director of MAS reports this was less of a problem in 2002 than when the Goodman Project first began.

Table 5.4

Average months spent at selected stages before adoption for children looked after before the age of 12 months (year ending 31 March 2001) (England) compared with concurrent planning (CP) cases

	Time from last care episode to confirmed placement for adoption (Care Order for CP cases)	*Time from placement (Care Order for CP cases) to Adoption Order*	*Total time last care episode to Adoption Order*
England: under 1 year	15.5 m	11 m	26.5 m
Concurrent planning cases*	7.0 m	5.7 m**	12.9 m**

* Excludes the only case over one year old at the start of care.

** Excludes two children who returned to birth families.

Figure 5.3

Average months spent in selected stages to Adoption Order: England under 1 year and concurrent planning cases

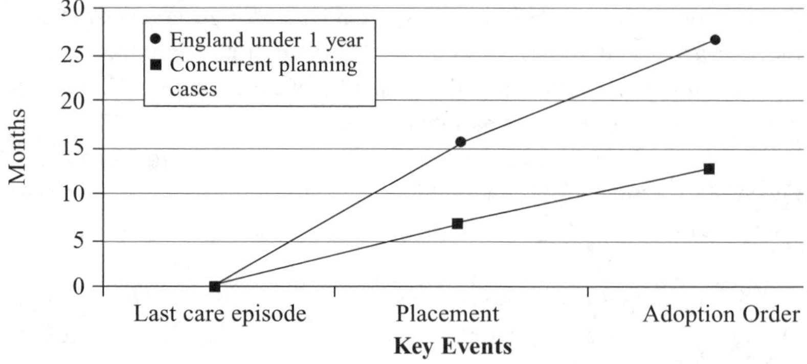

Returning to the present sample, it should be noted that in the Trafford sample the children whose cases had not progressed to full Adoption Orders already showed some tendency to have spent longer between the start of the last care episode and placement for adoption. At the time of writing, six Trafford Adoption and Permanency Team children's placements had not progressed to the granting of Adoption Orders, but all had been matched and placed for adoption. For these six children, the time between the start of the last care episode and the adoptive placement was on average 23.4 months compared with 15.4 months for the 15 children with Adoption Orders. It is possible that the six without full Adoption Orders may have been particularly hard to place, and that the adoptive parents subsequently met problems with the placements that meant they preferred or were advised not to progress to an Adoption Order application until the children had settled down. It is sometimes the case that adoptive parents prefer to leave the responsibility for the children's well-being in the hands of the local authority and the family social worker who knows them best, and only when initial problems have been settled, do they complete the adoption applications that would transfer that responsibility to the local authority where the family lives.

In the MAS Adoption Team sample, the opposite was true: the average wait in this early stage (between coming into care and placement for adoption) for the seven children who had no Adoption Orders was 18.7 months, compared with 23.3 months for those with Adoption Orders. Five of these seven cases entered the evaluation study later on; it is possible a longer follow-up time would have seen the granting of Adoption Orders.

The length of time in impermanent care

Part of the picture given above concerns the amount of time spent in impermanent care. The difference between the three placement groups is marked. We have seen (Chapter 4) that a high proportion of the concurrent planning cases were placed with their concurrency carers from hospital, and, with one exception, all were placed with concurrency carers before age 12 months. However, technically this placement is still impermanent. Any comparison with the children placed by Trafford and MAS Adoption Teams assesses "permanence" not from the concurrency placement, but from the Care Order that confirms where the child will live permanently. Legally they remain as foster placements until the final hearing and the Care Order.

The MAS and Trafford Adoption Team placements, on the other hand, were significantly older when they came into care, and many more of them were in sibling groups (Chapter 4). Almost by definition, therefore, these children would have been harder to place; the extended time in impermanent care is therefore less surprising. Table 5.5 shows that the MAS and Trafford Adoption Team children spent significantly longer in impermanent care than the concurrency cases.

Table 5.5

Months spent in impermanent care before adoptive placement (MAS and Trafford Adoption Teams' cases) or Care Order/final hearing (concurrent planning cases)

Placement groups	*Number of children*	*Mean no. months in impermanent care*	*Std deviation*	*Range*
MAS Adoption Team	23	18.96	6.52	6–30
Trafford A&P Team	21	16.52	4.83	9–25
Concurrency projects	24	7.20	2.44	3.5–12
Total	**68**	**13.99**	**7.20**	**3.5–30**

F 37.76, 2df, sig. <.001.

The difference between the length of impermanent care experienced by the MAS Adoption Team cases and that of the Trafford Adoption and Permanency Team cases is not significant. The length of time spent in impermanent care by the concurrency cases was, however, significantly less than either the Trafford cases (F 71.9, 1df, p<0.001) or the MAS cases (F 66.03, 1df, p<.001).

As we have noted in Chapter 3, the concurrent planning cases have a particular set of milestones (Key Events) that do not have exact parallels in traditional adoption cases: this makes it difficult to compare the intermediate stages on the route to permanency. The closest parallels that can be found are in the length of time from the date of the last care episode to the final hearing for the concurrency cases (at which the Care Order for permanence is established), and the date of the last care episode to the adoption placement for the MAS and Trafford Adoption Teams' cases. Even in this, the comparisons are not strictly valid: the concurrency cases carry a much higher risk of not going through to an adoption hearing after placement with the concurrency carer (in the data from LSS, Seattle, the proportion of children returning to birth families runs at roughly 15 per cent) than the adoption placements do of failing.

Cases referred but not accepted into the Goodman Project

Bury and Salford SSDs provided information on the care careers of some of the children who were referred to the Goodman Project but (for the reasons reported in Chapter 4) were not accepted into concurrent planning. Information was not available for all these children: Table 5.6 gives the numbers for whom information was or was not available from the authorities. The researchers did not obtain similar information on children referred, but not accepted, into the other two concurrent planning projects, but there is no obvious reason why the pattern of the children's care careers would be significantly different from those of the Bury and Salford children.

Using the same tracking system as for the concurrent planning cases, we tried to assess the outcomes for the Bury and Salford children who were not accepted into the Goodman Project. For a number of cases the information[8] was minimal, but it appeared that, among the 46 children

Table 5.6

The availability of information for children referred by Bury and Salford to the Goodman Project, but not accepted

	Bury	*Salford*
Referred but not accepted by Goodman	32	51
i) information available	21	25
ii) untraced	11*	21* 5**

* Original referral had no name or date of birth attached (usually pre-birth telephone enquiry).

** Original referral was named but no subsequent trace in LA records.

[8] Information accurate at end March 2002.

for whom information was sufficient to track some part of their care career, the following pattern emerged: 12 children were rehabilitated to family members,[9] 14 had moved to adoptive placements, and 17 children had Adoption Orders granted. The average time between coming into care and the adoption placement was 11.2 months and 18.9 months up to the Adoption Orders.

It can be seen that the results for these children were closer to those for the Trafford Adoption and Permanency Team's cases than the MAS Adoption Team cases. At the time of referral to the Goodman Project by Bury and Salford social workers, these children had tentatively been identified for adoption, although obviously with the rider that intensive work with the birth parents might lead to their return home. A quarter (12/46) were returned home by the two local authorities. Although the reasons why they were not accepted into the Goodman concurrent planning project may have been more to do with the absence of suitable concurrency carers, it is also possible that the Goodman team would not have found the cases suitable for concurrent planning. It is not possible to quantify this point.

Measuring the children's development through the evaluation period

We next turn to the more direct and individual measures used to record the children's behaviour and development at the start and end of the evaluation period (12–15 months).

As we have noted (Chapter 2) the Looking After Children checklists that we used to record the children's capabilities are not designed to identify the "normal" or "abnormal" child (*cf*, the Strengths and Difficulties Questionnaire (SDQ) – see below). The LAC checklists are designed to record the current capabilities and behaviour of the children in different age bands. The LAC checklists used in the present survey were for the following age bands:

i) Emotional and behavioural development: aged under 12 months; 1 and 2 years.

[9] Although dates and legal status were missing for 11 children.

ii) Attachment: aged under 12 months; 1 and 2 years; 3 and 4 years.
iii) Self-care skills: ages 1 and 2 years; 3 and 4 years.

When children moved from one age band to another, in terms of these checklists, the new checklist was used. The checklist items for the under 12 months, and the 1–2-year-olds are substantially the same.

For children over four years, the SDQ was completed by parents (foster, foster-adopt, or adoptive) and when appropriate (and with permission from parents or the local authority) by teachers or nursery staff.

The attachment questions from the LAC Assessment and Action Records remained the same for children in all age bands (see Appendix B).

First interviews and follow-up interviews

MAS Adoption Team

Fifteen adoptive families who were recruited by the MAS Adoption Team were interviewed by the researchers, representing 77 per cent of the families recruited by the Adoption Team in the three years of the evaluation study. All these families were interviewed shortly after the placement of the 23 children who form the MAS Adoption Team sample. Only 13 families with 17 children were seen at the 12-month follow-up; four children were placed with two families too late for the 12-month follow-up interview to be included within the research timetable. In the year-end interview the 13 sets of parents were interviewed and data were collected using the same questionnaires as at the start of the study. Parents were also asked about the dates of Key (adoption) Events and about the health and behaviour of the children, how long it had taken to settle in, and what help they had received from the child's local authority or the adoption teams.

Trafford Adoption and Permanency Team

Twenty-one looked after children and their foster carers were seen at the time of the referral of the children's cases to the Adoption and Permanency Team, i.e. before the adoptive placement. At the end of the year, four children were still with their Trafford foster families, who completed the questionnaires, for the second time. The remaining 17 children had been placed with adoptive parents, and the majority of these new parents completed the questionnaires and were happy to be interviewed. However, three families (with five children) declined to be interviewed, although one family nevertheless completed the questionnaires (while preferring not to be visited).

Concurrency cases

In all there were 24 concurrent planning cases across the three projects.[10] Because the numbers within each project were relatively small we have chosen to combine the results. Statistical comparison of the children in the three concurrent planning projects was not feasible with such small numbers, but the general impression was that they were not dissimilar in their demographic characteristics (gender and age), and the course of the care arrangements was similar.

All 24 concurrency carers except two were interviewed within eight weeks of the placement of the child. These two concurrency families were seen several months after the child had been placed, because one project joined the evaluation at a later stage. It was judged inappropriate to collect data retrospectively on the development and behaviour of the two children placed in these families. Eleven of the 24 concurrency families were seen at Time 2; for most of those who were not seen the follow-up date lay well outside the research timetable. This reflects the relatively slow build up of cases in all three projects.

The parental assessment of children's behaviour and development: the younger children

As the checklists and questionnaires were age-specific, it was not always possible to use exactly the same questionnaire at the start and end of the study. If, for example, a child was aged three at the time of the first interview and aged four plus at follow-up, the SDQ would be used at the second visit, but could not have been used at the first visit. By contrast the attachment questions were repeated because they were the same for all age groups.

[10] Three cases in the Goodman Project were used to pilot the interviews and questionnaires; they have been excluded from the following analyses.

Table 5.7

"Looking After Children" checklists used for children under 5 years in three placement groups: Time 1

Age groups of Looking After Children checklists	*Trafford placements with foster carers*		*MAS placements with adoptive families*		*Concurrent planning placements with carers*		*Numbers of children rated on LAC checklists*
	N	*%*	*N*	*%*	*N*	*%*	
Under 12 months	4	24	2	12	21	95	27
1 and 2-year-olds	6	36	11	65	0	0	17
3 and 4-year-olds	7	41	5	29	1	5	13
Totals rated on LAC checklists*	**17**	**100**	**18**	**100**	**22****	**100**	**57**

* The remaining children were assessed on the SDQ only: i.e. 4 Trafford and 6 MAS children.

** Two children were not assessed on the LAC checklists, but were under 12 months at placement; they were seen by researchers too long after placement to collect this information.

Table 5.8

"Positive scores" given by parents and carers on LAC checklists: Time 1

	Number of children rated by parents and carers	*Total possible score*	*Cut-off point*	*Children scoring "Positively"* *N*	*%*
Emotional and behavioural scores					
Children aged under 1 year	27	45	37/38	22	81.4
Children aged 1 and 2 years	15	30	25/26	12	80.0
Everyday skills					
Children aged 1 and 2	16	12	7/8	6	37.5
Children aged 3 and 4	13	14	8/9	12	92.0

It is worth recalling that the numbers in each age group (under 12 months, 1 and 2-year-olds; and 3 and 4-year-olds) were unevenly spread across the referral groups: 21 of the 24 concurrent planning cases were rated on the under-12 months checklist at the first interview (Time 1), compared with only four Trafford cases and two MAS cases (total = 27). The figures for each age group are given in Table 5.7.

At Time 1, the LAC checklists were completed by foster carers (in Trafford), MAS adoptive parents and the concurrent planning concurrency carers six weeks after placement (with the exception of two concurrent planning cases already mentioned). There are no established norms for the LAC checklists so we have chosen not to present the results in terms of how many children fell into a category that might cause concern to professionals.[11] It became clear, however, that the very large majority of concurrency carers rated the children and babies at the first interview as having almost no serious behavioural or psychological problems, although some had medical problems. Table 5.8 shows the proportions of children who were rated "positively" on the LAC checklists by their parents and carers (the working definitions of "positive" scores are given in Chapter 2, but the total possible scores and the cut-off points are included in the tables below as an *aide memoire*).

At Time 2 very similar proportions of the children were rated positively by the parents and carers (Table 5.9).

Parental assessment of children aged 4 years and over: the Strengths and Difficulties Questionnaire

The SDQ was used to rate the behaviour, mood and sociability of the children aged four years and over (N = 23). The pro-social scores are identified separately from ratings that indicate the presence of difficulties; the latter four sub-scores are added together to give a score of Total Difficulties. The expectation is that in a community (i.e. non-clinic)

---

[11] Bailey *et al* (2002) sought information on which looked after children in one authority might be "causing concern", in the sense that their progress was "below average" or "poor", but this information was gained from other sources in addition to the LAC checklists. They clearly considered that the LAC checklists would not, by themselves, provide sufficient information for social workers to make the necessary judgments.

Table 5.9
"Positive scores" given by parents and carers on LAC checklists: Time 2

	Number of children rated by parents and carers	*Total possible score*	*Cut-off point*	*Children scoring "Positively" N*	*%*
Emotional and behavioural scores					
Children aged 1 and 2 years	19	45	37/38	15	78.9
Everyday skills					
Children aged 1 and 2	19	12	7/8	4	21.0
Children aged 3 and 4	14	14	8/9	14	100.0

population, roughly 80 per cent of the children would have "normal" scores, 10 per cent borderline and 10 per cent "abnormal". As the children in the present sample would generally be regarded as "at risk" of behavioural difficulties, the "cases" have been identified as those with a high or borderline score (Goodman, 1997). Unlike the LAC checklists, the SDQ has established cut-off points determining the range of "normal", borderline or "abnormal" scores (Table 5.10).

At Time 1

These data were collected from foster carers (Trafford) or adoptive parents (MAS comparison group). None of the concurrency children were over four years at placement.

It is important to be reminded that these Time 1 data were collected when the children had only been with their new families for about six weeks. Among the SDQ ratings at Time 1 that reveal disturbed behaviour, the proportion with "borderline/abnormal" scores was well over the 20 per cent that would be expected in a community population for hyperactive behaviour, conduct problems and the domain of peer relationships. Only on emotional symptoms did the children score near the level expected within a community group. Interestingly, the children's pro-social scores were also close to those that would be expected from a community sample. The children were particularly likely to be showing evidence of conduct

Table 5.10
Normal and abnormal/borderline scores on the Strengths and Difficulties Questionnaire for children over age 4: Time 1 (N = 23)

SDQ sub-scales	*Parents' SDQ scores*					
	"Normal" scores		*"Abnormal" or borderline scores*		*Total number of children*	
	N	*%*	*N*	*%*	*N*	*%*
Pro-social behaviour	18	78	5	22	23	100
Hyperactive behaviour	14	61	9	39	23	100
Emotional disturbance	17	74	6	26	23	100
Peer relationships	15	65	8	35	23	100
Conduct disturbance	11	48	12	52	23	100
Total scores for disturbed behaviour	**15**	**65**	**8**	**35**	**23**	**100**

problems. As is often noted in the literature on adoption, several were reported as having found the move to the adoptive home very stressful. Equally, some adoptive parents were in turn stressed by the arrival of children – for many this was the first time they had lived with children in their household (see Chapter 6). However, even with the disturbed children, most parents found that the pre-adoption preparation work gave them the means to ride out the stress. We were told that one child with marked behaviour problems in the early weeks had settled reasonably well after six months:

> *The first few weeks were very hard work and sometimes we wondered what we had done. [The child] was very demanding and we had to adjust to having someone else in the house. But now we have a good relationship. She was mine the moment I clapped eyes on the photo. I thought we would get a raving barmy child, so it's been great.*

At Time 2

SDQ scores were available for a total of 29 children, including some children who were not old enough for the SDQ rating at Time 1. Ratings at both Time 1 and Time 2 were available for only 19 children. The

Table 5.11

Comparison of adoptive parents' and carers' Strengths and Difficulties Questionnaire scores for children over age 4 at Time 1 and Time 2 (N = 19)

Parents' and carers' Strengths and Difficulties ratings	*Wilcoxon signed ranks tests:* Z	*2-tailed significance*	*Effect size* r
Pro-social scores	–1.57	.116	0.36
Hyperactivity	–.75	.452	0.18
Emotional problems	– .35	.724	0.08
Conduct problems	–1.93	.054	0.44
Peer group problems	–1.79	.073	0.41
Total Difficulties Scores	**–1.31**	**.191**	**0.31**
Number of children	19		

important issue for parents and carers was whether any problems they faced at Time 1 had remained as problems or diminished over the following months, and for this it was necessary to look at the scores for the 19 children for whom we have a SDQ record at both data collection points. Although the overall picture for the group looks promising, a comparison of the scores at Time 1 and Time 2 for each individual child established that there were no significant improvements over time on any of the sub-scores or on the Total Difficulties score. However, the conduct problems scores at Time 2 came close to being significantly reduced compared with Time 1 (Table 5.11). The size of the sample provides some confidence in these results; medium effect sizes can be observed for pro-social scores, conduct problems, peer group problems and Total Difficulties scores.[12]

For the group of 19 children for whom there were scores at both Time 1 and Time 2, conduct problems were reported in fewer children (from five children (26 per cent) to one child (5 per cent)), and the number of children with "borderline/abnormal" Total Difficulties scores had reduced from six (32 per cent) to two (10 per cent). Hyperactivity remained as the one area in which parents still reported relatively high levels of

[12] Cohen (1988) has suggested that 0.20, 0.30 and 0.50 represent weak, medium and strong effect sizes respectively.

disturbance, with an identical number of children (seven: 37 per cent) showing "borderline/abnormal" scores at Time 1 and Time 2. Deutsch *et al* (1982) noted that a significantly higher proportion of adopted children meet the diagnostic criteria for Attention Deficit Disorder, and Fahlberg (1994) suggests that these children, even when very young, may be hypersensitive to external stimuli. Only one child still showed a "borderline/ abnormal" score on the pro-social scale.

Teachers' assessments of the children aged four years and over on the SDQ

The teachers of 12 children over the age of four years completed the SDQ at Time 1; two children over four years were not in school or nursery class. At Time 2, eleven children were rated by teachers. As with the parental ratings, the important issue is whether the children had individually made progress during the follow-up period. Unfortunately, teacher ratings were available for only six children at both time points. The results are therefore insufficiently robust to draw any conclusions, but are given in Table 5.12 as indicating the direction of the children's progress.

Table 5.12

Comparison of teachers' SDQ scores for children rated at Time 1 and at Time 2

SDQ sub-scales	*Teachers' Strengths and Difficulties Scores*			
	Abnormal and borderline scores		*Abnormal and borderline scores*	
	Time 1		***Time 2***	
	N	*%*	*N*	*%*
Pro-social behaviour	3	50	1	17
Hyperactive behaviour	4	67	3	50
Emotional disturbance	0	0	0	0
Relations with peers	2	33	0	0
Conduct disorder	3	50	3	50
Total Difficulties score	**2**	**33**	**2**	**33**
Total children	**6**	**100**	**6**	**100**

For this small group of children, hyperactivity and conduct disorder behaviour stand out as not improving so much as the other items on the SDQ. There was no evidence of significant improvement for the six children on any of the items over the follow-up period.

Parents' and carers' assessment of the children's attachment to household members

In the BAAF Practice Note, *Planning for Permanence* (1996), attachment is presented as the first of the key arguments in support of seeking permanent families (p 3), and is identified as being at the core of the child's emotional development. Trafford foster carers, MAS adoptive parents and concurrency carers were asked to rate the level of the child's attachment both to the parental figures and to any other children in the household on the simple attachment questionnaire included in the LAC assessment records. The results were very positive.

Table 5.13 shows that, at Time 1, the very large majority of children and babies were reported as "closely attached" to their mother carers, to their father carers and to the other children in the household. This was despite only having been in the household for about six weeks before the Time 1 interview. The brief questionnaire was filled in by mothers, which may in part account for the slight disparity in the scores for mothers and fathers. Both at Time 1 and Time 2 there are different totals for "mothers", "fathers" and "other children" in the households; this reflected the fact that some children were in the care of single parents and carers, and for one-third of the 68 cases there were no other children in the household.

Again it is important to bear in mind that information was not available for all the children at Time 2. In addition, when considering the Trafford children placed with adopters during the year, the parent or carer who did the second rating was a different person from the foster carer who rated them at Time 1.[13]

It is noticeable that the attachment ratings, both at the start and end of the follow-up period, are remarkably "positive". This may arise from using a measure that, for the babies and small children (the majority of

[13] Except for the four Trafford children for whom there was no new placement, who were rated by the same foster carer as at Time 1.

the sample), was not particularly sensitive. The results may therefore be reflecting the inadequacy of the measure to pick up all the nuances in the attachment between the carers and these babies and toddlers. However, all these families were seen face-to-face for nearly an hour and the younger index children were nearly always present.[14] The researchers' observations, though not systematically collected or co-rated, appeared repeatedly to confirm what the carers were reporting: a high level of "engagement", mutual responsiveness, the child showing pleasure in the carers' company, and general contentment. The concurrency carers were, almost without exception, delighted with the arrival of their "new" baby or toddler, and lavished considerable attention and affection on them. With these young children, this adult

Table 5.13

Attachment of children to household members reported by mothers six weeks after placement (Time 1) and at follow-up (Time 2)

Attachment with:	*Proportion "closely attached"*			
	***Time 1** (N = 66)*		***Time 2** (N = 48)*	
	N	*%*	*N*	*%*
"Mother"	51	77	44	92
Total "mothers"	66	100	48	100
Attachment with:	*Proportion "closely attached"*			
	Time 1		***Time 2***	
	N	*%*	*N*	*%*
"Father"	40	66	39	89
Total "fathers"	60	100	44	100
Attachment with:	*Proportion "closely attached"*			
	Time 1		***Time 2***	
	N	*%*	*N*	*%*
Other children in the family	39	83	34	92
Total other children	47	100	37	100

[14] Parents and carers sometimes chose to see the researchers when the index child was at school.

behaviour seems to have elicited strong and engaged responses from the children, if not immediately, then after the first few weeks of living together. The researchers were probably seeing the Positive Interaction Cycle graphically described and illustrated by Fahlberg (1994, p 29). The following quotations illustrate this point.

"Traditional" adoptive mother: *I used to worry that I wouldn't be able to love an adopted child as much as my own, but this child has given rise to such love and affection. It felt like I had a whole new bundle of love. We have just grown to like each other.*

Adoptive father: *It feels like we have always had [the child] – I wouldn't be without him. He loves being around us, and likes to help, but if he's tired he comes for a cuddle.*

Mother: *H. is an affectionate child and loves being kissed and cuddled. When H. first came to us, she didn't want any contact with me, having been more used to having a closer relationship with the foster father. But now H. has latched on to me, and doesn't like me to leave. H. is fine if going out with my mother, and leaving me in the house, but I cannot leave them both here and go out. But after only three months we think she is the perfect child for us, and it feels as though she has been here since birth, and is just ours now.*

Mother: *J. is very loving and genuinely happy, has a good sense of humour and enjoys teasing us. J. likes physical affection, and is very closely attached to us both. The foster placement was definitely not a negative experience, the best, given that she could not be placed with us from birth. There were lots of big hugs and learning to share with other children.*

Fahlberg (*ibid*, p 30) has described how, in infant adoptions, 'the processes of attachment and bonding are similar to those which occur when a baby' remains in her own family. She notes that the child occupies a place of 'particular value to the family', and the researchers can report that this appeared to be the case in the present study. With the exception of the Trafford foster carers rating children at Time 1, all the children were being rated by adoptive parents or concurrency carers who hoped to adopt the child. The pleasure in the newly arrived child may be particularly acute for these families and, in turn, may have contributed to the positive ratings on attachment. However, it is worth noting that there was no statistically significant differences at Time 1 between the three placement groups in the proportion of parents/carers who reported "close attachment". Ninety per cent of the Trafford foster carers reported the children as closely attached, compared with 70 per cent of the MAS Adoption Team placements and 74 per cent of the concurrency placements. The Trafford foster carers were responsive to the children's needs, but they were also experienced and it is less likely that their ratings of attachment of the newly placed children were distorted by placing any particular personal value on the child's responses to household members.

When there were difficulties in the attachment of a baby, the concurrency carers sometimes put it down to medical problems, such as continuing drug withdrawal symptoms. Looking at the adoptive children as a group, not just the concurrency cases, some parents specifically chose to report attachment difficulties with the "new" child in the first interview. They were alert to individual differences. If the children were placed as sibling groups, parents sometimes commented on how one child had become more quickly attached than another, and this might be described as reflecting the child's reaction to the parents' own style or personality. When parents had the experience of adopting more than one child, they were frequently clear about how the individual personality of the children might lead one to "attach" more quickly than the other(s). These parents saw this as natural, and nothing to worry about, which may have been a reflection of the fact that they were also not reporting extreme difficulty.

> At Time 1: *We have a lot of good days and only a few bad. [Older child] is attaching well, and we are very fond of her/him. [The younger child] was very affectionate from the beginning, so now it's already like we have always had the children.*
>
> *I felt a little unsure [of younger child] when we met at the foster parents' house. We both found it hard to "connect", and he was a bit subdued. But that may have been because he didn't have much language and was too young to realise what was going on. He's a bit cautious, thoughtful, which I like. But he likes a cuddle. I suppose I warmed to*

[the other child] immediately, who is bouncy and very interesting; lively and always with something to say.

At Time 2: *I found it easier to relate to [the older child], because we can talk. My husband is closer to [the younger child], so it all works out.*

In other families with more than one adopted child, individual patterns might develop, though each child showed confidence and close bonding. In one interview the younger child went frequently to the adoptive mother for comfort and a cuddle, or to show her what she was doing. The older child was also reportedly quite closely attached, particularly to the mother, calling her "Mummy" spontaneously from the start of the placement, but not needing the constant physical proximity that the younger sib required.

There were, however, some isolated examples of very real attachment problems reported by the new parents in all three placement groups. At Time 1, three new mothers and six new fathers reported that they felt a newly-arrived child was "not close" to them.

Mother at Time 1: *We have found it difficult. A. is showing very few signs of attachment to us, and we have not warmed to [this child]. We are concerned that [this child] takes up too much of our attention. We have had some support from the manager of the children's home. We are not feeling any love for these children yet, and we are not getting it either.*

At Time 2 none of the adoptive parents or concurrency or Trafford foster carers described the children as "not close", but there were four adoptive mothers and five adoptive fathers who said a child was only "quite close". Three of the four mothers, but all five fathers, had lived with the child for the full year of the research. However, the very large majority of the adopted children about whom we had follow-up information were clearly contented and attached.

At Time 2: *She settled well and seemed happy as soon as she came to us. She is a smiley child, wonderful and gorgeous really. She likes to be held and cuddled and sometimes lies with her head on my shoulder. She is so vulnerable that you bond immediately. The family feels right now; this is my family.*

Among the MAS comparison adoptive families, who received 23 newly adopted children during the evaluation period, six had older adopted children and two had older biological children. In the 24 concurrency families, five had previously adopted children and six (more) had older biological children. While the majority of the Trafford children had started in foster placements with several other children (including their own sibs in 15 cases), none were placed for adoption in families with existing older children. At the time of the first interview after placement, low attachment scores were less likely to be reported in relation to other children in the household than in relation to the adults. For example, at Time 1, 23 per cent of the children were not "very closely attached" to "mothers", and 33 per cent of them were not "very closely attached" to the "fathers"; this compares with the children not being close to 17 per cent of the other children in the household. At Time 2, the difference had disappeared.

Although we have noted that a child might be more attached to one "parent"/carer than the other, there was a tendency for the "very close" attachment of children to the "mother" to be mirrored in their "very close" attachment to others in the household. Table 5.14 shows that the very close attachment to the "mothers" is significantly related to very close attachment to the "fathers" at Time 1.

The same pattern was apparent at Time 2 in the 44 families for which data were collected for both "mothers" and "fathers": all the children who were reported as showing "very close" attachment to their "mother" also showed "very close" attachment to their "father" ($\chi^2 = 34.3$, 1df, $p<.0001$). Interpretation is not obvious; it is possible that both partners (mother and father) together generate and elicit closeness with the child(ren), reflecting the quality of the relationships common to all the members of this household. But it is equally possible – at least in theory – that the child is responding to both adults in the same way because of some aspect of his or her own personality. The shared type of response has been found in other studies; Rutter (1979) noted that children securely attached to one parent are likely also to be securely attached to the other.

Harwin and Owen (2002) have noted that among children whose placement plan had been fulfilled by the follow-up date, 65 per cent had made "good progress", compared with only 40 per cent of the children

Table 5.14
Comparison of "very close" attachment to mothers and to fathers at Time 1

	Attachment to "mothers"		*Attachment to "fathers"*		*Totals*
	N	*%*	*N*	*%*	
Very close	37	93	8	40	45
Not very close	3	7	12	60	15
Totals	**40**	**100**	**20**	**100**	**60***

$\chi^2 = 19.6$, 1df, $p<.001$
* The remaining eight children were in one "parent" households.

whose care plans were still unfulfilled. In the context of their study, "good progress" meant that the child had either entered the study with no problems and maintained that status, or that initial problems had been ameliorated. Fulfilled adoption placements accounted for the highest proportion of the children who made "good" welfare progress. As we have seen, the very large majority of the concurrency children in the present study would have fallen into the first of these categories. The advantages of a childcare model that emphasises speed of placement and decision-making are clear.

The General Health Questionnaire (GHQ): adoptive parents and concurrency carers

One of the background features of the children's new placements is the mental health of the new parents. For many adoptive parents and concurrency carers, the arrival of the index child was the first time they had carried responsibility for a child, and for many families this new child was a very young baby; some of the babies had health care problems deriving from the drug or alcohol addiction of their mothers at birth. In Chapter 6, the new adoptive parents and the concurrency carers report on this experience, referring to loss of sleep, loss of freedom of movement, and having to think of the needs of the baby or very young child. They had sometimes had some weeks to adjust to these possibilities, but when it came to accepting the child, may have had literally only a few days to make the final arrangements. Inevitably, as they told the researchers, the tensions were considerable.

Forty-one of the new mothers (adoptive and concurrency carers) completed the GHQ, among whom 34 per cent reported scores over the accepted cut-off point (4/5) indicating some mood disturbance. There are no thresholds for the four subscales, which tend to be used by clinicians for providing individual profiles. At the time of the placement of the index children, there were no differences in the total GHQ scores of the MAS Adoption Teams adoptive parents and the concurrency carers (foster parents in Trafford were not asked to complete the GHQ). There was a significant reduction in the total GHQ scores for the 21 mothers for whom Time 1 and Time 2 data were available, but since this was less than a third of the total sample of mothers, it is of little value except as indicating a likely trend. The qualitative interview material also suggested that parents and carers who had variously reported themselves as exhausted, anxious or under a good deal of strain at the time of the placement were nearly all reporting normal levels of mood disturbance by the time of the follow-up interview. The exceptions were those concurrency carers who had not been able to finalise a Freeing Order or an Adoption Order.

Summary

- The concurrency children spent significantly less time in impermanent care compared with the adopted children in the MAS and Trafford Adoption Team samples.
- The concurrency children moved less often before their final placement compared with the adopted children in the MAS and Trafford Adoption Team samples.
- Because the children in the concurrent planning projects were significantly younger than the children in the other two groups, the progress of the former was compared with children aged under one year when entering care in England in 2000/1. This showed that the concurrent planning cases (excluding the only child over one year at entry into care, and the two who returned to birth families) moved significantly faster through the various stages from last care episode to

Adoption Order. The Adoption Orders were granted in less than half the time taken for the same age group in England.

- The selection into the concurrent planning projects appears to have been partly dependent on the number of Strengths in (birth) Families detected by the concurrency teams. Jones (2002) has given details of the factors associated with success and failure in reunifying children with birth parents. But he has also made it plain that it is not possible to derive a *score* from such lists of parental characteristics that will enable the courts and practitioners to say exactly what the chances are of success with one or another action. Practitioners' judgments on qualitative issues will continue to be important.
- Although professional judgment contributed to the selection of concurrent planning cases, the availability of suitable carers also influenced which children could be taken on by the projects. To that extent there were no established criteria in any of the three projects about which cases were suited and which were not suited to the concurrent planning approach. Weinberg and Katz (1998), in a review of the use of concurrency in the separate states in the USA, also noted that states' statutes tended to avoid any definition of which cases might be suitable.
- The children under the age of four years for whom the Looking After Children measures were used to record behaviour and development showed few problems at the time of placement, and fewer still at the time of the researchers' follow-up visits.
- The parents' and carers' ratings on the Strengths and Difficulties Questionnaire for the children over four years also showed some improvement when considering the group as a whole, but for individual children these changes were not statistically significant. The small number of children for whom there were ratings on the same checklists at Time 1 and Time 2 made it difficult to study change. Hyperactivity was the most commonly reported problem and showed virtually no improvement between Time 1 and Time 2. Improvement on conduct problems came close to being significant. However, since the initial ratings seldom showed serious problems, there was little room for substantial change for the better. The results stand in their own right: the majority of the children being

represented as presenting virtually no difficulties to their carers and parents.

- The attachment ratings at Time 1 were clustered at the positive end of the possible scores. There was some evidence of an improvement in the proportions of children showing "close attachment" to both mothers and particularly to fathers by Time 2. In retrospect, it would have been more discriminating to have asked for ratings of the "bonding" of parent(s) to child, as well as the attachment of the child to other family members (Fahlberg, 1994).
- Two children (8 per cent) in the concurrency sample returned to their birth families. This number is too small to draw any firm conclusions. Over a 10-year period, 15 per cent of the Lutheran Social Services concurrency team's cases returned to birth families, and in one programme in Minnesota, during 1999–2000, 58 per cent of the children returned to a member of the birth family.[15] It seems likely that each concurrent planning programme will achieve different rates of rehabilitation into the birth families, and these will largely be dependent on which children are selected into the concurrency projects, rather than being "built-in" to the concurrent planning approach.

[15] Personal communication: Rob Sawyer, Director, Child and Family Services, Olmsted County Community Services, Rochester MN.

6 **Negotiating the routes to adoption:** the voices of the carers and adoptive parents

In the first part of this chapter, we set out the views of the concurrency carers about their experiences of being part of a new approach to finding permanence for young children. In the second part of the chapter, we report the experiences of those families who chose to follow the traditional route to adoption, either through MAS or when adopting children from Trafford SSD. The latter group of adopters were scattered across England, and used several different adoption agencies for their training, selection and subsequent support. Unlike the MAS adoptive parents, the Trafford adoptive parents did not have an option of choosing to join a concurrent planning project.

The carers in the three concurrency projects were very aware of their role as the ground-breakers; sometimes this seemed to them to mean that they were not getting as much support from professionals as they would have expected if they had been following the mainstream route, because the professionals themselves were feeling their way. At other times, and for some individual families, the procedures ran smoothly, and there was a feeling of relief that "their" new child, the birth family and they themselves had sorted things out with speed and fairness. Very few concurrency carers had previously adopted children using the "traditional" route, but when they had, they were asked to compare the two procedures. In most cases, their view was that the "new" system was likely to be better, as they anticipated that it would be speedier, but they recognised, as we shall see, the burdens to themselves of the risk that the child might return to his or her birth family.

This is not a chapter in which statistics are given; a choice has been made to record the opinions and experiences of those who were involved in the day-to-day effort of taking into their families a new and often very young child. For the concurrency carers there was an additional set of tasks: meeting with the birth parents and their families several times a week, being committed to advancing *their* parenting abilities, facing the risks inherent in being a concurrency carer, organising their lives around the contact sessions. All this was experienced while not, many of them felt, being in any sense an ordinary foster carer. Here the aim is not to judge the concurrency carers' views. Their thoughtfulness and sensitivity to the issues that faced them speak for themselves, even when – occasionally – they had negative experiences either with birth families or with professionals.

In the first section, the views of the MAS adopters who had decided not to follow the concurrency route are included to highlight the reasons why families choose one route or the other. For all families, we have disguised as much as possible the individual circumstances, while preserving the thoughtful and useful descriptions of feelings and events they had experienced.

Deciding to become concurrency carers

The processes by which the three teams sought to recruit concurrency carers have been described (Chapter 3). At the end of the day, however, the choice between the concurrent planning route to adoption or the mainstream, traditional route was in the hands of the potential adopters themselves. At all stages, the concurrent planning carers were told that the nature of their task involved some risk – though small overall – of the child returning to their birth family. Some carers mentioned that they had been told that the likelihood of this happening was 50 per cent, although most were aware that in the Seattle project the figure was reported as 15 per cent. In one project at least, carers were reminded that this figure referred to numbers over several years: in any one year the figure might be anything from nil to 40 per cent. Nevertheless, carers were alert to these inherent risks.

> *I first thought, 'Good God, I'm not doing that. It would be a total gamble.' Then the other side began to kick in, and I could see it would help the adopters to get to know the birth parents, and it would be better for the children. It's not in the forefront of your mind that the child could return.*

Among other characteristics, therefore, they needed emotional strength to help them to cope with possible loss. Eighteen of the 24 concurrency carers families (75 per cent) were seeking to adopt children because they had been unable to have any biological children, although five of these families had previously adopted children. The majority had been through several years of trying to have children of their own. Loss and disappointment was a familiar, but not distinctive experience for many: it was also reported by those who chose the "traditional" adoption route. However, this experience in itself was exactly what made some families realise that they had the strength to take on the role of concurrency carer.

Unfortunately loss is a familiar feeling. So I know what's going to happen to me. I will retreat, I will be very sad, I will probably internalise quite a lot of my grief and pain. But I do know I have got good support and I hope that I would then struggle to go on and adopt another child. But I don't think I would want to use concurrent planning again.

We're used to dealing with loss, and with disappointment.

Clearly, outweighing the obvious risks, the strong possibility of having a baby rather than a toddler or older child placed with them was an incentive for many families to join the concurrent planning provision rather than mainstream adoption. Katz (1990) also noted this as one reason why the Seattle project had few problems with recruiting carers.

We wanted to adopt a new-born baby, so when we heard that the concurrency team could place very young babies, we went for it. We knew it would be a big risk, but we went into it with our eyes open.

There was often a strongly altruistic element in the choice: the idea that the children would gain, even if they themselves lost, or would be at risk of losing. The carers were also attracted by the notion of a service that was totally child-centred, and gave the children "the best of both worlds" in terms of preserving attachments and promoting the return to the birth parents within appropriate timescales. For some applicants, including those from ethnic or religious minority backgrounds, the support for birth parents to care for their own children was crucial. Commenting on the early years of the Seattle project, Katz (1990) reported that many of the foster-adopt families recruited into concurrent planning 'wanted to help prevent the well-known harm to children adrift in temporary care for long periods' (p 222). Thoburn *et al* (1986) noted that a combination of altruism and fulfilling one's own needs (for a family) was common in prospective adopters. Likewise, Groothues *et al* (1998/99) reported that over a quarter of the parents adopting Romanian babies and young children mentioned an altruistic element in their motivation.

> *If the child returned to the natural parents, that was a risk for us. But the positive aspects of that were explained to us. OK, while we might be bereaved, disappointed, upset, we would also, hopefully, feel we had taken part in a positive process and that if the child did go back to the parents that was the best thing. I think we both knew that really [concurrency] was the better route. Perhaps not for us, but for the child, yes.*

> *We heard that it would be better for the child, and that's what really influenced us. We were struck by how much children move around in the care system – knocked about – before they get adopted. If they move less, that makes it easier for us adopters as well.*

For some concurrency carers, their own childhood experiences influenced their choice of concurrent planning. One described the loss of a parent during his early childhood, which meant that he had no personal memories; this was confounded by the surviving parent's reluctance to talk about the past. He felt he could understand the feelings of an adopted child denied knowledge of his/her birth family. For this parent, and many others, the decision was a balancing act: wanting to help a child to avoid some of the pain that he had experienced in his own upbringing against the likelihood of the child returning to the birth family, and therefore having to absorb more pain himself. Another concurrency carer said that all his family had suffered from the unpredictability of a parent whose presence was totally unreliable. He recalled how this had been a regularly upsetting feature of his childhood. This carer wanted, above all, to provide stability for the new child in their family.

This highlights, again, that the carers had very varied backgrounds and had often themselves had troubled childhoods. Many had experienced difficulties in recent years, over and above loss and distress, and they typically exhibited remarkable levels of coping and resilience. Friends and family figured strongly in their reports of how they would cope with the child going back to her birth family (see below). Many concurrency carers said they understood that a child adopted through the traditional route often experiences several moves before placement. Adoption in these circumstances also risks breaking close relationships that might have developed with foster carers: 'We'd have been seen [by the child] as the enemy a little bit.' But it should be stressed that this was a minority view. The traditional adopters who rejected concurrent planning clearly felt such problems could be overcome, or were not significant.

One or two concurrency carers mentioned that the existence of other children in the family would have a buffering effect on their own grief if the new baby had to return to its birth family.

> *I wouldn't have done it if I hadn't got [another child]. Because I felt that whoever came to us, and whatever had happened, it would have been lovely. And if it hadn't have lasted we would have had that experience. I don't think I could have coped – I wouldn't have thought like that if I didn't have a child already.* Later this mother added: *I felt that for [older child] it would have been really sad not to have known what it was like to bath a baby or see one learning to crawl or walk. They are all things [older child] would never experience if we did not take the risk.*

Others drew attention to the benefits they and the newly-placed child would derive personally from the experience.

> *And we felt we would benefit even if the baby did not stay with us. We thought that once the child was with us, and we were getting to know him it would be very difficult to give him up. But, it would give us an understanding of what birth parents go through a little bit, and that would be a helpful thing to go through – not nice – but helpful. And we felt sort of, well, if it happens we just cope somehow. It would be terrible and we can't imagine what it would feel like, but we would just have to deal with it.*

The concurrency carers' reports on their own internal resources

As we have seen, the carers were fully aware of how many demands would be made of them, and honest about their capacity to meet the likely difficulties. Most knew that they would need a lot of help to face the risks associated with being in a concurrent planning programme. They had strong families and friendships on which to call; they had been selected, at least in part, by the concurrency workers for these characteristics.

> *To be on the receiving end is quite hard, to be that generous . . . it requires a bit of almost religious . . . [but] we are both quite bold and resourceful. You have to have the resourcefulness to cope, and that is a strength we have.*
>
> *Our way of coping would be to go to [wife's] parents. When things have gone wrong in the past we have gone to them.*
>
> Mother: *Oh, yes it would be Mum, but friends and other family as well.*
>
> Father: *But friends were a mixture. Some said, 'What will you do when the baby goes away; that's going to be really hard.' While others would say, 'Are you really just a baby snatcher? What about the poor mum?' But we had been told that she wouldn't be going into concurrent planning if it was something sudden. It has to be a persistent problem and these really are the last chance situations.*
>
> *The [team] get you to suggest how you are going to deal with it [risk], to be honest, by suggesting how other people have. They don't tell you: 'This is how we recommend you plan to deal with it.' They get you to come up with your own strategies.*
>
> *We would draw our strength from God should that happen. And the support of friends and family. We made sure we explained it all to our parents and our family and friends, and particularly close friends . . . Standing with us and knowing the full risks that were involved and knowing that they would be there for us should it go wrong.* (Partner added: *'from our point of view'*).

Traditional adopters' views on concurrent planning[1]

The prospective adopters in the MAS Adoption Team comparison sample were asked for their views of concurrent planning,[2] since they had been given the option of going down this route. Concurrent planning did not appeal to all, and it is instructive to consider the views of those who opted *not* to join the programme. The risk of having to hand the child back to the birth family after several months together appeared to be a major deterrent for some.

> *It didn't take us long to decide not to go down the concurrency route. It seemed to be adding a whole layer of risks and we wanted to minimise the legal risks in the adoption. It seems to make you more of a foster parent and we know we want to adopt. We might form an emotional bond and then lose the child anyway.*
>
> Partner: *It seems a good idea, but best for very young children, and that isn't really [the age group] we want.*

Much like the concurrency carers, there were traditional adopters who were initially attracted to concurrent planning because of the obvious advantages for the child. For example, one wife favoured it because she thought the child would be "less damaged". Her husband was less convinced, and the younger age of the concurrency cases was not important to either of them. For them the deciding factor was related to the logistics of arranging contact three times a week, particularly as there were already school-age children in the family who needed to be picked up at set times. These carers believed contact would be disproportionately complicated and very demanding on both children and adults in the family. Other families raised the issue of sustaining this high level of contact with the birth parents over some months. One or two adoptive families lived at a considerable distance from the concurrent planning project and realised that organising contact up to three days a week would involve a great deal of driving in a large city.

---

[1] The views on other issues of the adoptive families that chose not to use concurrent planning are given in the second half of this chapter: see p 148.

[2] The views of the Trafford adoptive parents, seen at the end of the follow-up period, were, of course, not relevant: they had not had the opportunity of choosing concurrent planning.

In essence concurrent planning is a good thing, but it will only work for children under three (when they are likely to be in all-day nursery), and only if the carers are very local. We don't see how it can work with lots of siblings placed together, or if you live far away from the contact centre.

In one or two families it was the anticipated level of contact with the birth families in concurrency that was daunting or unattractive. Sometimes, previous adoption experience deterred people from wanting to meet the birth family any more than was strictly necessary for a closing down of the relationship. This former experience may have been wholly negative: in one case the birth mother of older children already in the family had never met the adopters and made no use at all of the "letter-box" arrangements for cards and photographs.

For the MAS adoptive parents, the potential advantages of concurrency were sometimes outweighed by concerns about the perceived risks, either to themselves, or to other family members, of the child's return to the birth family. The needs of the children already in the family were clearly important. The high contact rate in the concurrent planning cases, theoretically never less than three times a week, could mean less time spent with older children, complications about picking up from school or could necessitate arranging baby-sitters for holiday periods. Where they already had adopted children, parents felt strongly that if the concurrency child was "handed back", this would convey a very negative message to the children already in their family.[3] For this reason one family chose traditional adoption for their second child specifically in order to protect their older child: 'It would be too much of a risk for [the older child]. We feel quite protective towards [older child].'

The idea of concurrent planning was appealing, because the child wins. But if we had a concurrent planning child, we couldn't hand them back. That would give quite the wrong signals to the other children.

---

[3] This point of view was borne out later when one concurrent planning child returned to the birth family and the concurrency carers reported the profound grief and sense of loss their older child experienced.

While acknowledging the enhanced possibility of getting a baby through concurrency, there were adoptive parents who felt they could not cope with the prospect of losing the child after a few months. So it seems as though such decisions are taken very individualistically:

> *The attraction is that we might get a baby, but we couldn't bear to lose it after a few months. It might be bearable if we had another child, but . . .*
>
> *We didn't need to think about [concurrency], because we were told we could get a suitable placement through ordinary adoption. And we didn't think we could cope with going through the business of putting our hearts into it, knowing the child might go back. We've been through too much loss to be able to face more.*

In the same way that concurrency was being chosen by carers who wished to adopt babies or very young children, some families chose to remain with the MAS Adoption Team because they wanted older children.

> Father: *I prefer children who can speak and understand when you talk to them; we would prefer school-age children.*
>
> Mother: *It [traditional adoption route] involves less contact with the birth families, which makes me feel more comfortable.*

The value of concurrency for the children was often explicitly recognised, but other pressures in the families pulled them back to traditional schemes.

> *I heard about concurrency right from the start, and I could see the advantages for the child and for us. We would get a younger child, and the younger ones have suffered less. The children also go straight to someone who wants them, and we would know something about the child's background to help us to help the child to adjust. But we had to reject this route because we couldn't afford it. If I could have had 12 months off we would have loved to do it.*

The concurrency carers' views on the training programmes

Returning now to the views of concurrency carers, we explore first their views on the additional training and information they received. In all three projects the concurrent planning carers were offered extra training sessions in addition to the routine adoption preparation groups so that the particular demands and requirements of concurrency could be addressed. These sessions were mostly well received. However, some carers felt that it was not always helpful to use training material from the Lutheran Social Services project because the cultural gap was too wide.

> *The videos from America are not very good. For one thing, the one on returning the child to birth parents is about a three-year-old and ours are nearly all babies. We should get some British videos about the difficulties and so on.*

One other couple felt strongly that they would have preferred to be given information on all the "hazards", as they called them, from the start, with the implication that this had not happened. But this was unusual. Most carers reported that they were given an honest picture from the start.

> *Sometimes I had the feeling that they thought we wouldn't be able to cope with all the nitty-gritty bad luck stories. So I challenged one of the groups and said: 'Look, I really feel we need to know the worst,' because anything else is then a bonus.*

> *The point about the child going back was raised on a lot of occasions. But I think it's necessary, it has to be in your mind all the time, it is part of concurrency planning. Yes, we knew that children wouldn't be placed unless the chances of them returning were quite low, so the prognosis for that wasn't good.*

One couple was particularly appreciative of the assessment process, feeling it had made them think very positively about what they had to offer: 'Our social worker made us see our good points – and she followed that with good advice later on.' It was widely reported that the preparation groups gave everyone the opportunity of thinking about the consequences of taking on a child or baby from a disadvantaged or abusive background. Two project teams included "sculpting" in the preparation programme for carers. This was reported by many as a very powerful way of conveying the likely feelings of all the "players" in concurrent planning – the birth parents and family, the child, the social workers, the carers and others.

We were "playing" the social workers, and the child and the mother and the boyfriend who was a bit aggressive and then the fosterers. You could see the dynamics and how it could be absolutely awful. I think they were trying to tell us that you could get into a confrontational situation very easily. That helped me to see that you had to face the fact that the mother might fight. They told us the truth didn't they? You wouldn't want to snatch a child away from a mother who was crying her eyes out, would you? I think they wanted us to say it, and it was painful, that you would give up a child if things were going really well with the mum, and she could cope . . . We must be prepared to consider it, knowing that we were all quite desperate for a child . . . They were as brutally honest as necessary.

It made you think about a lot of new issues that you don't realise are involved. They don't pull the wool over your eyes, not for one minute. You have to know what you are letting yourself in for. We heard about how you might be down the hall and you can hear the baby crying with the birth parent and you are dying to get in there and say 'give it to me', but you can't. You know it's going to be difficult in that sense.

However, there were gaps: more than one carer mentioned that there should be more specialised advice on child development. Where possible, concurrency teams asked experienced parents to supply much of the detail that the prospective new parents wanted. Reading lists were kept to a minimum, which some carers felt was right, as few people pick up their parenting skills from reading ahead of their eventual hands-on experience. Being able to talk to carers who had completed the adoption was reportedly very helpful: 'We could see in the flesh someone who has done it and lived to tell the tale.'

One concurrency carer felt vastly reassured by the information that was given on the issue of nature versus nurture, and about the extent to which her family would mitigate any adverse aspects of the child's family history. This was felt to be important by many carers as they were frequently taking on the care of babies and young children with family histories of drugs and alcohol abuse, and previous child protection issues. Other concurrency carers brought up the issue of not knowing the child's full genetic history. For example, they may know who the mother is but not the father, and there may, therefore, be genetic "problems" lurking to be discovered in later life.

> *There is the whole thing of not knowing the genetic side [of the Dad]. Every time I take [the baby] to the doctors and they say, 'Is he allergic to penicillin?' Or is there a history of this or that, it brings it home that I don't know. But that is quite common with adoption, not just [for us].*

At the same time this parent saw how not knowing the background of her new child opened up quite exciting opportunities in the family.

> *You don't know if the baby will turn out to be interested in arty things or be more physical. I've got no preconceived ideas so maybe I will be more open and follow her more [than with older child]. Who knows?*

This was quite apart from the advantages they perceived from meeting the birth parents, and passing on some information to their new child. One family regretted not being able to meet the birth parents, who had failed to attend any of the contact sessions.

> *Some of the other carers said how lucky we were not having to face contact sessions, but although part of me does not want to meet her, part of me does, so that we can see what she looks like and what she is like. And she turned up once and said she'd like to meet us, but she disappeared again. It is sad because I feel like we have missed out in one sense. And it's the baby's long-term well-being, and we cannot fill those gaps.*

Sometimes, however, the training material was not presented in ways that would make sense to new parents, or people who were not familiar with the finer points of child development. On one occasion a video was presented of the Strange Situation experiments,[4] in which young children are exposed to the presence of a stranger while alternately in the presence and absence of their parents. Only after the prospective adopters asked what the purpose was, did the concurrency team explain the distinctions between attachment models that were being illustrated. One carer felt that

---

[4] Ainsworth *et al*, 1978.

a full discussion about attachment in the group would have served the same purpose more effectively.

The size of the training group appeared to be important for some carers. Everyone recognised the difficulty of anticipating in advance the precise size of a training group, but more than one parent felt quite daunted.

> *Personally, I didn't like the big group. I think they should have made them smaller. I'm not shy, but I find it very intimidating with lots of people trying to talk about anything. There are some extroverts around, but just because you're going to adopt doesn't mean you are one of them.*

All in all, carers were generally less critical of the preparation than they were of the subsequent adoption procedures, particularly when it came to dealing with the child's local authority. However, one person commented:

> *I suppose if I was going to be a little bit unkind, I mean they have been lovely to us, but we were conscious that everyone was on a learning curve, and that everybody was, sort of, learning this new business together. Sometimes we thought 'Why can't you do it a bit more efficiently?' But they're ever so nice and we do understand. It was a case of having no precedent, so you couldn't pull something out and say: 'This is the way it is.' Because nobody knew the way it was.*

Asked directly about how they saw the preparation groups once they had completed the whole concurrency "journey", the majority were highly appreciative, and felt they had been well prepared, but that some of the uncertainties remained. The next comment is typical:

> *I think it was good so far as it could be. How do you prepare someone for an emotional journey that's unknown really? They tell you that you will have ups and downs, but everyone copes differently, so you've got to prepare yourself.*

Looking back, more than one family said that they felt the need for an information pack, and that – coming close to the final hearing – they were still unsure of what was happening. We return to this point later.

> *I'm a bit floundering in the technicalities. Like at yesterday's meeting, there were comments on what was happening at the next court hearing.*

And I get a bit lost when we're talking about interim care orders, and what the various care orders are, and what the various proceedings are. We don't get told anything. And unless I actually try and ask someone, we get no information, which I find very frustrating. You are doing all the hard work, but getting absolutely no information about how it's going. And my social worker will be very placid and tell me nothing.

Concurrency carers' concerns about attachment

When we saw the carers before placement, many gave touching descriptions of how they would seek to protect themselves against becoming too involved with the child. This was an aspect of concurrency that individuals felt they would usually have to cope with for themselves. One father was clear that he would try not to get involved; but he thought it would be easier for him "to keep his distance" than for his wife, because he would be at work and she would have the day-to-day care of the new baby.

I will build a barrier just in case the worst happens. I would obviously like to keep [the baby] but I would cope if she had to go back. I am adopting a "negative" approach and assuming she will go back.

Others saw this as an impossible demand to make on oneself:

I don't think trying to keep yourself detached is a strategy [for facing the risks], because I don't think you can do that. I mean . . . looking after a baby for nine months without getting attached?

Later, when a baby had been placed with this family, the same carer commented as follows:

I think we are holding back to a certain extent, but I don't think it's a conscious thing. As far as giving her love, we are not holding back, but if you said to me she will be going back in a couple of months, I think I could cope with that. I think we do guard against it a bit.

Interestingly, in a survey of attitudes to adoption and fostering – including concurrency – in California respondents similarly reported that attaching to a child and then not being able to adopt her would deter them from applying to the concurrent planning programme (Alcalay *et al*, 2001).

One or two parents who already had children in the household took a pragmatic view of these early stages, but only in retrospect. Their experience with their existing children meant that they were comfortable with the apparently slow process of developing a fully bonded relationship.

> *To be honest I hadn't really bonded with the baby [in the early weeks]. It didn't happen like that. A two-month-old baby doesn't snuggle in to you. They might fall asleep on you, but they will fall asleep on a cushion. Six months is when it happened for me.*
>
> *I don't think we held back during the time we were only fostering him. My other child definitely attached immediately and adored [the baby]. In my quiet moments I loved the baby just as much and didn't hold back. I think that maybe was because I thought there was only a miniscule chance of him returning to the parents. Perhaps it would be harder for people who haven't got another child.*

Some concurrency carers described an immediate bond between themselves and the baby; for others it took longer. The carers without any previous experience of being a parent seemed to have very high expectations of what they *ought* to be feeling. For several there was an added complication of having to look after a baby who was still suffering some measure of alcohol or drug withdrawal. These babies were exceptionally sensitive and restless. Some were reported as screaming much of their waking time, and were very difficult to settle. This could disturb the pattern of developing love, not least because the carers were physically exhausted by the amount of care the babies needed.

> Mother: *I think if someone had taken [the baby] away in the first few weeks I would have lived. He was very demanding. He had colic and there was this endless screaming.*
>
> Partner: *Psychologically you weren't bonding.*
>
> Mother: *But once [the baby] became more jolly, you couldn't have given him up. Once you start having that feedback . . . I think we didn't have to try very hard to love him. He just came and that was it.*

I wanted to love her but I couldn't, I didn't know how to. It was so very hard and I felt like I'd failed because I couldn't bond with her, but something in me . . . I just knew we had to keep going with it and I couldn't give up. So once I'd got through that it was OK.

One family, looking back over the previous year of uncertainty, reported how they and others in their support group were able to allow that last bit of bonding with the child to reach its full expression only when the Freeing Order was agreed, or even at the final hearing that confirmed adoption as the care plan.

One of the other [concurrency] mums, whose case had just gone through and a full Care Order made in their favour, she said: 'Oh, I could kiss them for the first time.' And we were quite surprised by that, but you could feel the relief in the room, and other parents were saying: 'Yes, we had the same thing. We just kept this little bit back.' And inside there is still something, that kind of safety net I suppose, a self-preservation thing that just meant . . . a bit of something that we held back.

The placement arrangements for the concurrency children and babies

For many concurrency carers, as for the adoptive families (see below), the time waiting for a possible "match" was very stressful. These couples were not critical; indeed they fully understood the reasons for the delay, but this did not prevent some considerable strain. Outside the control of the carers or the concurrency team, the delays could arise in the assessment process, or the submissions to panel. Again, the carers understood this, but it was they and their families who shouldered the strain. One team leader remarked that, once approved, carers seemed able to cope with a limited waiting period only. This may be true overall, although the numbers "lost" to mainstream adoption seemed very small; perhaps it is important to remember that, together with the time taken to decide to adopt, the assessments could take more than a year.

At the end of assessment we had to go to two panels, and you just have to wait for the right date. Then one of the panels decided to defer a

> *decision.* [sighs] *I mean, it's OK, it's just a little bit of delay, like everything else. Our worker happened to be on annual leave and someone else went with our papers, and couldn't answer a question about us. And the panel said: 'Oh well, we will have to meet again.' And that was the second panel so we couldn't quite understand why they deferred. It feels like a lifetime when you are waiting.*

Similarly, the actual placement of the children could be fraught with complications, or handled with an apparent lack of sensitivity by local authority or hospital social workers, that was as upsetting for the carers as it was for the birth parents. However, the most commonly reported complication was the very short notice that some carers had that a child was ready for placement. This was equally difficult for the concurrency teams to handle when babies were slightly premature. In some cases, carers had literally one or two days to get themselves, and perhaps other children in the family, ready to receive a very young baby. Mothers, in particular, compared this with the eight or nine months of a normal pregnancy.

> *. . . we have had two weeks. It has been very scary actually, but thrilling as well. A bit like . . . you have won this incredible prize and it is being delivered in two weeks' time. Anyone doing concurrent planning is in that frame of mind that you have got to move quickly.*

> *We took [the baby] out and then came back here. And suddenly we got a phone call saying the mother had unexpectedly turned up at the foster mother's house and had gone mad that her baby wasn't there. The social worker said perhaps we should keep [the baby], and although we had everything ready I was looking forward to one more night without a baby in the house, and the foster mother had wanted to say goodbye. So it was all rather shocking though only one day different from the arrangements.*

Carers were sometimes shocked by the impact of a new baby on the household, even if they had an older child. The reality of a newly arrived infant could be even harder when the family had no previous experience of babies or if the child was suffering from the effects of drug or alcohol withdrawal.

When we finally got her (aged under two months) she was very, very distressed. She knew she was somewhere different, with different people and for a couple of weeks she just cried, screamed solidly and there was nothing we could do to comfort her. I longed for this little bundle and suddenly this baby was screaming the whole time. We knew it was going to be hard work, but nothing had prepared us for how awful it was.

For many people there were issues surrounding the timing of one parent giving up work. Employers seem to have been reasonably flexible about the amount of notice required, but often the person who was to be the main caregiver had to work out a notice period. Unlike a conventional pregnancy, the foster-adopt families frequently had no idea of an impending match with a concurrency baby or child. We also observed that carers rarely went through an extended introductory period with the child, in contrast with the traditional adopters. Occasionally, it was possible to visit a baby in hospital before placement, but this also was rare.

We had about one weekend's notice, because it was a matter of the hospital deciding when to let her go, as well as the local authority agreeing concurrent planning. I couldn't get out of work fast enough for that, so my partner had to take over.

Meeting the birth parents

Part of the preparation before becoming a concurrent planning carer involved thinking about meeting the birth family. Many carers felt apprehensive about this, not least because they recognised that it might be their first encounter with a parent from a background that was likely to be very dissimilar to their own. The unknown could generate genuine alarm. Aware of the long-term advantages of telling adopted children about their birth parents, they nevertheless saw the meetings with them as a major challenge. The word "scary" was used over and over again.

We will see her [birth mother] before the baby is born, which will be great. But with a mixture of feelings. I feel sad and scared and hopeful she will like us and that we cannot be, in some ways, seen by her as a threat.

. . . the prospect of knowing the birth family is really scary, and you think, 'No, no, I don't want anything to do with the birth family.' But it's really important for adoptive people to know as much as possible about where they come from. So, yes, it was good in the end.

The idea of close contact with the birth mother was quite scary. We were sort of apprehensive. I knew that I wouldn't be on my own, there would always be someone else there. So there was safety in that. And I had asked my Mum to come too.

But the advantages were also apparent to many concurrency families. While the perceptions some held of "traditional" adoptions may be slightly inaccurate, this concurrency carer clearly felt that the programme offered advantages over traditional adoption for all the family members.

I'm really glad I opted for concurrent planning, more glad now than then. How sad it would be for one child to know everything about themselves, while the other child had big gaps missing. I thought that meeting the parents would be good for us as a family, for me. It would dispel the fantasy fear of 'Oh my god, that woman has looked at me twice, she must be the birth mother' and rush out of Sainsbury's getting hysterical. To me it would not be quite right to bring up someone else's child, well your child, and you have never met the birth mother. I would always be wondering what they looked like, were they this, were they that? Suppose the child asked, 'Where was I then?' and all you could say was, 'You were with a foster family'.

This reflects one of the points made in the training material prepared by the Lutheran Social Services team in Seattle (Katz, Colacurcio and Cordes, 1994). In an early preparation group, these authors suggest that one of the reasons for the high level of contact between birth families and concurrency carers was that 'Birth parents can give the family and child information that no one else has (essential for present parenting and future life book information if reunification is not possible)' (*ibid*, p 23).

One family stressed the future benefits of telling children that their birth parents had been committed to trying to get them back, and had worked hard through the concurrency programme; even if they had not been successful, this would be a good model for the children.

Some concurrency carers felt quite calm about the prospect of meeting birth parents, no matter what their background or current problems. These carers all shared professional experiences that had brought them into contact with people from many different parts of society; as one carer said, 'We understand why some people end up in a mess.' For other carers, however, the reality of the birth families was a shock. They may have had a theoretical knowledge of the sort of troubled backgrounds the birth parents could have, but this was not sufficient preparation. The reality could lead to complete bafflement or real antipathy. The carers anticipated difficulties when explaining the qualities of the birth parents to their child later on when so little in their lives or attitudes was positive. These difficulties were not confined to the concurrency families. Several birth parents felt equally hostile towards the adoptive parents or carers, though probably for other reasons (see Chapter 7).

However, carers frequently expressed considerable understanding and sympathy with the birth parents. They commented on their disturbed upbringings, and the effect these experiences might have had. But they were also clear about the implications for the children.

Basically she's a child; a teenager, and she is very angry. She hates anybody in authority; she has been ruled by social services all her life. On the other hand she is quite vulnerable and immature, and I think it was asking a lot of her really, because she hasn't got any one special person to hold her hand. She hadn't [abandoned] the baby in a phone box or anything.

Obviously if she'd had her way she'd have kept [the baby]. It was sad she couldn't, because she was so nice, but at the same time you could see she couldn't manage, couldn't change her, feed her, comfort her – even in a short session. She wasn't interested in what I had to report.

Other concurrency carers felt the need to take a tough stance on the amount of sympathy they could afford for the birth parents:

I'm holding the birth parents at arm's length, I'm being civil, but I'm not allowing the opportunity of me thinking about them, outside of just the practical things. I don't think they warrant me thinking sympathetically about them. Which is probably a hard thing to say, but that is how I am.

The concurrency workers and the carers explained that these conflicting feelings were extensively explored in the preparation groups. In the training material produced by the Lutheran Social Services team (Katz, Colacurcio and Cordes, 1994, p 24) it is suggested that this issue is explicitly discussed. Our interviews reveal how such feelings endure, and are recalled sometimes many months later after contact with the birth family has been formally severed. This underscores the importance of a de-briefing session with concurrency project workers after the first meeting with birth family members when such ambivalent thoughts will be prominent and perhaps painful. At times, carers had to deal with aggression from the birth family. One carer described this in the following terms:

We'd go into the room and she'd be allowed to say whatever she wanted to me, and I wasn't allowed to retaliate . . . it was very hard to sit there and take everything on board. And I'm thinking, 'Hang on, you know, I've put up with a lot and you are the social workers and you should be putting up with some of this.' I mean we were the ones who had been up all night, and just to sit there and get all the mother's aggression. I never wanted it not to work. It would have been nice, just for [the baby's] sake, to have built up some sort of rapport [with the birth mother]. But that just never happened.

Set against these varied encounters with birth parents, there were a small number of concurrency carers who never met the birth parents. In three cases the birth parents seemed to "disappear" and despite the best efforts of social services, the courts and the concurrency teams, they simply never turned up for contact. In its way this was a major disappointment for the carers. It also caused the carers to question whether these were appropriate concurrency cases. Three families commented, for example, that they were disposed to use concurrency a second time on the grounds that the first placement had been so "straightforward": no contact and relatively rapid advancement to final hearing and Freeing Order. But they all suggested their experiences had not been "real concurrency".

Other concurrency carers also suspected that "their" case might have been inappropriate for concurrent planning, usually when they understood the full extent of the birth family's difficulties. One described the use of concurrency as "ludicrous" in their case, even though the birth parents were turning up for contact, and were opposed to the possible adoption. This was not an isolated reaction.

Support for the carers from the concurrency teams

Generally speaking, the carers reported feeling well supported by the professionals in their training and preparation for concurrency. For example, the respect encountered at the first enquiry to the concurrency project often contrasted with feelings of being "fobbed off" during a telephone call to a local authority adoption service. The sound relationship between the concurrency workers and carers underpins any possible strains that the concurrency work might impose in the ensuing months.

> *We both feel incredibly well supported and informed; at every stage [the project worker] will ring or we will have a conversation. I have heard how good they are way down the line when things hit you when the kid is 13 or whatever, from people who have adopted through [the project].*

> *We have been thrilled with [the concurrency team], and certainly having experienced a little bit of the [local authority], they come out tops in their support for us. They were very focused and they wanted to help.*

When things went smoothly through the courts, the contact was regular and the relationship with the birth parents was pleasant, the concurrency carers had little about which to complain or be anxious. But in some cases, carers had a particularly hard time, for example, if guardians or the courts appeared unsympathetic to the need to get the – often very young

– child into a stable setting. At such times of stress, a case might be made for independent counselling. Carers took pains to point out that the other parts of their lives had to continue against the background of the drama being played out with the concurrency team and "their" child. Relatives might become ill or die, they might lose their jobs, or have to move house, and they were expected to tolerate a high degree of uncertainty about something as important as the future of the child, alongside these other stressful events, without professional support.

> *Definitely we should have the right to see an independent counsellor. No matter what traumas you are going through, your friends can't necessarily understand it all, and it's not fair to have your partner take the whole stress on, is it? And it's a real thing of being very, very helpless, an absolute outsider to the programme. There needs to be someone there, not necessarily a social worker.*

Some of the carers reported that they felt well supported by the local authority social workers, and in one case by the child's guardian. It seemed that – in these instances at least – the professionals outside the project felt less constrained when advising about the progress of a case and its likely outcomes. This openness "gave heart" to the carers, and was reported in the follow-up interviews with appreciation.

A small number of concurrency carers felt that they were kept in the dark about what was happening at crucial times in the concurrency process. One carer complained of a general lack of information about what was going on; the family had no idea which stage they had reached in terms of the process of concurrency, the assessment of the birth parents, the court appearances or the legal processes. They felt that they "struggled to make sense of" many aspects of the concurrent planning process, and what the function was of the "Care Order", the "Freeing Order", the various forms E and F and the Schedule 2 report. They were not aware that there would be a directions hearing every month, nor did they understand what it was for. Their (then) foster child's guardian enlightened them about much of this, but not until a home visit just before the final hearing. When this family asked questions, they claimed that they were made to feel they should already know the answer or that they were just being "difficult". The important point was made that, if it was hard for carers to understand the process, it was likely to be even harder for birth parents, with the additional emotional stress of losing a child, perhaps not for the first time. Learning difficulties might also contribute to birth parents' difficulties in understanding written material.

At times, it was clear that uncertainty was compounded by delays occurring in local authorities completing their reports, or not answering urgent phone calls. For two cases, at least, this led to deadlines being missed and court reports not being completed. Generally, the concurrency carers reported much less satisfactory relationships with the local authorities than with their Project team workers; this was not true in the Brighton & Hove families.

Carers who were going through this type of experience advocated the development of an information pack, produced in straightforward language, that would explain how each stage of the concurrent planning process was organised. The pack would include timescales and critical dates, which could be filled in appropriately for each family and updated regularly. The carers would thus be aware if the timetable was slipping and why. More importantly, the information would give them a sense of control over their part of the process, and a means of ensuring that professionals keep to an expected timetable.

Support groups for the concurrency carers

The waiting period between finishing the preparation groups and home study, and confirmation by the permanency panels for adoption and fostering was difficult. Support for carers came almost entirely from professionals and family during this time, although as soon as they were approved they could, in all three projects, join other approved carers in a support group. This apparently helped carers to cope with the second waiting time: from panel approval to placement of the new child. Sometimes experienced members of the support groups volunteered to help with the preparation groups: "telling their story", although some carers preferred to derive support from close family, such as siblings or parents, or even from their friends, rather than from other carers.

I don't really like support groups. I know it's selfish because I ought to be there for the new people, but it's two-and-a-half hours and I would rather be doing the ironing or watching telly with [partner] . . . my feeling is . . . adoption doesn't define me, and I don't want it to define my adopted child.

In one geographical area many of the carers have stayed in touch, phoning and meeting informally; all the projects have special days – summer picnics or Christmas parties – when carers and children meet. By and large, this was seen as a bonus. In the Coram Project, a group was set up for the relatives of concurrency carers, which many appreciated.

The final decision about the child's possible return to the birth family

Concurrent planning is "a roller-coaster ride", said one carer. The concurrency carers were very aware of the likely impact on the birth parents – nearly always mothers – of the final recommendation by the team and the decision of the court that the child should stay with the carers. Of the 24 children in the three concurrency projects, only two children were returned to their birth families. In order to preserve confidentiality we have not included any direct quotations from these cases concerning the way the decisions were reached or the impact on either the carers' families or the birth families.

The carers, like the birth parents, were acutely aware of the importance of the birth parents' attendance at the contact sessions, and the equal importance of completing any other educational or therapeutic programmes that the teams organised for them. In the contact sessions, attendance was only part of the task; the carers knew that the quality of the birth parents' "performance" during contact was equally important (see Chapter 7 for the views of birth parents, and Chapter 8 on contact). It is therefore not surprising that the concurrency carers often had ambivalent feelings about the birth parents' behaviour during the contact sessions.

It is inevitable that the carer doesn't want the contact to go well, because that would go against keeping the baby. But we don't want it to go badly either, because that is hard on the child.

. . . to be quite honest, now, because you really hope, you really want

to adopt, actually her not coming . . . you think, well this really increases our chance of adopting.

The final decision either to return the child to his or her birth parents, or to agree that the care plan should be adoption, is taken by the court. The final hearing date is frequently set at the first hearing. Concurrency carers and birth families are thus aware of the timescales to which everyone is working. Concurrency carers perhaps understand more readily than birth families the motives behind the timetable.

During the months before the final hearing, some of the birth parents moved towards relinquishing their children, sometimes unexpectedly, sometimes after talking through the details of their action with the concurrency team workers (see also Chapter 7).

We were not a text book case, or there probably isn't such a thing. It all happened very suddenly. I just turned up for contact and was told that [the birth mother] wanted to relinquish. All the social workers were out and there was just a student in charge, who said: 'Oh, [the birth mother] wants a word with you, she's decided to relinquish [the baby].' But she didn't want to talk to anyone but me. It was such a brave thing to do. Her plan was to say goodbye . . . and we were all crying. I am going to cry now, remembering. It was very emotional because she was sitting there crying and there was no-one there who knew what to do. That was the awful thing. There were no social workers present.

There was considerable sensitivity to how birth parents might be feeling. The following is typical of what several carers reported.

I really wanted to know how she [birth mother] was, and I wanted her to know that we cared how she was, and that we weren't leaping up and down because we had her baby.

The "traditional" route to adoption

In the first part of this chapter the views of the concurrency carers on their experience of concurrent planning and the reasons why some prospective adopters did not choose concurrent planning were reported. In this section the views of the adoptive parents following the traditional route are given on several other aspects of the procedures, to balance the reports of the families who chose concurrency. Twenty-three children were placed with families recruited by the MAS Adoption Team, and 21 children were with Trafford foster families at the start of the research. Of the latter, four children had remained with foster carers at the end of the follow-up year, but 17 were placed for adoption during the study period (see Chapter 5 for details).

After the decision to adopt

Several couples reported a lack of sympathy from the local authorities that they had contacted – 'a very rude and tactless reception' said one couple – as well as little or no encouragement to continue with their adoption plans. In contrast, a large number of adoptive parents said that they had been "delighted" by their reception at MAS and other voluntary agencies.[5] At the start of the evaluation, central government had already recommended a change of attitude towards the use of adoption from local authorities, and had stressed the importance of their supporting prospective adoption applicants. It is disappointing to find that unfriendly experiences still prevailed during the evaluation period.

Preparation groups

The information we gained about preparation groups for traditional adoption relates exclusively to groups run by voluntary adoption agencies. The families that adopted children from Trafford Social Services attended groups in their respective localities. All the preparation groups were highly thought of:

> *The groups were good. You go into adoption because you want children. You are so naïve at the beginning; you don't realise what they may have gone through. But you do learn that children are survivors.*

[5] This was also reported by adoptive parents of the Trafford Adoption and Permanency Team cases who were seen at the follow-up interviews. These parents had contacted a wide range of local authorities in their own geographical areas, and subsequently been prepared and supported by several regional voluntary adoption agencies.

We also liked to build up relationships with the other adopters, and find out that adoption was so normal.

Like some concurrency carers, there were prospective adoptive parents who found the training quite challenging.

I found the training sessions terrifying, especially the "ice-breakers" at the start, but we found the information was great. At the time, because our assessment had not been completed, we found some sessions were a waste of time, but the material on child behaviour was good. We have tried to put some of the things into practice now with [placed child]. We find it a bit hard to remember exactly what was said, but we can always ask.

Adoptive families waiting for the placements

The adoptive parents had many anxieties in the weeks before they heard about the children. Some anxieties were about the possible medical problems or behaviour problems the children would bring into the family, sometimes about the "gaps" in the children's histories, sometimes about the purely practical issues surrounding the arrival of young children.

Adoptive father: *I know the next six months are going to be extremely hard, changing from comfortable calm surroundings, learning to bond and adapt to the children.*

Adoptive mother: *I am worried that I may not be able to remember what I have been taught [about parenting].*

The wait is horrendous. You can't pace yourself. It's like waiting to be hit on the head.

Well, we had been turned down for three children, and it felt like eternity before we heard about [this child]. It's a stressful time.

Meeting the birth parents in mainstream adoption

Like the concurrency carers, many of the parents using the traditional route to adoption had a sense of alarm about meeting the birth parents or grandparents. When we interviewed the MAS adoptive parents before a placement, these meetings were only in prospect, but the Trafford adoptive parents who were seen only at follow-up also remembered their concerns about this part of the placement arrangements. But to balance that feeling, there was widespread appreciation of the importance of the meeting that would provide them with a small amount of information to pass on to their adopted child in later years.

> *We felt it was important for J. to meet and then have some ongoing contact. We were worried that J. would have difficulty understanding why [the mother] had given him up at birth and had not wanted contact. But the grandmother does, and both sides have got to feel the need for contact [i.e. not just birth family].*

> *I know it's silly, but I feel very ambivalent about meeting the mother. I would find it much easier to meet and talk with a young, unmarried mother who was obviously unable to cope with bringing up a child, than to meet and "be nice to" a parent who was responsible for neglecting or abusing "our" children.* After meeting: *We thought they were "nice people" and could almost have been friends if the circumstance had been different.*

In one family meeting the birth parents left the prospective adopters completely cold. They had been warned to expect some hostility from the mother, which was largely what happened, but by keeping "cool" managed to achieve a reasonable farewell meeting.

> *I can't say we have any feeling or sympathy for them. He's a druggy and she's weird. I came away thinking they were a sad pair, but did not feel they had any connection with [newly adopted child]. I don't think much was achieved by meeting them.*

Like the concurrency carers, the adoptive parents who found that it was not possible to meet birth parents very much regretted it. Their perspective was very similar to the concurrency carers, and they held very positive views of the value to their children of knowing more about their parents in future years.

> *We are keen to meet, not just for the children, but also for us. We have sent the letters but not got anything back. But I am happy to do this, because it may help the children in the future.*

The contrast with the experiences of the concurrency carers is marked. While the latter had weeks and months of intensive contact, during which the outcome of their own support to the birth parents might contribute to the final recommendations to court on whether the child stayed with them or returned to the birth family, the traditional adoptive families only had to deal with "farewell" meetings. In traditional adoption, there is no suggestion that the adoptive parents should provide any particular support to the birth family, and certainly not on an ongoing basis. For the adoptive family the decision had already been taken when the child was matched, and the courts had confirmed adoption as the care plan. In one sense, it scarcely mattered how successful these meeting were for the participants, although it was obvious that the majority of adoptive parents were keen that they should be rewarding.

Introductions and placement of the children

The children going through the mainstream adoption procedures either with the MAS or the Trafford adoption teams were, without exception, placed from foster homes or children's homes into the adoptive family. They were significantly older than the concurrency cases at the time of their placement into a permanent family (see Chapter 4). It was therefore not surprising to be told that several of the children had become quite attached to their foster carers. Sometimes this presented problems at the time of moving to the adoptive family for both the adoptive parents and foster carers, even if the placement was eventually judged successful. There was considerable variation in how the adopters reacted to being called "Mummy" or "Daddy". Some were clearly delighted and felt it showed how the children had accepted their new families. Others were critical of social workers or foster carers who introduced them with these names, and who did not make allowances for how the children might naturally grow towards using these names in their own time.

Well, we felt the foster parents were really too attached, and were almost obstructive during hand-over. They seemed to be reluctant to let us get at all close when they were there. And they had already got [the child] calling them Mum and Dad. It made me a bit doubtful, but we kept going.

We found the introductions very hard, because the foster mother found it hard to "let go". She was often emotional and weepy and was very reluctant to let us hold [the child]. They were good and caring, and she has had a stable start to life. But it was not an easy time.

The majority of adoptive families, however, did not face these early complications, and were appreciative of the transitional work done by the foster homes, or by a relative.

The foster parents were very professional and helpful at the time of the introductions and the move.

Support systems

Support came from the adoption teams, but also from relatives and friends. Adoptive parents recorded that they had good support from MAS in the form of practical advice, and the Trafford adopters recorded support from a wide variety of voluntary adoption agencies. In a number of families the adoption worker's support was described as excellent:

Well, we have one another, and lots of family and friends, so we talk to them about our worries. We will go to them for advice too, when the children appear.

However, the support groups were not universally enjoyed or valued equally by all the adopters. One family commented that the couples that attended were all at different stages, and were sometimes not very friendly or open with the most recently arrived members. These reactions are bound to be very personal.

In the next chapter we report the views of some of the birth parents to concurrent planning and the alternative experiences arising for them in traditional adoption.

Summary

- The experiences of those seeking to adopt through concurrent planning were not – at least in the early days – very different from the experiences of those adopting by the "traditional" route. The initial enquiry, attending training, the home study period, building relationships with the adoption teams or concurrency teams, and finally going through Panel were all shared experiences, as were the difficulties associated with arranging the time to leave work.

- However, the concurrency carers also had very considerable *extra* demands made on them: the frequent and close contact with birth parents, and the continuous uncertainty about whether the child might return to the birth family. Many of them felt they could not throw themselves into the role of parent in the whole-hearted way that adoptive parents can.
- While the concurrency carers should be able to access considerable support from the concurrency teams, the evidence from this early study suggests that on occasions this may not have met all their needs. Equally, some of the adoptive families reported that they could have done with more support once the child was placed with them. Although there should have been regular local authority visiting up to the date of the Adoption Order, this did not provide for all the parents' needs.
- At the intermediate stage – waiting for the Freeing Order and then waiting for the Adoption Order – delays and bureaucratic mistakes affected some families in both groups. Neither group should have had to shoulder the added burden of bureaucratic bungling when they had so many other potential sources of anxiety with which to deal. The best social work practice would ensure the availability of appropriate support, for which the Quality Protects Briefing Note 5 (Thoburn, 2002) provides excellent and detailed advice.
- Our findings on the outcomes for the children, reported in Chapter 5, indicate that the time from placement to the decision on permanent placement was very considerably shorter for the concurrency children than for the children going through the traditional adoption process. Nevertheless, the experiences of the two sets of prospective adopters were not dissimilar in-so-far-as they both need high levels of support and understanding.

7 Birth parents' experiences in the adoption of their children

It will not surprise workers in this field of childcare to hear that it was not possible to see all the birth parents. Adoption agency social workers tried to persuade them to participate, but with limited success. The letter from the researchers that was given to birth parents by the concurrency teams and Trafford social workers seldom produced a response. Home visits and telephone calls were slightly more successful, but the response rate remained very low in two projects. Contact was usually successful when the researchers were in the concurrency offices at the same time as the birth parents.

We recognise that the birth parents probably saw the research interviews as intimidating. Frequently they were reported as having difficult relationships with "authority" and may well have seen the researchers as part of that world, not least because the request for an interview was made through the social work teams. Hunt (1997) has described birth parents' reactions to the case conferences and court procedures; theoretically, they were more involved in these after the Children Act 1989, but they still reported the occasions as "intimidating, depersonalising and demeaning". If that had been a common view during the years of the current research, it would explain why some birth parents would not have wanted to meet more professionals. On the other hand, some parents, as we will see, had very positive views of the concurrency team workers.

Table 7.1 shows that ten (42 per cent) out of the 24 birth parents of concurrency cases were interviewed but a much smaller proportion from the other two placement groups. The 21 looked after children in the Trafford sample came from 12 families. Only one birth mother was seen; six refused to participate, and five mothers were "not available". This category included some who had, according to the Trafford social workers, "disappeared". Others were seen occasionally by social workers, but seldom predictably, and frequently they did not have fixed addresses. The children placed by the MAS Adoption Team had often been parted from

Table 7.1
Interviews achieved and not achieved with birth parents/families

Reason why birth parent was not seen by researchers	*Concurrency Projects' birth parents*		*Trafford Adoption and Permanency Team birth parents*		*MAS Adoption Team birth parents*		*Total birth parents*
	N	%	N	%	N	%	N
Birth parents contacted but refused interview	1	4	6	50	2	13	9
Birth parents "not available"/ no contact	10	42	5	42	8 (14 children)	53	23
Birth parents interviewed	13	54	1	8	4 (6 children)	27	18
Local authority refused contact	1	4	0	0	0	0	1
Total parents	**24**	**100**	**12**	**100**	**15**	**100**	**51**

their birth parents months or years before they were referred to MAS, and contact had been lost with the local authority in a high proportion of cases. The MAS Adoption Team have found that local authority social workers are not always keen for contact to be renewed, but the Team sometimes manage to make some professional contact later.

It had been intended to see all the concurrency birth parents within a few weeks of the placement of their child with the concurrency carers. It was seldom possible to organise this within the planned timeframe, and in the event, the interviews were held at various times in the concurrency process up to, though not after, the final hearing. Inevitably this distorts the results, because, while a birth parent might feel optimistic about the return of their child at the start of the concurrent planning programme, they might have changed their minds about whether they wanted to have their child back as the months went by, or become aware of the increasing possibility that they were not going to achieve the targets set out for them in the concurrency plan. We will highlight this when it was obvious from the interview material that changing circumstances had led to particular views being put to the researcher. As much as possible, this issue was explored in the interviews. In the course of these interviews the birth parents were encouraged to speak about their feelings and opinions of the concurrency planning process they were going through, with promise of confidentiality. In reporting their views anonymously this promise is not being breached: personal details that might identify the family have been taken out of quotations from the interviews and the gender of their child has sometimes been changed.

The following results should be read with these caveats in mind, but we believe that the views of the birth parents are particularly important when considering the overall picture of concurrent planning. We report what they said in the interviews and did not check on their stories: their words are their own.[1]

---

[1] Provided in confidence and wherever it is necessary we have disguised the family circumstances.

Characteristics of the birth parents

The Strengths in Families and Poor Prognostic Indicators

These checklists, designed by Katz and her colleagues for use in concurrency cases, were completed for 59 children.[2] The reasons why the forms were not completed for some birth families were often not clear. Sometimes the reason given by the social workers was that the family had not "engaged" with the team in the assessment. Among the 23 children placed by the MAS Adoption Team, the checklists were not completed by the local authority social workers for four families with seven children. For these children social services were contacted directly by the researchers, but the social workers with sufficiently detailed knowledge of the original family to complete the questionnaires had apparently moved.

The variations in the characteristics of the birth families in the concurrency projects, compared with the families referred to the MAS or Trafford Adoption Teams, have been discussed in Chapter 4. To summarise, there were significant differences in the scores on the Strengths in Families checklist, with more of the parents in the concurrency cases showing more positive characteristics.

By contrast, there were no differences between the concurrency cases and the two comparison groups in the frequency with which social workers reported the Poor Prognostic Indicators. All the families appeared to share very troubled backgrounds and high levels of current problems. On this checklist a high proportion of the families in all three placement groups showed substantial parenting deficits and evidence of dangerous or criminal lifestyles. The characteristic checked most frequently on the PPI was a history of child protection services involvement and the removal previously of other children, with no apparent change in the domestic circumstances in the interim. Among the 59 parents for whom there was a completed PPI, 19 (32 per cent) were reported as addicted to drugs and/or alcohol; of these, four obtained their main livelihood from dealing or prostitution. Twelve mothers (20 per cent) had continued to take drugs and/or drink to excess during the recent pregnancy. Addiction problems at the time the index child was taken into care were not significantly different in the three placement groups. Domestic violence had been

---

[2] See Appendix C for the full checklists.

experienced recently by 17 birth mothers (29 per cent), varying from one-fifth among the cases placed by the MAS team, through 30 per cent among the Trafford team cases to over one-third in the concurrency teams' placements. Case notes (often voluminous) also indicated the high levels of stress experienced by the birth families across a range of social indicators such as multiple disadvantage in the parents' own childhoods, inadequate or unstable housing arrangements, long-term unemployment, and frequent changes of partner.

General Health Questionnaire results

The interviewed birth parents (all except one mother) were asked to complete the 28-item GHQ, and ten did so. Of these, seven showed total scores over the 4/5 cut-off point recommended as indicating moderately severe mood disturbance (mean 11.8, SD 10.22) (Weneke *et al*, 2000). The profile of the whole group derived from the subscales suggests that these ten birth parents suffered from considerable anxiety, but depression was also common.[3] As we only saw the birth parents once, we have no way of knowing whether these responses were stable over time, or were temporary reactions to the stressful events surrounding them when we held the interviews.

For three further reasons, these results are of little value in describing systematically the levels or types of psychiatric disturbance among these birth parents. First, it is a very small sample; second, a substantial proportion of the birth parents were not seen; and third, it did not prove possible to see the birth parents at a standard point in the adoption process. Some were seen within a few weeks of the placement of their child in care or in an adoption placement; others were interviewed some months into the process. Their mood was thus likely to be influenced by a range of external events over few of which they appeared to have any control. There was no evidence on whether the events surrounding the removal of the index child had triggered the mood disturbance or whether it had also existed in a similar form and at a similar level of severity before the child started being looked after.

---

[3] Mean anxiety score: 9.6 (SD 6.77); mean depression score: 8.4 (SD 7.06); mean social dysfunction score: 8.1 (SD 4.46); and mean somatic symptoms score: 7.5 (SD 5.42).

Specialist support programmes for concurrency birth parents

In a recent Research in Practice briefing paper it has been noted that 'The paucity of research on services to birth parents reflects the paucity of the services themselves' (Thoburn, 2002). Weinberg and Katz (1998) also noted that the limited resources for birth parents could undermine a concurrent planning initiative.

In the present study, the numbers were collected of birth parents who were involved with programmes that would help them address the reasons why their child had been removed. This information was not always recorded in the case notes. Across the whole group of birth parents in the three concurrent planning projects, help from specialist programmes was not universally offered or available locally, and the commonest form extra help took was the work done in the contact sessions with the supervising community workers or social workers. These periods of one, two or three hours allowed the supervising staff to monitor how the parents handled and responded to their child, and to teach new skills. Such advice tended to be highly practical: hygiene, diet, sleeping or eating arrangements, learning to handle and play with children, management of disobedience, and so on. But as one concurrency carer observed, 'It is hardly rocket science to care for a baby of three months for two hours – a 12-year-old could do it.' Although family social workers could not be expected to endorse this extreme view, it was true that the contact periods did not make the demands on birth parents that all parents find to be a challenge: organising the day, getting children ready for school on time, fed on time, to bed on time; regulating the television watching of older children; dealing with more than one child in the household, and running a household as well. Neglect, lack of physical care, poor hygiene and abuse had all been cited as reasons for taking older children into local authority care from the same families, and although the concurrency children were all removed from parental care at very early ages, it was judged that they would have been at risk of the same levels of neglect and abuse if they had not been removed. However, in one case where the possibility of the child returning to the birth parents strengthened, the frequency and duration of the contact sessions were considerably increased in order to test the parents' skills with the ten-month-old child.

The number of birth parents in the concurrency programmes who received other and more specialised services appeared therefore to be small overall, although there was some variation between the projects. In one project, the team put considerable effort into finding services and enrolling their birth parents on them, finding that it was sometimes possible to get special courses set up for parents. In this particular project, finding appropriate services for men was very difficult, but local services for women were easier to access. These were available in Women's Centres and included groups for parenting skills, nutrition and cookery, and for victims of domestic violence. Finding services for men in this area was a challenge: it took 17 phone calls to get one man onto an anger management course.

The relevance of the special programmes was not always appreciated by parents. One birth family had been referred to a parenting group, but complained that this was designed for parents of two to four-year-olds, whereas their child was under one year old. They withdrew before completing the course. Clearly the advantages of having skills for the important years when their child was a toddler was lost on them. In this project, five other families attended courses in full. In another project one couple seemed confused about whether or not they had been offered help with parenting, one parent claiming they had, the other that they had not. This illustrates the advantage of written agreements with the concurrency team (lacking for this couple) with a named provider of the training. The more frequent response was that 'we didn't need any parenting class'. For the majority of parents, however, the supervised contact sessions provided the main opportunity to improve the care the parents currently offered their children. Even in this, the purpose of supervising their parenting skills was not always understood by the parents.

They don't want him to come home, they feel we can't parent him.

Interviewer: *Are you getting any help with learning about being parents?*

Birth parent: *They just sort of sit there and ask us questions; they're asking us to show them, because we bath him, and when we bath him we do it together, because one of the supervisors in the contact actually says it's good to do teamwork, so one does the bottle, one changes and then we bath him together. But they still don't think we can do it.*

One couple recognised the uncertainty associated with going on a parenting course, and the fact that it was not a guarantee of the child's return.

It is also important to reflect on whether the specialist services that were provided would deal with the underlying problems that many birth parents exhibited. It was, for example, suggested by experienced practitioners that attending anger management classes was unlikely to have a sufficient impact on parental behaviour to make them "safe" parents in the timescales set by the courts. There also seemed to be an absence of programmes that could address violence to children or partners for parents who did not have a criminal record. One project discovered that, to qualify for the local anger management courses, a parent would have to be on probation. We have noted that the incidence of domestic violence within the concurrency families was high. While it was true that some of the birth mothers had left the men who purportedly were violent, it is widely understood that such women are vulnerable to becoming involved with other violent partners. In one project, anger management courses were attended by six sets of parents. One project found a suitable group for survivors of domestic violence, but the waiting list for appropriate psychotherapy was longer than could be encompassed in the concurrent planning timescale. In part as a substitute, some personal counselling of the birth parents was done by the concurrency team workers who had the relevant skills. The evidence from previous events and other children having been taken into care from the same family is properly given considerable weight in the final decisions about placement. In a small number of cases, the responsibility for severe harm to another child in the family was still being disputed by the parent(s), but the balance of professional judgment had to be on the side of the child's safety.

Some birth mothers reported having a succession of partners who were Schedule 1 offenders. The programmes that would enable them to remain as single parents, or learn to choose partners more wisely probably do not exist. The benefit system does not provide very generous support for single parenthood, so just at the level of family budgeting, the option of moving away from the Schedule 1 partner is not attractive. The intensive parent support programmes are also absent from many areas. Many of these families are severely disadvantaged and require particularly supportive childcare services, such as day care for all the children, and that may not always be available within reasonable distance from the parent's home or at the time she or he needs such support.

As noted above, drug addiction was also common. In one project, three birth mothers (two with the birth fathers as well) (out of seven families) were referred to and accepted immediately into local drugs projects; they attended erratically or not at all. In another project addicted parents of five children were referred to specialist programmes, but it was not clear how well they attended: they were not deemed capable of parenting the index child by the final hearing date. In the first project, one mother (out of seven cases) was also referred to a specialist parenting assessment centre and attended for all the sessions.

Birth parents' views of the concurrency projects

Thirteen sets of birth parents[4] from the concurrency cases (54 per cent) were interviewed in the research, and, judging by the reasons why people could not be seen or why they had refused an interview, it is very likely that this was not a representative sample. This group of birth parents, for example, were more involved in contact, and had relatively stable housing arrangements.

Being well-informed about concurrent planning

While all the concurrency carers had actively chosen to join the concurrent planning projects, it was not always clear that the birth parents had been in a position to make such a positive and well-informed choice. Some of the birth parents felt that they had been "bounced" into accepting that concurrency was an appropriate model for them.

We agreed because we could see that the baby wouldn't hang about in the system; that he wouldn't be moved around, and that he wouldn't get

[4] Some parents were seen singly, but some in couples.

> *hurt or harmed. But a meeting should have been arranged with our solicitor beforehand to be told about concurrent planning. The worker should not just have "popped up" in the court. There should be direct discussion "person-to-person with parents and workers".*

Eight parents could remember being given written information about the concurrency projects. The rest either said they had nothing in writing or had forgotten. Seven of the eight recalling the written information thought it had been helpful. One couple had two weeks to agree to joining the concurrency project: while one might believe this gave them plenty of time to think of the advantages to them, they were in the middle of the court procedures surrounding the placements of their five other children, and this took considerable energy and time. The baby was slightly premature and taken away at birth. They considered they were 'being pushed into things; it was difficult to take everything in', but later came to have a more positive view of how they were treated. After three or four months, when their opinion of the concurrency team had become very positive, this remained as their only criticism.

Another couple, also hearing about the concurrency project for the first time in court, claimed they were not given any written information, and very little time to absorb this novel idea. Their solicitor recommended they accept the programme because it would give them a better chance of the baby coming home to them. This couple certainly misunderstood the ideas underlying concurrency planning, believing it was only a matter of time until the baby returned. They maintained to the researchers that they only heard about the possibility that the baby might be adopted by the carers after about three months attending contact at the concurrency project.

> *We thought it would be like a family centre where the children came home after a time.*

This couple had an overall poor relationship with the concurrency workers, and a very poor opinion of the concurrent planning option. But they were also resentful and lacking understanding of why their child had been taken into care in the first place. Since it is highly improbable that they did not have the possibility of adoption explained to them in full from the start, their criticisms could be explained by this generalised hostility.

They are always criticising, watching every move we make – we get a lot of "sarky" comments. We don't get a chance to show good parenting. Everything is done for the foster parents and nothing is done for us. They got given a buggy for the baby, but I wasn't given anything. The [concurrency] building is always dirty. [Worker] controls everything in our lives and tells us that the contact appointments take precedence over everything else – attending the job centre, or seeing the probation officer.

One other couple also said they had been given no written information about concurrent planning. Written material was available in this project, but since both partners had severe reading difficulties, it is possible they had not read it. They both recalled being told about concurrent planning but had retained only a hazy idea of its purpose.

However, many birth parents were clear that they had been given the information and had it explained to them by concurrency workers, even if it was difficult to absorb.

We were given written information about the project, and given two weeks to think about it. It was difficult to take everything in at first. It was all going too fast. We had a lot of questions we wanted to have answered. We got the answers from the Project, which was good.

This view might be contrasted with that of a birth father from a traditional adoption case, who felt that everything went too fast for him, and that he received no support from the professionals involved in his children's case. It was clear from a lengthy interview that he had some difficulty following what was being proposed for his children or the timetable for the decisions and court procedures. His reactions will be familiar to many social workers in contact with such troubled families.

[The social worker] pushed for adoption – she didn't give me a chance. She doesn't care about me, and the distress she's caused me. The guardian was a "waste of space", he just went along with social services. He didn't take the children's interests into consideration. I reckon they planned it all between them: the reports were just the same. They didn't give me a chance to sort my life out.

In contrast to the birth parents who had not understood the purpose of concurrent planning, and had no clear view of the consequent obligations and expectations laid on them, many parents tried to work to the goals that were agreed with them by the concurrency teams. Early in the life of one project, it was noted in an advisory group meeting that the birth parents 'were expected to work co-operatively with the concurrency team', and that most viewed "very positively" the option of concurrent planning, and the clarity of the expectations. The research interviews supported this professional view that some parents made good sense of the aims of concurrent planning for their child.

> Father: *It's different, because it's like – concurrency carers. And I actually felt good about that because I thought, if they are going to foster them temporarily that means they are going to build up a bond between them, and . . . Finally they have to be moved until they find the right home. This way they build up a bond, and they would also, then, live there for the rest of their childhood.*

The views of the birth parents on what was being offered by the concurrency teams had an important bearing on their wider perception of what a concurrent planning programme had to offer. There was a group of birth parents who were all interviewed close to the end of the concurrent planning period who held very positive views (five – 39 per cent of the interviewed parents). Eight spoke of the benefits of contact with their child and three more of the benefits of the specific programmes they had to follow.

Views about the project workers

The parents who were interviewed reported widely varying views about the concurrency teams. Interestingly, they nearly always contrasted the concurrency workers with "social workers", with whom they had almost universally had hostile relationships and negative experiences in the past. When they spoke of "social workers" they always meant local authority staff, and they often implied that the concurrency workers were not social workers. It was as though the professional background and training was not what mattered, but rather the responsibility that social services departments carry to protect children, which was perceived as intrusive and punitive. Those who expressed hostile opinions of "social workers" were largely drawn from the group who had older children, many or all of whom had been taken into care at one time or another. These parents reported the concurrency workers as being more approachable and helpful. However, even when they said the concurrency workers had been more responsive to their perspective, this did not necessarily lead them to feel more involved in the decisions about their child. While ten (77 per cent) of the concurrency birth parents who were interviewed felt they had been involved in the preparation of court reports, half still felt excluded from *long-term* decision-making about their child. Fewer than half were satisfied with what the assessments concluded. Nevertheless, of 13 parents, five (39 per cent) came out of the concurrency programmes with a more positive view of the adoption placement, and half said they would like to be involved with concurrency again if another child was born. The numbers are small, but these responses paint a positive picture of overall or longer-term success with only a minority of these very disadvantaged parents. The reasons for the less positive views are explored below.

Not given a chance

The importance of being "given a chance" was very clear from the concurrency parents' interviews. There was a common perception by the parents that they were not being treated fairly by social services, and they were not getting a chance to prove that they could manage with this child, even when they had failed with others. There was a strong undercurrent of grievance, with which many family social workers will be familiar. As in the study by Freeman and Hunt (1998), the birth parents who were interviewed mostly understood the reasons for their child's removal, though they often disputed details of their own child protection histories. Their sense of injustice came either because they felt they had tried to change or their circumstances had changed or because they intended to change, but that social workers did not give them credit.

> *When they first said concurrent planning, I was against it. I dunno why, I just don't like it. They were saying, 'Right, he's going to concurrency carers'. That's like saying, 'Well we're not going to give you a chance'. We thought we were getting a chance, and everything was going all*

right [while with first foster carers], until [social worker] said he's going into this foster care and adoption. And I thought well, that's not giving us a chance.

Birth parents can't win; they set us up to fail. They have got to learn that birth parents are more important than [foster carers]. Carers don't get assessed like we do. They talk down to me, like I was a child. We're not given any respect. I don't know why I bother; we are being criticised all the time. And we don't get to see [the baby] nearly as much as we should.

These mothers frequently expressed the view that they were 'not being given a chance' with the concurrency child. When saying this, these birth parents nearly always meant that it was the local authority social workers, as opposed to the concurrency workers, who were not giving them 'a chance'. It is important to see this in terms of the high level of support that the birth parents were given in the concurrency projects, and the fact that these were new relationships. The concurrency team workers told the researchers that, hearing these views of social work, they had themselves made sure that the birth parents understood that team members were also social workers. And it is clear the birth parents did often understand this, but still reported their more positive views of the concurrency teams in contrast to the local authority social services. Most of the birth parents interviewed by the researchers saw their previous contact with social workers in very negative terms. The following view is not untypical:

I've never liked [social workers]. I've had them ever since I was a kid. I was in care up to [age] 17. And when we had the older kids here they were always round the house, and they used to sit there and stare. And they are always lying to you. But [the concurrency worker], I could get on with her really well. I could sit down and talk to her, and she would listen. I just felt she was a nice woman. But she wasn't a social worker, she was from the concurrency team, you know. She was very supportive.

Below is a longer extract from an interview with a mother and her partner. It reports several aspects of their perceptions: that the mother thinks she is trying but is not understood or given credit for this; that the partner thinks his inability to read is being held against them both; their feeling that they are not trusted with the welfare of their own child; and that they feel social services have not let them prove their capabilities. This couple had four previous children taken into care. There is no suggestion that the concurrent planning placement was ill-judged, nor that the assessment that this couple continued to show signs of inadequate parenting skills was wrong. These quotes are simply the parents' perceptions and valuable as an indication of the extent of misunderstanding between some birth families and the concurrency services, and the scale of the task facing the concurrency teams.

> Mother: *I am trying to make a new beginning, but they keep shoving it in my face that because of my past, I will never be able to parent a child properly. So because of that, they've put me through for therapy. Well I'm not being funny, but I feel as if I'm trying to move forward, but social services are knocking me backwards. It's not me doing it, it's them. You know, it's your fault, you know because of your past, your mum dying and all that, you've had a sad neglectful childhood, but no, they're not letting me try and move forward at all. And then they are trying to say that I was dependent on [partner]. If I was dependent on him, I wouldn't have gone to work. So far, they keep saying I haven't [moved forward], not sufficient enough to parent a baby.*
>
> Partner: *Not really no, but again, I can't read and write. Well, I can read, a little bit, but they're going on that as well.*
>
> Interviewer: *Do you feel that you're not getting the information?*
>
> Partner: *Yeah, we are getting information, but we're not given the chance to prove it.*
>
> Mother: *I mean they won't let us have her for even a day by ourselves. You know, it's stupid. We're not going to try and make a run for it, or anything.*
>
> Interviewer: . . . *mother and baby placement?*

Mother: *We asked for that, and they said no. A psychiatrist came round and told us we would not be able to cope because the baby is so demanding. Which she is not. She lets you know when she wants her bottle, she lets you know when she wants to cuddle, otherwise she's content.*

Interviewer: *Do you find her demanding in the contact?*

Mother: *Not at all.*

Partner: *No, not really. No.*

These views are an important reflection of the concurrency teams' styles of working and contrast with the response of parents to authority that is frequently reported in child abuse studies (Corby, 1987). They reflect the findings of Masson *et al* (1997) that birth parents value in social workers a willingness to listen and being treated with respect. However, it needs to be remembered that many of the birth parents were not seen by the researchers, mostly because they refused to participate, and these missing parents may well have expressed more hostile opinions about the concurrency teams. It should also be recognised that, where the outcome was that the child should stay with the concurrency carer and the plan was for adoption, it is not improbable that the birth families change their attitude to the concurrency workers. This has been reported when family attitudes were tracked through the year following the discovery of severe abuse (Sharland *et al*, 1996). In this latter study the initially positive reports about social workers had deteriorated into increasing disappointment. Some birth parents in the present sample had also changed their minds about the concurrency worker as the months went by.

Sometimes the project worker is helpful. But underneath she's just a social worker, and she's starting to behave like all the others now. To begin with she was: 'We want to give you a chance, we want to see your baby coming home,' and now she's saying: 'Sorry, he's not coming home'.

We got told everything was going brilliant by the currency [sic] team, and then four weeks before the court hearing we got told: 'You're not doing your job.' And I said, 'Hold on a minute, you just said in the reports we were doing brilliant, and then you say we're doing nothing'. They don't know about looking after people or their kids, they just like taking them away. And they had said to us, 'Oh, you've got a good chance. You're going to get [the baby] back.' We were doing everything they told us to do. But currency planning is [rubbish].

The same birth parents nevertheless took a very favourable view of their own concurrency worker: 'She's polite, she's understanding . . .' Such positive reactions were not uncommon and frequently extended to wishing they had been able to use a concurrency team with their older children.

I would have loved to have gone there [the concurrency project] with [first baby]. Then I wouldn't be in this pickle . . . When I've been depressed [team leader] has always been there for me. Whenever you are stuck you can just give them a ring, and they'll help to sort it out. I think they're brilliant. They are honest and straightforward, not like social services – they are a load of rubbish.

In the court I was given leaflets, which said about contact and that. Which is quite interesting for me. I knew what the place was about. Helping families, not being against them like the social workers are . . . It seems to be that people want to help . . . to get [my baby] back. It's not just being left in the hands of social workers . . . I don't understand why I couldn't come here in the first place [when two older children were taken away] . . . they should have been here a long time ago . . . they speak to you properly as well. They speak to you like a person not like a client sort of thing.

One couple were unusually clear in their high opinion of the concurrency project, and were able to list the benefits it offered them.

We found our concurrency worker very honest and direct. Everything was written down clearly for us, and we knew where we stood. They explain everything in everyday language. You are treated with respect, like a person – you get greeted as though you were friends. They will do a brew when you arrive. We were listened to and we were heard. At the end of the day it was our decision. None of this has been our experience of working with social services – they lie through their teeth. [Get rid of] social services: they are just ignorant. Put the money into the concurrency project.

Some families clearly understood that the concurrency teams were very obviously and practically giving them the chance to get their child back.

I did understand what they were saying, that A. would not be safe, but I didn't have a chance to talk to them proper. They [LA social workers] were already talking about adoption right then, in the hospital, and I didn't think that was right. I don't agree with the adoption even now, but then at the end it wouldn't be my choice. But here [concurrency project] people want to help me get A. back. It's not just being left in the hands of the social workers.

Parents' understanding of the purposes of contact

An important aspect of the concurrency work is the close involvement by a small team with the birth parents over several months when they attend for contact with their child. Of the 24 sets of birth parents in the three concurrent planning projects, 13 appear to have attended reasonably regularly for the supervised contact (see Chapter 8 on contact). A few birth parents turned up for one or two sessions and then "disappeared": 'making their decision with their feet', as one team worker neatly put it. One of the important tasks of the concurrency teams was establishing as soon as possible, often within hours of the failure to turn up for contact, the reasons behind this behaviour. The contact arrangements were subject to constant review and in most concurrency cases ended up by being reduced in number or duration as the birth parents increasingly failed to keep appointments.

There was a common perception among the concurrency parents that they were not being "trusted", and this showed most markedly when they spoke of the contact arrangements. For example, if their child had gone to a traditional foster carer (as had sometimes been the case with children previously removed from them), parents expected that they would have contact in the foster carer's home and more unsupervised freedom to take their child out of the concurrency project. The very different arrangements in concurrent planning did not make sense to some of them. The controlled contact arrangements in each concurrency project then tended to be resented by this group of parents. The reactions of birth parents to the contact arrangements are reported in more detail in Chapter 8.

It has been noted (Chapter 6) that many of the concurrency carers reported a sense that the scales were tipped in favour of the birth parents, because of the specialist services and the way in which birth parents will always get "massive support" to succeed. So there seems to be a tendency for each to adopt the view that the other is the favoured party, and this in turn appears to generate considerable anxiety in each group. This anxiety during the concurrent planning phase of these projects, up to and sometimes beyond final hearing, may be seen as one cost of a system that actively supports birth parents being given one last chance, but asks potential adopters to "hold" the child while the parents struggle to prove their capabilities. Clearly every case is different in this as in other characteristics, but the strain on both sides should not be under-estimated.

Parting from their child

The pain of parting with their children was apparent in several concurrency birth parent interviews – perhaps increased by so many being taken away at birth. One woman, who had previously had older children removed for serious neglect, had nevertheless hoped to be able to start a family again. Her sense of loss was particularly acute.

> *I had longer with [the older children], but I felt rushed into signing things with the baby. After I had [the baby] – this might sound bad – but after, I didn't want to hold him. Because I knew he'd be gone, and I didn't want a chance to try and love him, because I'd have been too much attached to him.*

> *I turned up [on the hospital ward] when the concurrent carers were there. I was supposed to go twice a day to see her, anyway. But I turned up at the wrong time, didn't I? I started to cry, you know, the way she was sitting there holding the baby and looking down, and that should've been me. So I had to go into another ward, I was very upset.*

Birth parents' views of the carers and adopters

The birth parents, not surprisingly, had very varied attitudes to the concurrency carers. Some were very positive.

> Mother: *At first I was a bit wary, because I didn't know them, but . . . yes, I did feel a bit angry, but when I met them I liked them. They're really nice people.*
>
> Father: *I was very impressed actually.*
>
> Mother: *They used to say hello, and tell us what the baby had been doing, and they say he's a good baby and sleeps through the night.*
>
> *I liked [the carers] when I first met them; they asked how I was. They knew about [first baby] and asked about her as well. They keep a diary for me of [the concurrency baby's] sleeping and feeding, and when he first went in the car seat and so on. They showed me the diary whenever we had contact.* Later: *I wrote to the judge saying that [the baby] could be adopted only if he could go to [the concurrency carers], as I know they love him.*

This fairly warm relationship did not prevent the build up of some resentment and sadness as the months went by; this mother found it increasingly "difficult" to give the baby back to the carers at the end of contact, and minded that the baby used to look round for the carers but never looked for her. But she told the researchers that she knew she had made the right decision. One couple decided as soon as they met the carers; though their solicitor had been very positive, they had been doubtful at first, but changed their minds at the meeting. The positive feelings continued throughout the contact period of several months.

> *When we met them, something clicked. We saw them and decided straight away [to join the concurrency programme]. Contact felt good. The foster mother always handed him over in a positive way. She explained everything that had happened since the previous contact, described his weight, what he'd played with, and gave us lots of details. I always felt comfortable handing him back. We have a good relationship with [the carers] – they have never foul-mouthed us. We've become part of their family and they are part of ours – because of our love of [the baby].*

Not all the relationships were so positive. Some birth parents seemed to feel baffled by meeting the carers, not knowing what to say or ask. This left them unable to form a clear view of the future of their child, and they were more likely to revert to their underlying hostility to what was happening to their child.

I just wanted to know – they could do their job properly.

Interviewer: *What did you think about them?*

Mother: *I dunno. But it does help to have met them – a little bit. But they're not looking after him well. He's going on ill all the time. We just see him, she never comes in; she just sits in the car. And he never says anything to speak of. Lets us know what's going on and that's it. They don't show us the record book, like his first foster carer did.*

Hostility was not uncommon, but rarely expressed as forcefully as with the following birth parents. They had initially had contact with their child with foster carers, but later the child was moved into the concurrency programme. The contrast for them was sharp; they saw the original foster carers as friendly and supportive, but disliked the concurrency carers from the start, and had no compunction in saying so.

We've met them, but we don't like them. Our [child] is like a rag-doll to them. It looks to me like they're looking after [another child], but not our child any more. Right from the start we didn't like them. One minute looking after our child, then pushing it to one side. It's their attitude. Well, you don't look down on the natural parents and you don't talk down to them. We give them clothes for the child, but they never use them, and toys. They treat us like dirt.

Birth parents' decisions about the outcome for their child

The majority of birth parents seen by researchers were the mothers. Very few birth fathers remained involved in the contact arrangements, or accessible to the researchers. Some birth mothers who were interviewed reported that they were unsure who the birth father was.

We have noted that half of the parents interviewed reported that they felt their views had not been taken into account when long-term decisions were being made about their child. But some of the mothers slowly came to realise that they were not going to be able to provide appropriately for their child.

> *I had a good think about it. At the end of the day I'm not in a position to care for him. I wrote a letter to the judge saying that I wanted the best for [the baby] and I cannot look after him just now.*

In one case the birth parents made the decision to relinquish the baby after a few months, telling their concurrency worker that they were deciding to go for adoption, provided it was with the carers, 'and no one else'. Another couple had clearly got on well with the concurrency carers and the mother decided in the end not to fight the case. She did not say, in so many words, that she was happy with the carers, but she implied this by her change of heart over the few months after the first hearing. The father also said he felt better about concurrent planning because he knew, after meeting the carers, that the baby was going to be well looked after.

> Mother: *It's never going to be easy, but concurrency is probably the best solution because at least you know where you stand, and you know where your children stand, and all the little things in-between. I'd say that to other people as well.*

One of the birth mothers who had reported that she did not feel she was being given a chance to show she could care for her baby, when asked whether she would contest the adoption if that was what the court decided, said:

> *I'd mostly go along with it [decision to place for adoption], as long as I could turn round to the judge and say that next time I have a child, I want to be given a chance. Not just for social services to say, 'we'll give you a chance', but I want them to* prove *that they can give me a chance.*

Others remained violently opposed to the carers and the placement for adoption through the final hearing and contested the Adoption Orders when the time came. Some were fundamentally pessimistic about their chances of getting the children back. One mother, looking into the future hoped to have her child back with one or two siblings:

. . . but that's not going to happen. I won't get [the baby] back. Because the social workers are very powerful. And they can have everything their way. Although so many times I've corrected the report, they don't bother to listen. Like how many times I have told them [the baby's] name and they still get it wrong.

Naming the children

All the children came to the concurrency carers with the name chosen by the birth family. Some carers wanted to change this even though, legally, the child was still known by the names on their birth certificates, until the Adoption Order. However, some names were changed, often to a second name given by the birth parent, but in four cases to a completely different name. Some carers appeared confused about what their rights were. In one project the issue emerged in a rather different way and was sensitively resolved. Two birth mothers wanted to show that they had chosen the child's name, and the project worker suggested a naming ceremony: and the project team arranged this for the birth mother and her chosen guests, the adoptive family and the project workers, followed by celebratory tea parties.

The views of non-concurrency birth parents

Five sets of birth parents were interviewed who were not in the concurrent planning projects (Table 7.1, p 156). They had been in contact only with their local social services, with which they mostly seemed to have poor relations.

Two felt that they had been given no warning by social services that the children would be taken away from them:

I had no chance to put my story and people were not believing what I said. They took one of them from the hospital and the other from school without me knowing. I wasn't allowed to see them alone, and the contacts were gradually reduced. I lost count of the court hearings and they were never in the same place. Other members of the family were never fully assessed, I know this. So when I realised that it was going to be adoption I just agreed. I wanted to see them to make sure they were the right people.

One mother felt that she had been left to fend for herself when she became very depressed, and that social services had been unsupportive throughout. She described how her GP, a counsellor and her solicitor have been the best people for her over nearly two years of care proceedings and placement. She found that she had to chase the social worker to finalise the contact arrangements: 'I shouldn't have to do that, she never rings back when I leave a message. I could do with some help with putting together a scrap-book for the children, but I can't get hold of her.'

Support systems

All the birth parents who were interviewed by the researchers said that they had help from someone, and could confide in someone, though this had not prevented some of them having at times quite serious depressive thoughts. Twelve of the 18 birth parents (67 per cent) said they could get help from their partner and nine (50 per cent) from their own parents or close relatives. A small number (four) said they had received help from professionals – their GP, their solicitor or social worker. Only two were supported by religious organisations. While eleven parents said they could confide in their partner (61 per cent) fewer said they could confide in their parents (six – 33 per cent). Friends and siblings were described as confidants by half those who were interviewed, and professionals by a small number. Some parents said these confiding relationships were very supportive, but most gave the impression of feeling helpless in the face of the decisions of courts and professionals.

Summary

- Not all birth parents were seen and there was little independent information that could tell whether they were representative of the birth parents overall.
- The extent of the birth parents' understanding about what was currently happening to settle their children's futures appeared to vary considerably. Most appeared well briefed, although some of the parents in the concurrent planning programmes did not seem fully to understand that they did have a chance of their child returning; these were

also the parents who did not fully understand what they should be doing to get their child returned to them. Some were definitely confused about the progress of the case even though they were well supported by their solicitors.

- The birth parents commonly reported having lengthy and poor relationships with social services departments, and contrasted this with the support and understanding they had from the concurrency workers. There were instances, also, of real appreciation of the small gestures by other people: the concurrency carers who really wanted to hear how the young birth mother was doing, the judge who arranged to have a photograph taken of himself, with both families. "Respect" was a word used many times when they described their gratitude for tempering the impact of their child being removed. However, anger and grief was often apparent in our interviews when they spoke of feeling that they had not been given a chance to parent the placed child. They interpreted this as "the system" being against them, but again, almost always saw the concurrency teams as helping them to deal with this.
- For many birth parents there appeared to be a gap between the assessments of parenting deficits that were recorded for the index child(ren) or those recorded for their other children previously taken into care, and the provision of educational or supportive services *once the child was in care*. While identifying this gap, it is not obvious how it could be filled: classes in bonding and attachment, or behaviour management are difficult to deliver if the parent has no child with them. The experienced social workers in the concurrency teams commented on how frequently there was a repetitive history of the same parenting problems cropping up with child after child. Previous services had not addressed the problems effectively, and there was no immediate evidence that some of the birth parents might not repeat the same mistakes again.
- The "high criticism: low warmth" parents present a particular challenge. In the present study, the concurrency projects' contact sessions (see Chapter 8) provided the main setting in which this work was done, although one project was particularly successful in finding special courses. This project also noted that some birth parents stayed with these local centres after the placement for adoption was confirmed.

- The present study did not determine the aims, the length, the content or the cost of the support services that the projects set in place for the birth parents. This is clearly an area for further investigation, not only to establish how effective such programmes are seen to be by the users or the social workers who subsequently judge the results, but also to find out if the content is appropriate for the particular task of improving parenting skills.

8 **Contact during concurrent planning procedures:** the arrangements and the reactions of concurrency carers and birth families

Contact in the field of adoption and fostering can take many forms. Birth parents may be in contact with their children, or with the foster carers, or with the adoptive families. Contact can take place before and after adoptive placements and can be in the form of face-to-face meetings or "letter-box" arrangements with the adoption agencies (or local authorities) acting as "post-box" and facilitator. Lowe *et al* (1999) have termed these "direct" and "indirect" contact. Contact with looked after children is set by the courts, and monitored by social services departments or agencies with special responsibilities for the task. The latter include the independent adoption agencies, two of which were involved in the present study.

Professionals vary in their assessment of the value of contact to adopted and fostered children. One of the few detailed studies of the effects of contact has recorded that the experiences of adoptive parents with the effects of direct and indirect contact between their adopted children and the birth parents are very varied (Lowe *et al*, 1999). For some adopted children and their families it was a wholly positive event, for others contact led to very disturbed feelings and was often preceded and followed by disturbed behaviour in the adopted children. The point was made that the contact arrangements in adoption were not always made with a full understanding of the child's interests (*ibid*, p 323); on occasion it appeared that the birth parents' interests were taking precedence over the child's. A study of foster carers' experiences with contact (Triseliotis *et al*, 1998) showed that nearly one in five reported that contact was almost never easy.

Fifty years ago, contact with any member of the birth family after adoption would not have been considered desirable. Adoption, which at that time was mainly of babies, was regarded by the courts as requiring a clean break with the past; the child would have the *advantage* of a fresh start. It was only when older children began to be placed for adoption that the issue of maintaining some form of contact with their birth families began to be discussed in more positive terms. Underpinning the modern perception that some form of contact with birth families is valuable is the understanding that these relationships are crucial in the normal development of the child. Nowadays, the guiding principles in determining the contact arrangements would be the importance of sustaining and developing a child's attachment to family members and her sense of personal identity, both of which contribute in later life to confident self-esteem and the ability to form strong personal relationships.[1] When contact is being organised for children in foster placements, where there is a possibility of rehabilitation, it is deemed essential to promote and sustain the attachment to birth family members. In addition, for older children, there is an intention to sustain the child's links with the family and community from which he came, and from which he will draw some part of his own lifelong personal identity. Oyserman and Benbenishty (1992) have stated that: 'if children are to return home . . . their emotional connection to their biological parents must be promoted. One important way to do this is via mutual visitation during the child's stay in foster care' (p 541).

When the care plan moves to permanent placement in long-term fostering or adoption, these perceptions of the purpose of contact appear to undergo a subtle shift. Contact is then seen to enhance the child's ability to form secure attachments in the new family. This shift is summed up well in a judgement given by Simon Brown LJ:

> *. . . contact may well be of singular importance to the long-term welfare of the child: first, in giving the child the security of knowing that his parents love him and are interested in his welfare; secondly, by avoiding any damaging sense of loss to the child seeing himself*

---

[1] Goldberg (2000, p 241–2) has warned of the danger of defining "attachment" so broadly that the relevant outcomes stretch over much of life, for example, to include school achievement, relationships within and beyond the family, or aspects of psychopathology, and suggested that the theory may lose its power if so many aspects of life can be reduced to a single early influence. In this chapter we confine our use of "attachment" to the simplest version of the theory that the child learns of the positive emotional and physical availability of the caregivers' nurturing behaviour.

> *abandoned by his parents; thirdly, by enabling the child to commit himself to the substitute family with the seal of approval of the natural parents; and, fourthly, by giving the child the necessary sense of family and personal identity. Contact, if maintained, is capable of reinforcing and increasing the chances of success of a permanent placement, whether on a long-term fostering basis or by adoption.* (1994) 1FLR 146–155 (pp 154H–155B); (*re RE Minor*) (Care Order – Contact)

However, there is some evidence that the current commitment to retaining contact between the adopted child and her birth family may need to be approached with as much care as the former reluctance ever to consider it. The evidence for a *beneficial* effect from a direct contact between the child, the birth parents and adoptive parents is not strong (Quinton *et al*, 1997). Rushton, Treseder and Quinton (1988), in their study of 18 adopted boys, noted that 'most distressing for some of the children were the arranged access visits' (p 70). There is no doubt that, for many adoptive families and the adopted children, contact can be a source of disruption and friction, which may last for days after each event, even if for others it was a positive experience (Lowe *et al*, 1999). Nevertheless, as Logan (1999) has pointed out, many practitioners now believe it is nearly always in the child's best interests to sustain face-to-face contact. We also need to remember that the links between early attachment and later outcomes is, as noted in Chapter 1, only modest (Goldberg, 2000). To use a concern about the need to sustain this family attachment as the sole argument for retaining contact would be to give this factor too much weight.

All the above comments concern the levels of contact that might take place between the child and her family when the adoption or other permanent placement has been settled. In concurrent planning cases the issues are different, particularly when the placements involve babies and very young children, as was the case in the present study. Good quality contact forms an integral part of the support for the birth parents while the child is placed with concurrency carers. Weinberg and Katz (1998) stated that 'Visits between parents and children are central to good concurrent planning regardless of the ultimate permanency arrangement' (p 14). They argue that contact must be a priority for the agencies and the courts.

Children who are the subject of care proceedings are likely to have either an insecure or a disorganised attachment or, as was the case for most of the babies in the present study, not yet to have an attachment at all within the birth family. In a concurrent planning programme, the carers are, legally, foster carers until the final hearing but there is a moderately high expectation that the care plan will eventually place the child with them for adoption. For the large majority of the children in the concurrent planning projects contributing to the present study, the experienced project workers expressed their doubts about whether the birth parents could meet the child's attachment needs and provide the continuity and predictability which is the hallmark of a secure attachment. A particular difficulty appeared to lie in providing a realistic timetable that the birth parents could manage, while setting a frequency of contact that would properly serve the child's interests, and allow for the development of a secure attachment to the concurrent carer. Thus it was necessary to encourage attachment both with the concurrency carers *and* with the birth parents – a difficult balancing act, and determining the frequency of contact was therefore not an easy exercise. There can be no prescriptive rules to govern the decision about contact, except the rule that the child's needs are paramount. Unfortunately, since those needs are always likely to be complex, it may not be easy to interpret how they should be assessed or weighted. In part because of this complexity, it is not uncommon for the contact arrangements to be re-organised as children grow up or their family circumstances change.

In theory, encouraging the development of close attachment both with the concurrency carers and the birth parents over the few months before the final hearing might not be difficult. As Rutter (1995, p 551) and Goldberg (2000, pp 106–107) have emphasised, it is usual for young children to develop attachment with a small number of people, and in many families this might involve (for example) relatives caring occasionally but regularly for the child. However, one must bear in mind that in concurrent planning, the two sets of adults (the main carer with whom the child lives, and the birth parent/s seeing the child for a few hours a few times a week) themselves have a unique and complex relationship arising from the fact that both wish to have the long-term care of the child. In addition, the "occasional" carer (birth parent) is likely to have difficulty in sustaining a secure attachment with the child because of their own unresolved previous losses and traumas, reflected in the frequently observed histories of poor parenting of their other children, of unstable relationships or of serious addiction problems.

In the concurrent planning programmes, the concurrency carers are expected to use the contact with the birth parents to help the assessment of whether rehabilitation is possible. In the present study this appeared to lead to considerable ambivalence about meeting the birth parents.

Frequency of contact – the dilemma

Arrangements for contact were laid down at the initial court hearing and included directions on the frequency and duration of sessions. Concurrent planning is, as we have seen, built around the idea of a high level of contact being maintained throughout the period before the final hearing. In the Seattle Lutheran Social Services model, this is Point 5 in the Steps in Concurrent Planning:

> *A visitation plan* (based on the child's age and developmental level) ***that ensures frequent, meaningful contact*** *is initiated, sustained and included in the court-ordered service plan' (original emphasis)*. (Katz *et al*, 1994a, p 14)

All three concurrency teams offered three contacts a week for sessions lasting between two and four hours. The arrangements set by the courts confirmed this in the majority of cases, but such arrangements were under constant review, and were varied depending on the progress of the case. In reality, in several cases, birth parents' contact was as little as one session per week from the outset, because it was agreed they would have had difficulty in managing anything more frequent. In almost all concurrency cases the frequency of contact was set at a lower level than would be offered by a local authority in "mainstream" cases when the child was placed in *short-term* foster care, and this was sometimes cited by local authority workers as a reason for not referring a child for concurrent planning (see Chapter 9). One senior project advisor commented, however, that in these latter cases there is often no attempt to differentiate between those cases where rehabilitation has a chance of success and those where there is a poor prognosis and the child's attachment needs to alternative carers have to be promoted at the same time.

The way in which early separation could contribute to very mixed feelings was vividly described by the birth mother of a six-week old baby removed at birth, with whom she was having contact four times a week for sessions lasting between one-and-a-half and three hours:

Well, she know who we are, but there's no bond there any more, because she's been taken away. It's gone, you know, we can't bond with her where she is now.

In another case the birth father of a one-month-old baby recounted that:

He didn't feel like our baby at all – we hadn't been able to hold him in hospital. Contact could be a bit draggy, spending three hours with such a tiny baby, who was often asleep most of the time.

Minutes of the legal sub-group of the Coram Family Project (November 2001) refer to a discussion about the possibility that the levels of contact offered by the concurrency teams may not be sufficient for birth parents, particularly since the first aim of the work is to see whether it is possible to achieve a permanent home with the birth parent. As little as two or three hours, three times a week, might both diminish the chances of a positive attachment and undermine the birth parent's confidence and understanding of the child's needs. Against this has to be balanced a concern that, because of the poor prognosis, the child's care within the placement has to be safeguarded. Frequent contact may be stressful for a young child. In most of the concurrent planning cases, contact involved the concurrency carers in travelling some distance several times a week (particularly stressful in inner city areas), and usually disrupting the baby or infant's normal daily routine. The concurrency carers often reported that children were fractious, upset or difficult to settle after attending contact.

One concurrency carer, who felt positively about contact with the birth mother, still commented on some negative effects that contact had on the child:

She's sleeping through the night now and she is normally settled and contented during the day, although the contact visits can unsettle her – not least because her normal routine is changed.

Another concurrency carer, who went on to adopt the child, recalled the adverse effects of contact on the child:

> *He was deeply upset by contact . . . he was very, very distressed and this took him months to get over.*

It is possible that some concurrency carers were particularly sensitive to any signs of distress in the children, and had a tendency to ascribe this to contact with birth parents. However, there was no doubt that contact sessions were unsettling for a number of children. This may not have been only a product of the contact *per se*, but of the surrounding circumstances: long car journeys, strange environments, disturbed routines. Perhaps not surprisingly, adverse reactions were reported to increase when contact had lasted over a number of months. The children were older and more strongly attached to their concurrency carers. They were increasingly likely to be awake during contact, but also to have adjusted to set routines of meals, people and places familiar to them on a daily basis. As these children became more aware of their surroundings, they became more vocal about changes of carer. Their reactions were very variously interpreted. Some birth parents believed that the baby cried because he knew they were his "real parents" and that he was going to part from them again in an hour or two. Other birth parents said that it was because the child's main attachment was now to the concurrency carers. Some concurrency carers thought they detected the general inability to parent a child properly when they heard the baby crying in the next-door room.

One birth mother explained how difficult the contact sessions could be for her and her partner:

> *I mean, the last contact we had, it was hard for us both, because we turned up there and she kept crying all the time, she didn't want to know me and her dad. She wanted X [the concurrency carer].*

An additional important consideration, however, in determining the frequency of contact was other demands on birth parents' time. While encouraging birth parents to maintain close contact with their child, the concurrency teams expected birth parents to attend programmes designed to address their own identified problems. Thus a parent might be on a drug dependency programme, attending parenting classes or anger management sessions as well as having appointments with other professionals, such as psychiatrists or psychologists as part of the overall assessment for the court. A small number of birth parents were in work or expected to seek work and had to change their shifts or attend interviews. However, this adjustment was no greater than some that the concurrency families had to make.

Birth parents did not always seem to understand the importance of other undertakings in the programme. For example, one birth mother attended contact sessions reliably and regularly for several months but refused to undertake any other programmes that might increase her chances of getting the baby back:

> *They all led me up the garden path, every one, you know. They said, 'You have got such good records with seeing your baby'. I have never let them down about seeing her, well one contact I missed but that was the flippin' bus services. So, everything was fine, you know, everyone said how well I'd done in everything but it obviously just wasn't enough.*

As Adcock has noted (1980) 'Much confusion results from our failure to define and distinguish the purposes of parental contact. Parental contact may facilitate discharge from care or it may be for the general well-being of the child who will not be returning home' (p 15). While each of the projects had detailed protocols, which included giving verbal and written explanations to birth parents, it was clear from our interviews that many of them had not fully understood or "taken on board" the fact that regular attendance at contact was not the only criterion by which a decision about rehabilitation of the child would be judged. Regular contact was necessary but not sufficient; the distinction was lost on some parents. Experienced practitioners will be familiar with families with whom it is hard to communicate effectively, but it was noticeable that several concurrent planning birth parents seemed to have especial difficulty in understanding what targets they were supposed to reach in the contact sessions or in other dimensions of their lives. This is no criticism of the concurrency teams, who worked hard to convey these expectations and how to achieve them.

The practicalities of contact

Concurrency carers were required to bring the child to contact and engage in the hand-over to birth parents. The preferred system was for contact sessions to be held at the concurrency project premises in a specially designated area. This might have included one or more rooms provided with baby equipment, age-appropriate toys and access to kitchen and toilet facilities. Some variations in arrangements for the contact sessions existed between the different schemes because of staffing or building constraints, but all three projects have ended up with contact facilities on the premises.

Not all contact took place at these premises. In some cases the court ordered further parenting assessments to take place in specialist Family Centres, usually over a relatively brief period. Contact would then continue in the concurrency centre. Whereas the latter were familiar and well supervised, with concurrency staff on hand at all times, the experience of some concurrency carers at the Family Centres was far less satisfactory, which they felt was because they were not known and their special role in relation to the child was not understood. This goes against the strong advice from Weinberg and Katz (1998) who have emphasised the importance of the quality of contact between parents and children during a concurrent planning programme.

Supervision of contact sessions

It was rare for courts to lay down a requirement for contact to be fully supervised but this occurred in two cases: one where a Schedule 1 offender was involved, and one where the contact took place in prison. However, all the concurrency teams provided a worker, who was a permanent member of the team, to be present during the sessions when contact took place on the team's premises. Two of the projects employed a designated worker with nursery nurse or similar training and experience (the Family Support Worker in the Goodman team and the Community Family Workers in the Brighton & Hove concurrency programme). In the other team there was no "dedicated" worker, but members of the team took turns to supervise contact sessions. The worker usually sat in during the session and might take an active part in what was going on, or might stay in the background, for example, reading or writing reports. This enabled the support worker to keep an eye on what was happening with the birth parent/s and child and to help out if parents required this. This apparently passive, watching role was misunderstood by some birth parents and regarded as unhelpful, which suggests that communicating what is needed in each session and their right to support might need repeated reinforcement. It also underlines the advantage of keeping reports as open as possible, so that parents can share the perceptions of the workers in what is going well in the sessions, and what is not going well. Other birth parents were endlessly critical of the way they were, as they saw it, monitored.

Set against these views we have recorded (Chapter 7) that many birth parents gained considerable support from the concurrency teams and felt that they were supported in ways that had not happened to them before.

Role of the family support worker

The role of the staff who supervise contact is a very important one within the concurrency team and ideally involves a dual function. The worker facilitates the contact between the birth parents and child and can help to consolidate this relationship. This may involve giving support, advice and encouragement to a parent in their handling of their child. At the same time the support worker is likely to be closely involved in ongoing assessment. This may include observing the relationship and the parents' handling of a child and, where appropriate, the relationship between birth mother and father. Intervention may be necessary in certain situations to prevent distress or risk to a child. One worker described how she had to intervene with one pair of birth parents who were arguing about and in front of their child. The worker told them that this was unacceptable and that they should leave the room. They did this but continued to shout in another room nearby whereupon the worker gave them a warning that contact would be terminated that day if they did not modify their behaviour appropriately. In another case a written/signed agreement was made with a birth parent about the level of drunkenness and/or smell of alcohol that would be accepted in the contact situation.

As described above, the family support worker's role is thus broader than simply providing supervision during contact but includes encouraging positive parenting as well as contributing to the assessment process.

The Goodman FSW was appointed in the early stages of the Project and was an important and fully integrated member of the team. She has summarised the key aspects of her role as follows:

1. i) Meet the birth parent/s prior to first contact to explain the family support worker's role.
   ii) Explain that observations and comments by the birth parents will be recorded and might be used in court reports.
   iii) Explain that intervention by the family support worker may at times be necessary and that s/he will give feedback to the birth parents, both positive and negative.
2. Having the same contact rooms is an advantage as it gives a sense of security to both children and parents . It may give them an opportunity to bring some sense of their own identities to the room.
3. Having the same contact supervisor is beneficial:
   i) It provides consistency for the child and parents as the relationship progresses.
   ii) Because of the above the FSW can undertake specific pieces of work that may be requested by the social workers e.g. household budgeting.
   iii) The FSW provides consistency in contact records. Social workers only need to seek out one person for information about a case.
4. The tools used for observation are: Contact monitoring sheet.

It was emphasised to us that "openness" between professionals and birth parents is an important characteristic of concurrent planning. This also applies to reports and records of contact: for example, the FSW reports in the Goodman team are available for birth parents to read. They are thus able to see that the records contributing to the final court report are factually based and unbiased.

Contact – the reality

Although designed to give birth parents the opportunity to see their child regularly at the same time as giving them help with aspects of parenting or other issues, in reality a number of birth parents in the present study appeared to find attending contact stressful or impractical. Out of

24 concurrency cases, four sets of birth parents (16 per cent) did not attend any contact sessions at all, and in one further case a birth mother attended only once. In one case the birth parents had had very regular contact with their baby while she was in a local authority regular foster home but did not attend any contact sessions once the child had been moved to concurrency carers. It is possible that these birth parents misunderstood the nature of the placement with the concurrency carers.[2] Another birth parent (who kept up contact very well) told the researchers that her child was placed for adoption – she also had not grasped the aims of concurrent planning.

For six further sets of birth parents, the contact sessions were so stressful that they were unable to maintain the commitment and opted out quite early, on average about three months after joining the concurrent planning projects. Among these parents were some who were not seen by the researchers, but it was known that their drug addiction contributed substantially to their inability to keep the contact appointments. While they reported finding the strain of attending the sessions too much to cope with, they also came to a realisation of what was entailed in "fighting" for their child. As one couple said, after having decided to relinquish their baby:

> *We could do everything we were told to and the Judge could still say 'no' at the end of it all.*

Again, this point raises the issue of what the birth parents understood by 'doing everything they are told to', and the problems of communicating successfully with some parents. Having made this decision, these birth parents found continuing the contact sessions particularly stressful and were anxious for the final hearing to be brought forward as quickly as possible. It has been noted (Chapter 7) that some birth parents relinquished their children for much more positive reasons.

Where contact sessions were missed, the concurrency workers tried to contact or visit the birth parent immediately so that the importance of commitment could be emphasised. Birth parents were given active help and encouragement to attend contact, but were reminded that

---

[2] This birth parent was not interviewed by the researchers.

non-attendance might be seen as an indication that they were considering relinquishment. Project workers' visits to encourage them to keep the contact going would sometimes produce no response; sometimes the house visit would enable the worker to establish beyond doubt that the birth parent did not want to continue with contact.

Another birth mother, whose baby was removed at birth, specifically asked for the number of contact sessions to be reduced. Ironically, her reasons were based exactly on the purpose of contact – to enhance the attachment of child and mother. For her it represented accumulating pain; the more she saw of her child the more painful would be the eventual break (which she saw as inevitable).

> *Then it got too much for me because I was getting attached to her all the time I was staying there and I said to them; 'Drop it down to once a week for about an hour' . . . They couldn't understand why I changed my mind. I said, 'I'm all confused at the moment' . . . My head was all over the place and I was under a lot of stress because of the little 'un and that, you know, I'd just had her and the next minute she's being taken away, you know.*

Some birth parents reported other aspects of contact as being difficult for them to cope with. They appreciated having the chance to see their child but resented the supervision and restrictions that were placed on them. After several months of attending contact, one birth mother said that she did not feel it was fair to assess her handling of her baby in such formal surroundings:

> *It feels artificial, it feels like you're being watched all the time. I do enjoy my time with the baby but it would be better to have more flexibility – to be able to go out and about. This isn't real. Sometimes it's like being in prison.*

The majority of birth parents were able to continue attending for contact up to and even after the final hearing. The time between placement with the concurrency carers and the final hearing varied from 5–11 months, but among birth parents who maintained contact there was wide variation in the frequency and reliability of their attendance. As the date of final hearing drew nearer, contact became more frequent or longer where the possibility of the child returning home was being considered, or alternatively reduced to once a week or less where the recommendation was to be adoption.

Some birth parents were positive in their views about attending contact. The mother of one child who had been removed at birth said:

I would like more visits. I wouldn't mind seeing her every day. I enjoy it when she's not upset because it's a bit weird, 'cos I don't know what she's used to, to settle her down now. Because she cries a lot. [But] she knows who I am – if they are already here and I walk into the room she starts kicking and bouncing up and down and smiling.

The relationship between birth parents and concurrency carers

This is an aspect of unique importance within concurrent planning programmes, which is designed ultimately to benefit the children, perhaps particularly if the final outcome of the placement is adoption. Through the contact sessions it is possible for both the concurrency carer and birth parents to gain from building up their knowledge and understanding of each other. The view is sometimes expressed by people who are unfamiliar with this way of working that such a relationship is bound to be fraught and characterised by rivalry, misunderstanding or lack of common ground. The findings in the present study suggest that it is the exception rather than the norm for birth parents and concurrency carers to experience a continuously negative relationship.

Birth parents ideally meet the concurrency carers before the child is placed so that both parties can begin to get to know each other. In practice this was not always feasible in the cases we studied, and for a small number the first meeting was when the concurrency carer took the child to the first contact session. In one or two cases, the concurrency carers met the birth mothers before the baby was born, which one couple described as a "strange feeling":

There was this lady sitting there heavily pregnant, and we were desperate to have her baby . . . We had already fallen in love with this child and it wasn't even born, and we didn't know the parents except from reports.

Both birth parents and concurrency carers expressed some anxiety about what the other family was going to be like, sometimes based on preconceived notions. One birth parent said: 'How can we compete with them, when they have a car and a house?' We have reported some of these anxieties in previous chapters.

Birth parents' expectations

Birth parents often described being rather overwhelmed and confused at the time of the first meeting. On the one hand they understood that they were meeting the "concurrency carers" who were going to be looking after their child; on the other hand, most of them were already aware that these were people who were hoping to adopt the child if he or she was not able to return home. One young birth mother met the concurrency carers on the same morning that she had her baby boy and, perhaps surprisingly, described this initial meeting as much more positive than she had expected.

> *They asked me how I was and about my other children. They showed an interest in me, unlike a lot of other people.*

Another birth parent talked about her expectations that the concurrency carers would be "stuck up" but was relieved to find that 'she was nice, you know, and didn't seem stuck up'. Another young and not very articulate mother was rather overwhelmed when meeting the concurrency carers proposed for her child. She was supported by her worker and encouraged to ask them questions about themselves:

> *I asked them about them and their family and if they have got any pets and how big is the house and have they got a garden and how strong is their marriage . . . you know, things like that.*

One couple thought there were definite benefits for their child and for themselves in the contact they had with the carers:

> *S. is too young to understand now, but it may help her in the future. But if she doesn't want to carry on seeing us as she gets older we will understand. It is great to see her and know that she is being well cared for.*

Concurrency carers' expectations

The situation for concurrency carers tended to be more complex and in interviews, before a placement was made, they often described conflicting expectations. All had opted to join a concurrency programme in the full knowledge that they would be expected to have regular contact with the birth parents. Lowe *et al* (1999, p 315) noted that some adoption agency workers had experience of prospective adopters who were not able to fulfil their early agreements on contact. This referred to post-adoption contact but a similar failure to fulfil the commitment to a high level of contact over several months would be extremely unlikely to occur within the concurrency framework. Training sessions and preparation groups for the concurrency carers made clear the legal obligations and expectations surrounding their status, and carers would have had explained to them the purpose of frequent contact and the structures in place to support the participants. Training had also helped them to understand the importance of knowing as much as possible about the child's background, particularly so that they would be in a position in future years to pass on the information to their child if the final plan was for adoption. Having the opportunity to meet and get to know birth parents was something that was mentioned as attractive by the majority of the concurrency carers. They saw benefits in this for themselves as well as for the children (see also Chapter 6).

> *You can use contact positively, to get a picture of the kid's background to help when they are 16 or so. It can take the worry out of the child saying they want to go off and find out what their parents are like as you will be able to tell them.*

> *You know, the fact that we'll have met the birth parents and we'll be able to tell the – if we do adopt – the child later on in its life 'Well we met your mum and dad'.*

On the other hand, before having a placement, almost all concurrency carers expressed understandable concerns about how they would get on with the birth parents. One couple, who were awaiting a placement, were very open.

> *You have a preconceived idea that birth parents are monsters – we imagined people with tattoos and ready for a fight . . . but our worker*

has helped us to see that birth parents aren't necessarily bad but people with problems or who are inadequate.

Another couple expressed quite widely shared concerns when they said that they had been quite worried about the prospect of contact with birth parents:

Were they going to be difficult and horrid with us? . . . We just didn't know what to expect.

In general, however, concurrency carers obviously felt able to face this challenge and tended to adopt a thoughtful, sensitive approach to the first meeting.

I haven't any qualms about the first contact but am just worried in case I upset the birth mother in some way.

Attitudes towards contact was something which distinguished many concurrency carers from the adopters in the Manchester Adoption Society comparison group, several of whom said that the high level of contact, and the complex expectations that went with it, were among the reasons why they did not opt for concurrent planning (Chapter 6). One MAS adoptive mother said specifically that she preferred the traditional adoption route, as it would involve less contact with birth parents. One prospective adoptive father who decided not to join the concurrency project, said:

I would find it hard to meet and be nice to a parent who was responsible for neglecting or abusing their child.

What the concurrency carers experienced

For concurrency carers the reality of meeting birth parents at contact was usually more positive than they had anticipated. For the four sets of concurrency carers who did not meet the birth parents at all, there was usually a great sense of disappointment. Concurrency carers had prepared themselves, usually for quite a lengthy period of contact, and were hoping to gain a better understanding of the child's history and family background. As one couple put it:

We were totally set up for it. We were utterly expecting it to happen and completely committed to doing it, with apprehension, but we were totally ready for it. So it was a surprise . . . we did feel quite, sort of cheated . . . It is her security and well-being and whatever and we haven't got that opportunity to explain things, we cannot fill in all those gaps.

Similarly, concurrency carers expressed mixed feelings about the occasions when birth parents failed to attend contact regularly. On the one hand some concurrency carers admitted a "frisson" of excitement that this might indicate a better chance that the child might stay with them permanently but there was also a sense of disappointment and even irritation that they had been let down.

Concurrency carers also found that they were pleasantly surprised by how well the meeting with the birth parents could go; one concurrency carer said:

She had made a real effort, with make-up and so on, looking grown-up and she handled herself well. She had come with a list of questions that she wanted to ask us. She wanted to know if we knew other people with small children. She told us why she had chosen [the child's] name and I found this very moving. It was really nice meeting her. We could get to know her as a person, her likes and dislikes. There is no room on Form E for a personality to show through. It was a rather awful document full of sad things. Just knowing what she looks like and being able to relate this to [the child]; and in future I will be able to talk to [child] about his mother. She has already sent a little present which we loved to have.

Attending contact – the handover

As we have seen, concurrency carers commonly found attendance at contact to be stressful. For some the logistics of attending the concurrency centre several times a week presented difficulties and there were additional pressures when there were older children, who had to be taken and collected from schools and nurseries, or cared for in the holidays. Filling in the time during the actual contact session could also be very difficult. Where concurrency carers lived too far away to return home, they either had to find ways of filling in their time, for example, going shopping, or had to wait in the centre where contact was taking place.

Almost without exception the concurrency carers achieved the handover over of the child to the birth parent in a professional and appropriate way. There is no doubt, however, that for most of them this was a more stressful activity than it appeared to be on the surface. One concurrency carer, who went on to adopt, said in a follow-up interview that she had felt sick every time she arrived in the car park when taking the child to contact. In spite of having built up a very warm relationship with the birth parents, each session was a reminder that the child was not actually hers. Another concurrency carer felt she could not leave the car park, when she discovered that the contact session, which was not in the concurrency centre, was not being professionally supervised. She was extremely concerned at the unreliable reputation of family members. However, it could be equally stressful waiting in the building if the concurrency carer could hear what was going on, for example, when the baby was crying, but could not intervene.

> *It was sometimes quite stressful seeing the mother juggling the baby and not being able to see her, not being able to feed her or calm her down. That was hard.*

In a small minority of cases, concurrency carers found it very difficult to relate to birth parents or other family members – either because of their perceived aggression, apathy or general lifestyle. We have noted (Chapter 6) that they sometimes felt that they could have done with more support from the concurrency workers, perhaps intervening when birth parents' behaviour towards them was seriously inappropriate. There was a perception among a number of concurrency carers that it was always they who had to be flexible and "give".

In spite of the stresses and demands made on concurrency carers, none gave up or failed to continue bringing the child for contact, even where there was a likelihood of rehabilitation. Almost without exception, the concurrency carers proved to be resilient and able to adopt an understanding and sensitive approach towards the birth parents. Concurrency carers seemed to give a lot of thought to the best way of responding and relating to birth parents. One carer said that she had been very careful not to give instructions to the birth mother:

> *I deliberately tried not to come over as being bossy so she couldn't class me with these bossy social workers. I deliberately tried to be different from that and only to be there when she wanted me to be there and things like that.*

Another concurrency carer, who went on to adopt the child in her care, said:

> *We had no problems relating to [the birth mother]. We feel sorry for her and we would never want to take the baby away if his mother could cope.*

The relationships of birth parents and concurrency carers over time

The concurrency workers in each project used a short questionnaire to rate the relationship between birth parents and the concurrency carers. This was designed to gain a picture of how this relationship might change over time. The concurrency team workers' ratings were based on the observations and knowledge obtained over the course of contact sessions and included assessment of the relationship at different stages of contact, as well as an overall rating for the "success" of the relationship. A summary of these ratings is given in Tables 8.1 and 8.2.

It is clear that the majority of relationships between birth parents and concurrency carers were considered by their concurrency workers to be successful. In most cases the concurrency workers' comments matched the opinions of the individuals concerned. However, in a minority of cases birth parents and concurrency carers implied in the research interviews that the relationship was less good than the concurrency teams had thought. Sometimes the adults concerned remarked that they held back some of their criticisms and concerns from their workers for fear of being judged adversely. Several concurrency carers, in particular, mentioned that they felt they should keep their negative feelings to themselves in case it influenced the outcome of the placement. Overall, however, the concurrency teams reported that positive benefits were experienced by nearly two-thirds of the adults involved in the contact sessions.

Table 8.1
Assessment of the relationship between birth parents and concurrency carers at the end of contact

Quality of contact and relationship	*Birth parents* *N*	*%*	*CP concurrency carer* *N*	*%*
None/not assessed	4	17	4	17
Hostile	2	8	2	8
Cool	4	17	3	12
Warm and friendly	14	58	16	67
Total	**24**	**100**	**24**	**100**

Table 8.2
Overall assessment of the success of the relationship between birth parents and concurrency carers

Success of relationship	*N*	*%*
No contact/not assessed	4	17
Unsuccessful	4	17
Fair	1	4
Good/very good	15	63
Total	**24**	**100**

Feelings of hostility were rare, but were experienced by a few birth parents. Sometimes it seemed that the "chemistry" between parents and concurrency carers did not work and birth parents were suspicious and resentful of the carer. This showed up in the way that they criticised the concurrency carers, perhaps for the way they had dressed the child or by an obvious failure to engage with the birth parents. Relationships tended to become more stressed as the placement progressed, particularly if there was uncertainty about the outcome. One worker observed that a young birth mother tended to rebuff the concurrency carers and would often not acknowledge their presence: 'Over time the concurrency carers became discouraged in the face of continuing hostility.'

There were, however, examples of birth parents feeling positive towards the concurrency carers and appreciating the care and affection they were giving the child, while still feeling some resentment. Birth parents were particularly sensitive to the attitudes of concurrency carers, especially as exemplified during the handover period. One birth mother appreciated the fact that the carer always handed over in a formal way.

> *She says that I am his mum. [The carer] tells me that she is just looking after him for me, but I thought they would fall in love with him and fight me every step of the way for him . . . yes they do love him and they have bonded with him and he has with them.*

Another birth mother who decided to relinquish her baby after three months described the mixed feelings she had, that were also experienced by other birth parents.

> *I didn't like giving him back to them [the concurrency carer] at the end of contact. Also he used to look round the room for them not me. But I like "X" and "X". They're honest with me. They keep a diary of his sleeping, feeding, when he first went out in the car seat and so on. They showed me his diary whenever we had contact.*

It was often this quality of the relationship that helped the birth parents come to the decision to relinquish their child. One set of birth parents said that they knew the concurrency carers could give their daughter 'a very loving home, with more than we could offer her'. We have discussed this aspect of the outcome of contact further in the Chapter 7.

These observations by the birth parents, by the concurrency carers and the ratings of the concurrency workers suggest that the contact sessions and arrangements were seen as "successful" by nearly everyone. The remaining question, however, is what exactly is meant by successful, and there is some suggestion that the different players might have different reasons for rating the contact as successful or unsuccessful. These were not explored in the present study, but should form part of any further investigation of the effects of contact in concurrent planning. The only "players" who could not be asked were the children and babies, and there was certainly quite a substantial amount of evidence that, as they became more closely attached to their concurrency carers, the contact sessions became much more stressful for them.

Involving other birth family members

Contact could also involve other members of the birth family, including the child's grandparents, aunts or siblings. In one case a great-grandmother also attended some sessions. Birth relatives sometimes came to contact as part of the assessment process, but were more likely to attend to give support to the birth parent or just to have their own chance to spend time with the child. Potentially this could have been an additional stress for concurrency carers, but in most cases they valued the opportunity to meet other relatives as this gave them a direct opportunity to get to know more about the child's background.

Post-adoption contact

All the concurrency projects were ready to facilitate post-adoption contact. For one project, the detail was not in place as no children had been adopted at the end of the research period, but the plan was clearly for this contact to be facilitated by the team. Several concurrency carers were ready to accept a small amount of face-to-face contact, but for most, "letterbox" was their preferred choice. There were already, before freeing orders or adoption orders had been made, some difficulties being reported by concurrency carers about whether they or the birth parents should initiate the letter writing or the sending of photographs. This did not arise in the adoptive families, where contact arrangements had already been settled by the courts; it is likely that the final arrangements in the concurrency cases will resolve such problems.

Research has suggested that a flexible approach should be adopted when deciding which system of contact is best for the families (Logan and Smith, 1999). In the present study it was clear that all the concurrent planning carers and the majority of birth parents who were interviewed were receptive to the idea of letterbox contact and life story work. Knowledge about their birth families is important for children adopted in infancy, even though they will have no memories of that family (Neil, 2000) and at this early stage, our findings would suggest the form of contact experienced within the concurrency projects is likely to enhance the prospects of effective communication. It is too soon to say whether these contacts will be maintained, but the concurrency teams see it as a vital part of their continuing role with all involved in these cases to give the support and facilities for good communication to continue.

Summary

- Involving birth parents and concurrency carers jointly in contact is an essential component of concurrent planning. It is clear from this study that it is a demanding aspect of such a programme, both for the birth parents and for the concurrency carers. Most of the adults involved were able to identify both positives and negatives from the contact experience.
- Nearly all the concurrency carers saw substantial advantages, even though the practical organisation needed to maintain contact was often stressful.
- Overall, there had been a successful outcome to contact in the majority of cases, i.e. in terms of it leading to the development of a non-adversarial relationship between birth parents and concurrency carers. In the short term this can be seen to benefit the child.
- One aspect of the success of contact in some of the concurrency cases was illustrated by the voluntary relinquishment of the children, and the positive identification by the birth parents of the advantages to their child of being with the particular concurrency family.
- In contrast, non-attenders among the birth parents added to the complexity of some cases, as it was difficult to assess their intentions in relation to their child.
- The resilience of the concurrency carers and their commitment to this aspect of the programme was particularly striking. This may reflect a combination of factors: the initial training; their personal characteristics including the ability to empathise with birth parents; and, probably of major importance, the very strong desire to "stick with" the programme in the hope of finally being able to adopt the child in their care.
- There was clear evidence that the concurrency carers understood the legal requirements of their role, but this did not reduce, indeed at times seemed to increase, the level of stress involved.

- The contact arrangements made practical and emotional demands on all those who were involved. There is some evidence that concurrency workers sometimes underestimated the stress that concurrency carers felt about contact. It is thus important that workers remain sensitive and aware of the responses of concurrency carers and continue to offer appropriate support and advice throughout the period of contact.

9 The local authority context of the concurrent planning projects

All three concurrent planning projects under evaluation were operating within a wider framework of changing government policies and local circumstances. This chapter shifts the focus beyond the immediate boundaries of the projects, to consider the local authority context within which they were established. It explores how the local authorities came to be committed to concurrent planning, and what their expectations were in doing so. At the outset, no one had anticipated the time it would take for the first project (Goodman Project) to set up, or how long it would be before the first placements were made. When the later two projects were taken into the evaluation, the researchers decided to interview some of the local authority social workers early on, in an attempt to shed light on some of the difficulties related to embarking on a concurrency project. A total of 18 semi-structured interviews were undertaken with social workers from Camden, Islington and Brighton & Hove.[1] This chapter draws primarily on the material gathered from those interviews, and does not explore the views of the local authority social workers in Bury and Salford.

The interviewees were largely randomly selected from individuals known to have some experience of concurrent planning. With one exception, all of them had referred cases directly to the concurrency projects, or had managed social workers who had referred cases, or had some close involvement in setting up and overseeing the projects within the local authority. They ranged in experience from less than one year working in children's services to in excess of 15 years. Our objective in undertaking these interviews was to examine the perceptions of both field social workers and senior managers during the early stages of a concurrent planning project in order to gain insights into the issues raised for the local authorities. Interviewees were asked about their understanding of concurrent planning as a concept, their views on the procedures related to

---

[1] Throughout it needs to be borne in mind that we did not speak to social workers in Salford or Bury, where the concurrency work was initiated with the Goodman Project.

its implementation, the adequacy of their preparation and training for working in it, and their experience thus far. Their responses, supplemented by data from a small number of interviews conducted with Guardians, also gave insight into the roles of the various participants – the Guardians, the courts, and the other agencies – and the ways they were working together.

The introduction of concurrent planning

The conference held by Manchester Adoption Society (MAS) in 1997 at which Linda Katz was a keynote speaker attracted a great deal of interest in social work circles. We could trace links between both the Coram Family and the Brighton & Hove concurrency projects back to this event, when senior social workers and managers attended and first heard about concurrent planning as a new route to achieving permanence for young children. As one social worker described it:

> *At the time, we were very aware of the number of moves that our children had and it seemed like such a sensible way to work in terms of young children. So, I was impressed by the idea, in terms of it being very child-centred, and you know, came back thinking 'what a good and sensible way to work'.*

Linda Katz returned the following year and a senior manager from Brighton & Hove persuaded her to conduct a workshop in the area. This was directed at social work staff and managers, senior key managers from other agencies, the judiciary, guardians and local children's panel solicitors. Approximately 50 per cent of Brighton & Hove Children's Division staff attended the event. At Directors' and Assistant Directors' level, it was not the details of concurrent planning that prompted commitment to supporting a project, but simply the fact that it meant significantly fewer moves for children and that, in the long term, children would be potentially less damaged. A senior manager from one of the London authorities expressed a similar sentiment:

> *Anything that moves children through the system quicker was worth trying.*

This view coincided with developments in central government, notably the introduction of the Quality Protects programme (Department of Health, 1998)[2] and the subsequent *Prime Minister's Review of Adoption* (Performance & Innovation Unit, 2000). Thus, the initiative within these authorities was driven by senior management. At more junior levels, as we shall see, it met with mixed reactions.

In Brighton & Hove a senior manager readily admitted to 'a certain amount of opportunism' when referring to their use of Quality Protects money:

> *The funding opportunity became a possibility via the Quality Protects grant. We needed to go for it there and then, and establish some posts because otherwise we were going to lose it.*

Knowledge of the concept of concurrent planning

All of the social workers had heard of concurrent planning, though some had only come across it as a result of involvement in a particular case, perhaps when a supervisor had suggested it might be appropriate, or because they knew of the existence of their local project team. Two of the younger Brighton & Hove workers had been introduced to concurrent planning during their professional training at Sussex University, and referred to the fact that the tutors on the course had links with the Goodman Project. In London, literature was "going around" from Coram Family, although some social workers said that they had no previous knowledge of concurrent planning. In London, it also appeared that senior social workers were more likely to have come across concurrent planning in the social work press, or to have known about the work already going on in Manchester.

Most of the social workers grasped the key issues in concurrent planning: the focus on the child, the promotion of permanence by reducing the number of moves, and the concurrent exploration of the two potential outcomes –

---

[2] Objective 1 of the Quality Protects initiative as defined by the Department of Health aims to ensure that children are securely attached to carers capable of providing safe and effective care for the duration of childhood. Add to this the expectation that it should also support developmental work and the grant offered an ideal source of funding to finance a concurrent planning project.

a "built-in contingency plan". By placing the child with concurrency carers as early as possible in the process, preferably straight from hospital for a new-born baby, one social worker noted that he/she is provided with 'consistency and stability through a difficult period, but hopefully the adults absorb and manage the tensions'. One social worker mentioned the way concurrent planning puts a tight timeframe around the work that is done; another talked of the importance of decision-making within the child's timescale. Some of the field social workers admitted they were unclear about the distinction between parallel planning, twin tracking and concurrent planning.[3] However, most of the social workers seemed very aware of the dual role of the concurrency carers, as foster carers and potential adopters. Only two social workers mentioned the element of supporting families to change:

> *It is also to work closely with birth families to give them every chance and opportunity to mend their ways really and to look at their parenting and improve it, if that is at all feasible.*

Several took pains to identify the sequential procedures that are traditionally followed leading up to adoption, and the drift and delays which so often occur:

> *You try one thing, then you try the next, try rehabilitation, then try extended family, then you try to start looking for an adoptive family, which can take months and months and years and years, so concurrent planning kind of crams or condenses that process.*

Several senior social workers identified that the courts can also contribute to delay. The move to prospective adopters, should adoption be the outcome, cannot occur in traditional cases until after the final hearing:

> *Everything is agreed in principle without wanting to pre-empt the Court and the findings of the Court. So you are stuck in that limbo situation where you can't proceed until that has happened and I think more and more often, the Court exacerbates delay with children. And then the finger is pointed at everyone else when it is actually them that have put it in place.*

---

[3] See page 42.

However, one senior social worker described how, from his experience, the delays continue, even after the plan for permanency has been agreed by the court. He asserted that the introduction of Quality Protects had not yet managed to resolve these problems. He identified a typical scenario thus:

> *With traditional adoption, the emphasis in social work is very much towards the Care Order to get the child permanently moved, if that's the plan. And then the drift creates because the child is in a placement and then I think the emphasis gets lost. I don't think it should do, but I think it does get lost because the demands of the social work time on other things and, of course, you're passing a stage of the adoption process – the traditional adoption process – over to a different team which you have no control over. So from a management perspective, you have no control over some of the placements, except for sending an e-mail to say 'has the child been advertised?' And you've then got the demand of the other social worker on your own social worker, who may have a new case coming in. So, if the E Form hasn't been done, you may say you have to prioritise that. If they've got a court statement to be done on another case, it gets second place. So there's a conflict within the childcare team and there's a conflict within the family placement team.*

A hospital social worker referred to the general lack of urgency she considered existed within the family placement services, and which she felt was shared borough wide. She described it as 'an ethos which failed to recognise the urgency of placing children quickly, securely and safely'. She considered that, historically, social workers have tended to balk at the idea of speeding up the process. Thus, concurrent planning demands a huge difference by way of tighter planning and thinking, and clear decision-making early on in the process.

Some workers remained slightly suspicious of concurrent planning, believing that the recruitment of concurrency carers would be difficult because of the risks inherent in the role. It was suggested that, unlike traditional foster carers, the concurrency carers could be said to have a vested interest in the outcome, namely, that they wanted to adopt the child. It was questioned whether they could reasonably be expected to work with the birth parents toward the rehabilitation of the child.

Another source of doubt related to the matching in concurrent planning. It was pointed out that the small "pools" of both carers and children could be said to limit the choice of placement. In addition, by presenting the case to the adoption panel for approval *after* the placement has already been made, the outcome could be seen to be a foregone conclusion. In Brighton & Hove this problem is addressed by "endorsing" the match at the adoption panel before making the placement.

One of the London senior managers defended the case for concurrent planning, 'insofar as, from the child's point of view, you are actually [placing] the child in a very secure, planned path which lots of other placements don't afford'. But he acknowledged that for many social workers and other professionals, the ideology of concurrent planning is emotive. 'It switches on red lights, because it is seen as stealing babies from their families.' In his view, making the child's interests paramount has still not become ingrained in social work practice: families are still given too many chances, and the child is not at the centre of decision-making.

The benefits and risks in concurrent planning

Benefits

For the child, the benefits of concurrent planning were readily apparent to the social workers, and were rooted in the fact that the programme is child-centred. If the placement with concurrency carers goes on to become an adoptive placement, this is achieved at an earlier stage in the child's life, with potentially fewer moves and disruption preceding it. One of the greatest benefits for the child then was the potential for a strong attachment with an appropriate carer from a very early age. One senior manager pointed out that this approach encourages the courts to be more child focused. In the past the focus has tended to be upon parents and rehabilitation – 'it [now] allows them to have the child in a secure placement whilst also giving the parents the last chance'.

The clear timescales and the tight requirements of concurrent planning were also seen as a benefit for *the birth parents*, together with the recognition that they are being given a constructive chance:

> *We have to be much clearer about why we are concerned and what we expect them to do to get the child back. We have to be much clearer about our contract and the agreement with them, and the expectations, what will happen if they cannot meet the expectations.*

Added to this, many social workers thought that the opportunity for birth families to meet and form a relationship with the concurrency carers was in itself a potential benefit that "demystifies" the process for them. Ideally, however upset or angry the birth parents might feel at first, the relationship established with the concurrency carers might give them a degree of confidence by offering them firsthand knowledge of who is bringing up their child. This, in turn, might also facilitate ongoing contact between them if adoption is the final outcome. However, some social workers recognised that this face-to-face contact might not always work in a positive way (see also Chapter 8).

Social workers reported that, for *the concurrency carers*, the opportunity of knowing the birth family might be seen to be equally beneficial, dispelling fantasies about what they might be like. But many social workers saw that the main benefit for concurrency carers lay in getting a child as young as possible, and ideally from birth. The opportunity to adopt a baby was thought to be the real "carrot", with all of the advantages that this brings.

Local authority social workers were seen to benefit both in the short and the long term. For the right cases, where the prognosis is poor, concurrent planning was seen to offer clear plans and tight timescales, work that had clearer boundaries, which for the field social workers was potentially more satisfying:

> *It feels much tidier and a much more organised way of doing something. You actually feel like you are doing an OK job. Whereas when you have to move children quite a lot, you know that they've got attached to people, it is just like, 'Oh my God, again', adding to further problems, but you know that is the way you have got to go in terms of the overall plan for permanency, where this feels a much more satisfactory way of working.*

The local authority would avoid the cost of the long drawn-out process of looking for suitable adopters at a later stage, when the child is more damaged and therefore harder to place. Theoretically, the local authority is spared the need of having to provide for some of the more difficult children. However, the local authorities had all made a relatively high investment in the concurrent planning projects at the outset, which had to be offset against any short-term savings. The more far-sighted senior social managers were able to recognise that outcomes might be measured in other ways than counting child placements. For example, the senior manager of one London authority referred to the lessons that had already been learned from the experience of working with the Coram concurrency team, despite the fact that set up costs for the concurrency programme had been high, and the number of placements was low.

> *It has helped us develop our thinking in our frontline staff around adoption, so there has been a training and a development, and a knock on, to such an extent that our adoption performance this year is very, very good, and I think it has been partly due to the fact that, with concurrent planning being a contract that we have been discussing with staff, it has raised the profile . . . We were looking at things differently, so I think that what you get back has added value really.*

A senior manager in the Brighton & Hove project pointed to the difficulty of accurately measuring the savings from concurrent planning:

> *You're going to need to know that these children are going to be more settled, more stable, less likely to make demands on future social services or mental health services or whatever . . . You could argue that you would imagine that it would be likely to lead to less contested adoptions and even less contested care proceedings. We've had one example where that is exactly what happened and where, a little bit into the care proceedings, because the birth parents had met the foster adopters they could see that they were able to do things they couldn't do, and they decided not to fight the care proceedings. So there's a measurable saving there in terms of court time and legal expenses.*

In those terms, senior managers responsible for departmental budgets could more readily appreciate the benefits of concurrent planning. Like the London senior manager quoted above, she acknowledged a benefit in more than simply the number of placements achieved:

The myth is that there's two-and-a-half senior practitioners sitting around and not doing much and only supporting two or three families. And that may be true at any one time, but whether people have really taken on board the amount of court work that that very small team have done, and the number of successful – fingers crossed – permanent placements . . . because they haven't all been resolved as adoptions.

In Brighton & Hove it was explicitly recognised that the concurrency team also contributed to pre-birth assessments, exploring kinship care, and, if the concurrency team took on the case, taking over full statutory responsibility.

Many of the social workers thought concurrent planning would benefit *the courts*. They pointed out that the targets set by Quality Protects did nothing to tackle the frequent court failings. Benefits to the courts would arise from clear, time-limited targets set for birth families. Social workers referred to the way in which courts constantly call on expert witnesses, or demand assessment after assessment. Concurrent planning could potentially reduce the number of court appearances.

Risks

Generally speaking, social workers and managers had difficulty identifying any specific risks in concurrent planning for any of the parties. Some felt that the tight timeframe, which was frequently identified as a benefit, especially for the child, made it all the more important that everyone should have a fair hearing.

Risks for the birth parents were thought to lie in the possibility that, in placing the child with concurrency carers, it could appear that the outcome had already been decided before the case gets to court. Several referred to allegations made by solicitors that concurrent planning was 'adoption by the back door', and could be seen to breach human rights under the new legislation: 'Defence lawyers will argue that the stack (*sic*) is against the birth parents.' Parents might feel that there was not enough time for them to make the necessary changes in their lives, and they were not being given a fair chance. Some social workers stated that the timescales in concurrent planning might be deemed too short to be realistic for the birth parents, particularly given the sort of problems many of them have, such as drug addiction, alcoholism, inadequate parenting skills or a long history of child protection intervention.

> *I think once the decision has been made to put a child in for concurrent planning, actually what we are saying as a local authority is that the prognosis is extremely poor and there is a 99 per cent chance that you won't have this child rehabilitated to you.*

In defence of the timescales, one senior manager stressed that, since most of the families come with a history of previous contact with social services, they should have had adequate time to change in the past. In his view, timescales are focused properly around the needs of the child – 'when you are talking about a six-month old baby, you don't have two years'. And another pointed out that if it doesn't work when they are given a chance early on, then it probably would not work later. However, social workers did question the suitability of concurrent planning for young, first-time mothers, because of the limited contact it allows them with their babies, and the lack of opportunity it offers for them to learn the necessary parenting skills. Concurrent planning for them could be said to be both a first chance and a last chance, but not all birth parents could be expected to have the insight to understand what might be required of them in order to have their child returned (as we have seen in Chapter 7).

> *Any failures or misunderstandings in terms of the child's needs I don't think are given sufficient time for teenage mothers to go through and for their understanding to grow. Whereas if they were placed in a "mother and baby" residential or foster placement, maybe the prognosis may be poor, but you still have to go down that route for them, because (a) they have had no other opportunity of parenting, and (b) they won't understand in the future when they come to their second or maybe third child of what actually went wrong.*

The risks identified *for the child* related to the possible limited opportunities for the child to be reunited with the birth parents.

Hard to imagine risks – the only one is because of tighter timescales and the speed of the process, the birth parents might be given up on sooner, where if they had longer, they might have conquered their problems, but this really ties into the idea that new babies should have tight timescales because their development is so rapid. So if parents cannot meet the requirements, then it is better that the baby is placed with adopters rather than foster carers.

One social worker questioned whether the role of concurrency carers, carrying as it does the risk of the child returning, might impinge on their ability to attach to the child at the early stage. But others thought the risk for the child was more likely to be that the concurrency carers would not be objective in working towards the rehabilitation of the birth family and would therefore inhibit the child's return.

Social workers and their managers were agreed that the greatest risks are borne by the *concurrency carers*, because of possible loss of the child after getting attached, with all the associated emotional pain. Even if they are aware of the possibility that the child may go home, the social workers considered it was hard to know what sort of preparation can equip people for the reality of losing a child with whom they will almost inevitably have become attached. Only one senior manager commented on the potential risks for the concurrency carers of not knowing enough about the child's health status. At the same time, the risks for the concurrency carers were emphasised alongside the benefits, and as a result, several of the social workers commented upon the "exceptional" qualities they would have to have. One stated that they would need to be 'pretty special people to be able to cope with the demands', while another suggested they must be 'very sussed-out individuals'. Consequentially, it was seen that they must be carefully selected to be able to manage the potential conflict and pain related to the possibility of the child returning to the birth family. As one social worker pointed out, 'though everything is loaded in their favour, they would not feel happy for the child to go back, even if it might be in the child's best interest to return'.

For the local authority, it was suggested that there might be a risk of professional conflict if agreement in a case is not reached between concurrency workers and the field social workers. In London and Manchester, this risk was greater because of the voluntary sector status of Goodman and Coram Family working with the local authorities as statutory bodies. In Brighton & Hove, the umbrella of the local authority extending over both teams enabled them to collaborate more easily, and without cost implications.

Training for concurrent planning

All three projects had offered training and/or information sessions to other professionals – to the local authority social workers, children's guardians, and solicitors, but the take-up was very variable. In some authorities months went by before field social workers took up training places. In Brighton & Hove the concurrency team spoke about concurrent planning to the field work teams and collaborative work meant the latter gained knowledge. But:

> *More training would be really helpful. I think that, alright, they produce an information leaflet about their referral criteria but it has raised, certainly from where I see it, a lot of issues about what their referral criteria are, and why is it they take some cases and not others. I mean, I know the answer is usually they can match some children and not others, but I think it has been quite tricky at times . . . I think the service maybe hasn't done what people believed it might do.*

In London, Coram Family did a lot of preliminary groundwork, and later the concurrency team put on training days to which field social workers were invited. However, there was a marked difference in take-up between the two boroughs. In one borough, a senior manager had debated whether to make training compulsory for social workers, but decided against this. However, he considered that in his authority team leaders, both in the field setting and in the hospital setting, were committed to the concept of concurrent planning. As a result, he described how the 'culture had been built into the fabric of decision-making'.

> *We have made the decision that social workers need to know about it; that they have to consider it at a decision-making meeting, particularly at pre-birth conferences, and particularly at the first review after the*

child is born. So it is something that is on the agenda and is built into the process.

Only one social worker among those who were interviewed from this authority had not attended a training session. The others reported feeling well prepared and well supported by Coram workers and by their own senior managers.

At the time of the interviews, only two social workers from the other London borough, both at quite a senior level, had attended the early training sessions provided by Coram. They both felt that the preparation had covered the concept of concurrent planning quite thoroughly, but that at that early stage, the precise roles of the participants had yet to be clarified. One social worker considered that, one year on, a more sophisticated training programme was required, looking at what had been learned and the problems that had been encountered. Of the other social workers in this authority, some had already worked with concurrency cases, despite the fact that they had received no training – 'we have just had to pick it up and run with it as we have gone along'. Some admitted that things were not clear, and expressed an intention to attend a training day. Others claimed they were not aware of the programmes, or that they were too busy to attend. One hospital team had no social workers who had been to training, yet they were working with babies, many of whom might have been appropriate referrals.[4]

Both Brighton & Hove and Coram Family had put on training sessions for the local children's guardians and legal professionals. The numbers attending in both locations were relatively small, and the sessions particularly challenging for the concurrency teams, as there was widespread suspicion of the value of concurrent planning. The Goodman concurrency team put on training sessions locally but also provided information sessions for guardians in several other parts of the country. Our later discussions

---

[4] See also Chapter 3. Coram Family reviewed its approach to training in the light of the poor take-up by some of the field workers. One session had only three people attending; another session had eight social workers from one borough and only two from the other. In the latter borough, rather than inviting social workers to come to them, the Coram team subsequently went out to the local offices.

with some London guardians did not reflect this negative view. On the other hand, they did point out that they had not experienced any training as such, although all expressed interest in doing so.

Future concurrent planning work

One senior social worker favoured the Brighton & Hove model of locating the concurrency team within the local authority. Her argument rested on the grounds that it would make practitioners more aware of it. However, another worker supported the case for putting the concurrency team in an independent adoption agency like Coram Family. She feared the project risked losing its impetus if it were absorbed within the local authority.[5] Another senior manager in London believed that concurrent planning had become part of the social work culture in the borough, driven by the commitment of the team managers. Other social workers made the point that an independent agency might have greater credibility with concurrency carers.

Following this overview of the local authority context, the next chapter sets out some of the wider practice implications that can be drawn from the current evaluation study that could contribute to the planning of new concurrent planning projects.

Summary

- The more senior local authority social workers were well informed about concurrent planning, although many junior staff were not, certainly in the early stages of the projects' existence.
- Some field workers perceived potential risks which may have reflected entrenched beliefs and working practices and also, in some cases, an inability to understand the theoretical underpinning of concurrent planning. This lack of understanding existed whether the concurrency project was located within the local authority or within an independent agency being commissioned by the authority.

---

[5] One concurrency team leader also mentioned that some birth families have such poor relationships with local authorities that they particularly appreciate the involvement of an independent agency (see also Chapter 7).

- The systems that were eventually worked out to deal with referrals and the allocation of work were reasonably effective, although they took some time to "bed down".
- It would be inappropriate to use these interviews to judge whether the model of having a specialist concurrency team inside the social services department was more effective than having the team within an independent adoption agency. Both systems had strengths, although both led to some confusion at times, and there was an ongoing need for close co-operation between senior managers.
- The Brighton & Hove model, within the local authority, appeared to have developed a more complementary role for the concurrency workers alongside the field workers, and as such, seemed to pick up referrals earlier, and to have evolved ways of working together very effectively. On the other hand, arguments could be made equally for the benefits of working with an independent agency, in terms of the freedom and neutrality of practitioners operating outside the local authority structure.
- Generally speaking, there was optimism about the uses to which concurrent planning could be put, once the aims and working models were better known throughout the social services departments. The discussion of outcomes in Chapter 5 has indicated substantial support for this view.

10 Some practice and training issues for new concurrent planning teams arising from the evaluation study

In this chapter we discuss the practice issues that have arisen from the experiences of the three concurrent planning projects. The three projects were set up in varying social environments, and with slightly different models of working; these have been fully described in Chapter 3. The concurrent planning programmes are set in the context of UK childcare law, that may vary in significant ways from the legal structures in which the original and ongoing American programmes operate in the different states. This chapter explores these experiences in relation to the demands that would be made on new concurrent planning projects when setting up and carrying out the same work, while co-operating with groups of professionals possibly unfamiliar with the principles and practices underlying such an approach. Whether the projects are set up within local authorities (as the Brighton & Hove team was) or within voluntary adoption agencies (the Coram Family and Goodman teams) some major adjustments will be needed in the attitudes of concurrency workers and any professional who collaborates in a case. As Weinberg and Katz (1998) have pointed out, adopting concurrent planning 'requires some programmatic and philosophical changes (never an easy undertaking in large, complex systems)' (p 6). They have also emphasised that concurrent planning is best put in place as a unified programme, rather than a series of "add-ons" to existing adoption or fostering practice (*ibid*, p 15).

The following quotation illustrates this point from the experience of an agency making such a change:

> *You need to acknowledge all of the accomplishments within your agency. In order for them to be validated, you try to build on those accomplishments. If you don't, it would seem that everything done*

> *before was not valid, and you know you have done lots of things that are valid.*[1]

The issues discussed below have emerged from the present evaluation: looking at the outcomes of the cases, from the interviews with birth parents and carers, from discussions with social workers and guardians, and from the written reports of the projects to their advisory groups, funding bodies or internal committees. Although most of the issues were initially observed in the course of the research, they have been discussed in detail with the project teams, and the advice of senior practitioners and inspectors have been included. We would emphasise again the advice from Weinberg and Katz (1998) that we quoted in Chapter 1: 'The concurrent planning strategy uses traditional good social work practice.' The points we have included in this chapter build on this professional base.

We have assumed that the interest in the concurrent planning approach will increase. The results presented from this evaluation study suggest the considerable advantages for the children. Almost all the concurrency carers for almost all of their time with the projects also reported the advantages for them, even when they had also experienced anxiety and strain at certain stages. Among the few birth parents we were able to interview, there were positive responses that could certainly be developed by experienced concurrency workers.

It may be worth recording the picture reported by the concurrent planning teams before they started work. One team had identified the following as contributing to delays in placement for permanence in their area:

- lack of clarity about the care plans put forward by local authorities;
- prolonged unfocused efforts at rehabilitation (also by local authorities);
- delays in court proceedings;
- repeated challenges by birth parents;

---

[1] Frances Monroe, Program Manager, Santa Clara County Social Services Agency – addressing a Symposium on 'Concurrent planning – permanency for young children in high risk situations', 12 December 1997, University of Minnesota (see Wattenburg, 1997).

- delays in finding suitable adopters; and
- the complexity of meeting the needs of sibling groups.

The promise was, from this team, that many of these sources of delay would be addressed by the concurrent planning model, at the same time acknowledging that 'planning for children separated from their birth parent families is inherently difficult'.[2] The work of the three teams can be set in the context of these problems. Any new concurrent planning team will probably have detected some of these difficulties locally, although attitudes to achieving permanence have certainly changed in government, the childcare professions and the courts.

Setting up time for concurrent planning programme

The three concurrency teams all spent about a year on preliminary planning, setting up, and "networking" locally. All the teams commented on the importance of this period of establishing the framework for collaboration with other professionals and for making sure that the underlying philosophy and working practices are fully understood, before cases are accepted by the concurrency team.

It appears the main tasks in this period will include the following, each of which is discussed more fully below:

i) assessing need in the area: who are the children/families to be served?
ii) choosing who to bring on to the team /skills;
iii) preparatory work with professionals; preparation of information and information sessions with professionals;
iv) recruiting the concurrency carers;
v) developing contacts with programmes suitable for birth parents.

i) Assessing need in the area: who are the children/families to be served?

This is clearly the key issue to resolve before any other, not least because deciding which children and families will be eligible for the service will define some of the other early setting-up issues, like the skills needed on

---

[2] Coram Family Adoption Service, *Reducing Delay in the Adoption of Children under age 5 years*, September 1998.

the team, or the range of services that the birth parents may need. While the criteria put forward by the Seattle concurrency project (Katz *et al*, 1994a) have formed the basis of the selection procedures of the three projects reviewed in this research, there were some minor variations. A new concurrency team needs to investigate the perceptions of other service providers as to which children or birth families are most in need of permanency decisions being expedited. A concurrency team will not provide a universal service, so the workers and other local professionals need to be clear about what part of the looked after population they will be serving. This selection can be divided into decisions about which children should be included, and which families should be included.

a) Characteristics of the children

The reasons for setting particular age limits need to be discussed, and well accepted, by the local authorities that will be working alongside the concurrency team. The Coram Family concurrency project, for example, was explicitly intended from the start to prevent drift and delay in mid-childhood by making permanency decisions for the much younger age groups. This required the team to explain very carefully the link between early referral and decision-making about permanency, and the avoidance of later care proceedings and damage to the child. The early plans to select children under three years was revised to under two years. The Goodman Project originally intended to accept referrals of children up to eight years, but more recently revised this to children under six years. Brighton & Hove decided to offer the concurrency service to children under five years and later revised this to children under three years. As a senior manager in this local authority noted in an interview with the researchers:

> *These babies are matched as babies because of concurrency. They would normally not have been matched until they were older. This is partly because all the local resources would be put into placing older children where the bulk of the work is.*

The new concurrency team may be asked to justify their choice of children from younger age groups by local social workers and other professionals. In arguing for the specialist service for very young children, a new team could draw on national statistics that show that the primary school-age children in care are still very vulnerable to delay compared with infants (Ivaldi, 2000). This point was also raised in an advisory group meeting early in the life of the Goodman Project. It may be worth bearing in mind that some local authority social workers told us that organising adoption from birth is a task they see as one of the more straightforward and rewarding in their in-tray.

If a concurrency team plans to work largely with these babies or children under one year old, they may risk being challenged about the value-for-money aspects of their work, and possibly eliciting some professional envy from local authority family placement teams. One experienced team leader in the present study commented that he frequently heard it said that concurrent planning was too expensive, that the local authority systems were cheaper and only (*sic*) needed speeding up. The present study has certainly indicated that the children in the comparison group run by the local authority had to wait substantially longer than the concurrent planning cases before permanency was achieved. Although cost data were not collected, the likelihood is that the longer wait in foster care experienced by the children in the two comparison groups will have cost the state considerably more than the average for the concurrency cases, the majority of whom were in foster care on average for less than 12 months before the Adoption Order.

Close collaboration between a concurrency team and local authority practitioners on a range of assessment issues for younger children can reduce any potential difficulties. A concurrency planning team that is in-house to a social services department might, following the Brighton & Hove team, arrange to support the work of fieldwork colleagues by contributing to pre-birth assessments that do not end up as concurrency cases. This can be organised also from an independent agency, as the Coram Family concurrency team did in support of local authority social workers, but may take longer to reach an accepted pattern of working. One team leader also mentioned the widespread view in the local authorities that "babies can wait": he commented that, 'If they wait in a foster home for 12 months before placement for adoption, that is seen as successful'. A new team will need to be ready to counter these points of view when and if they meet them.

Another important aspect of establishing need in the area is the ethnicity of the children identified as likely to benefit from concurrent planning. This will guide the concurrency teams in their approach to and selection of concurrency carers. It may also guide their recruitment of their own team members. Some family characteristics are difficult to establish historically, but local authorities nowadays can provide exact figures about the proportions of looked after children with care orders in the chosen age group, for whom adoption became the plan, and how many have come from particular ethnic communities.

b) Characteristics of the birth families

One of the determining criteria for inclusion as a concurrency case is the possibility, even if slight, of real change in the childcare skills and the lifestyle of the birth parents. Concurrent planning is not a scheme for birth parents who have no hope of changing their parenting style or their lifestyle. Professional judgment about the capacity for change is thus of great importance (Hollows, 2001). Referring authorities need an opportunity to discuss this issue with the new concurrency team, and together set the likely parameters. There is no doubt that, in the present research evaluation, some families looked as though they were "set up to fail": a phrase used by a member of the judiciary in an advisory group meeting of one project. In the discussion that followed in that meeting, an experienced social worker agreed that the birth parents' own childhoods were often "appalling" and that they often lacked the social support networks or supportive partners that might enable them to achieve some essential changes. And it should not be thought that this is a perception only voiced by professionals: it was echoed by some birth parents themselves (Chapter 7) and even by some carers in the research interviews (Chapter 6). On the other hand, there is, at least theoretically, no reason why birth parents should not be able to make the necessary changes in the accepted timescale. A new partner or increasing maturity may offer an opportunity to professionals to encourage sufficient change in a birth parent to make him or her a "good enough" parent. Professional judgment will distinguish between ill-founded hope of change and the reality.

The concurrency teams in the present evaluation study recognised that inclusion in the projects was the last opportunity the parents had to care for this child. There has, therefore, to be *something* in the birth parent's characteristics or circumstances that can be worked on *within* the time-scales. It would be necessary for a new concurrency team to explain this point to local professionals, so that the same point can be made as early as possible to the parents. Katz *et al* (1994a) have emphasised the absolute necessity of having some positive characteristics in the birth family that could form the basis of the rehabilitation work that might lead to the return of their child. The new concurrency team will also need to search out the appropriate services that locally need to be accessible for the parents to make the necessary changes. This might lead, for example, to a team defining from the start that they cannot accept cases in which the central problem is drug addiction if there is no local detoxification programme.

Setting the criteria for accepting birth families into a concurrent planning project is thus an important part of the early planning. We have seen (Chapter 4) that the three projects were accepting families with varied characteristics. There is, at present, no clear definition of a "case" suitable for concurrent planning. Possibly correctly, the decision to include or not to include a case is dependent on professional judgment (at this point the other constraints, such as lack of suitable carers, are not being taken into account). In the present study, all the birth parents exhibited some positive features in their current or past circumstances, and the presence of these strengths significantly distinguished the concurrency cases from the traditional adoption cases. But the concurrency projects were also including a number of birth parents with the characteristics that have been identified as carrying very poor prognoses for intervention failure (reviewed by Jones, 2002). In an early study by Kempe and Kempe (1978), these factors included drug addiction, learning disability and a history of previous abuse or neglect of this or another child. In a more recent study of children reunited with their birth families, Terling (1999) found that previous involvement with child protection services, parents' substance abuse, an absence of social support and parents' failure to work constructively with professionals were critical in determining whether the child re-entered the childcare system.

In planning which families could be included, the new team will wish to consider the issue of compliance by the birth parents with previous interventions and treatment. A large number of research studies have suggested that non-compliance is highly related to poor treatment outcome in child abuse and neglect cases (summarised in Jones, 1998). In many birth families where the children might benefit from the concurrent planning approach because it brings early placement with a stable family, the parents' previous and current failure to co-operate with services appears more likely to persuade the local authority to put in place a traditional adoption plan. At a very senior level in the Social Services Inspectorate, it was suggested to the researchers that the single most important criterion has to be the ability of the birth parents to work with agency staff on their parenting. This view is supported by much research. For example, Jones (2002) has noted that: 'The families' recognition of a problematic parenting behaviour and their willingness to engage in work to overcome the problem are key factors for avoiding re-entry into the [childcare] system' (p 6).

However, while no one can doubt this is so, it is clear from the current study that for many birth parents their inability to work constructively with local authority social services departments does not predict an inability to work with the concurrency teams. One of the team leaders commented, in an advisory group meeting, that 'birth parents find it easier to be one step removed from the local authority . . . and can engage with the [concurrent planning] project'. The "one step removed" is the step away from the crucial legal responsibility for making decisions about their children, that is held by the local authority and not by the concurrency teams. In our interviews with birth parents, many mentioned their poor relationships with local authority social services, and contrasted this with the way in which they felt more respected in the concurrency project teams. It is our view that very great care must therefore be taken not to exclude parents for this reason alone: they may find or feel they have found a different professional environment within the concurrency project than they have found before (see Chapter 7). Since team members and local authority staff will largely share the same professional backgrounds, this perception by birth parents that there is a difference between the two emphasises how important the selection of concurrency staff will be: particularly their skills and experience in family work (see below, ii).

Despite these points, it is likely that there will always be a "grey area" between the cases where there seems almost no hope of rehabilitation and cases where there is categorically none. The greater the opportunity to discuss the criteria with local professionals and the judiciary, the easier it may be to reduce any uncertainties, despite each case being accepted on its merits.

ii) Choosing who to bring on to the team/skills

The concurrency teams consisted of social workers with considerable experience in family work, sometimes in adoption work, and in court work. In the Brighton & Hove model, a senior manager made the point that the workers needed 'to be strong on child protection issues, because they would carry those care proceedings through court. We deliberately recruited people who were strong on that end of the work, feeling that we could teach them the assessment work. We knew that they would be able to convince the courts; they had strong backgrounds in court work.'

In particular, the team members have proved their skill in identifying the central problems in the family that specifically prevented them from parenting successfully. The team leaders in the present study emphasised the importance of ensuring that the worker who has responsibility for the birth family should be different from the worker who has responsibility for the carer. At the same time, the researchers were told that people on a team should not become specialists with one perspective or the other: 'Everybody across the project should know where the birth parents are coming from and where the adopters were coming from.' One of the other team leaders commented on the fact that most social workers in local authority social services departments lack experience of integrated team work: field workers will do the assessments for court, another will support the foster placement, yet another may be involved in family finding, while the contact arrangements are supervised by a family centre. The concurrency projects, partly by their small size and partly because of the focused nature of their work, developed high quality, frequent communication and record-keeping that fed into proactive decision-making. The team leaders reported clear advantages when all aspects of their work were housed under one roof: contact, assessment of the birth family and family placement work.

We discuss below the importance of the skilled supervision of contact, but teams using community family workers for this part of the service told us how the team as a whole gained from their additional skills. New teams need to think in detail about the range of additional tasks that they may have to perform, such as bereavement counselling to concurrency carers if a child returns to the birth parents, or to the birth parents when – at the final hearing or adoption hearing – they learn they will not get their child back. While the events themselves can be foreseen, the strength of reaction is sometimes not easy to forecast. Sometimes, outside specialist agencies may provide the best service, but again need to be discovered and brought into the picture early in the life of the project.

iii) Recruiting the concurrency carers

The concurrency teams in the present study developed different methods of recruiting the concurrency carers to suit the needs of the children who were being referred to the projects. The Coram Family concurrency team used advertising in minority ethnic newspapers, but also recruited from the mainstream adoption team. The Goodman Project exclusively recruited their concurrency carers from among the families who approached the mainstream Manchester Adoption Society. In Brighton & Hove all the families who applied to adopt young children were visited by the concurrency workers, but some families were also recruited through advertisements in a local free paper. The new concurrent planning team will need to test the method that provides them with a steady stream of carers whose characteristics will match those of the referred children.

For all the teams in the present study there were underlying problems in keeping a "pool" of carers with whom the referred children could be placed. Training the carers tended to take place in groups; so it was often *groups* of carers who were approved by panel to become foster carers and adoptive parents. Meanwhile the local referrals had built up; once approved by panel, the foster-adopt concurrency carers might rapidly be asked to take a child. Once this small pool was used up, another gap appeared in the supply of carers. This gap in turn might influence the rate at which referrals were made to the team. Carers might find that they waited for months for a concurrency placement. Thus the teams tended to experience periods of intense placement activity followed by intense recruitment and training activity. The difficulty of retaining the "pool" of carers has been noted in some USA programmes. In Santa Clara County

Social Services, the Programme Manager has said: 'The biggest challenge most agencies will face is maintaining a pool of foster-adopt families.' (Wattenberg, 1997, p 7). Solutions, if they can be devised, will have to be found at the local level. The Santa Clara County service, for example, changed their recruitment to a single point of entry for adoptive and foster parents, enabling social workers to encourage them all to consider becoming a concurrency carer.

iv) Preparatory work with professionals outside the concurrency team

In Chapter 9 the views of local authority social workers about the value of concurrent planning for selected families were presented. These social workers were frequently responsible for the decisions about which families to refer, and were then responsible for working alongside the concurrency teams. It was found that senior managers endorsed the aims of concurrency, but that there was, for all three concurrency teams, some initial difficulty in liaising with frontline social workers. It was also found that locally, children's guardians and solicitors had little knowledge of the aims or structure of concurrent planning until they had taken a case on. Consequently, each team needed to do substantial preparatory work with professionals.

The team leaders told us that the involvement of local authority managers was particularly important for successful referrals to concurrent planning. Even at the end of the evaluation period, concurrency teams were still finding that frontline social workers made rapid judgments that a case was not suited to concurrent planning. Alongside limited understanding of what concurrent planning could offer the birth family, the local authority social workers frequently encouraged them to believe their chances of rehabilitation would be higher if they stayed with social services. It was noted by one team leader that most such judgments were still made on the basis of ill-founded optimism about the chances of a child returning to her birth parents – ill-founded if for no other reason than that none of the local authorities kept figures about the numbers of looked after children who did return home, and whether these returning children experienced long-term stability and successful child development. The concurrency teams reported that there was still a tendency for local authority social workers to agree later on that a case would have suited the concurrency approach. Strong management and leadership within the local authorities was needed to encourage a more open-minded assessment in the first two to three weeks.

For example, early in the life of the Goodman Project, the Director of MAS identified the 'widely differing levels of understanding of what concurrent planning entails and the project's actual role and remit.'[3] and our interviews with local authority social workers and guardians, though not systematic, suggested some of the same confusions existed some years later. At times these led to views that might not be helpful to the concurrency teams. While some social workers were apparently resistant to the idea of concurrency ("adoption by the backdoor") they then changed their minds after the referral to the concurrency project, starting to see no merit in even researching a return home. They appreciated the child being in a secure placement, but then argued that the outcome should immediately be adoption, even when the assessment of birth parents and their families was still going on. The concurrency team workers then had the task of insisting that – until the initial assessment was complete – they would not be in a position to recommend any particular course of action to the court. The team leaders reported that it was difficult, at times, to keep pace with local authority changing enthusiasms.

On the other hand, we were reminded by local authority social workers that there were several government initiatives that they had to manage during the period under review. In consequence, they felt that introducing yet another new way of working such as concurrent planning at the same time was unwise (the views expressed were stronger than this). One social work manager said that people could only consider a concurrency initiative once it had proved how effective it was: 'Until it has actually happened, and there is the experience of it going through then it will become something that people can consider.' This practitioner also felt that a concurrency project should undertake very extensive preparatory work before planning to open their doors to referrals.

We have described (Chapter 3) how each concurrency team contacted

---

[3] Goodman Project newsletter, No. 1, May 1998, available from 47 Bury New Road, Manchester M25 9JY.

the professionals in their areas, and the efforts they put into providing information sessions. There was some sensitivity around this issue. Some professionals said that they did not need "training" and we should describe what the concurrency teams were offering as "information" sessions. However, what was striking was that, whatever term is used, the sessions were not particularly well attended. In one local authority the attendance of social workers who would subsequently carry responsibility for referrals was so low that it raised an issue about management. The authority had a service level agreement; the project was new in the area, and only two others in England existed. It seemed surprising that the SSD management did not see that it would be advantageous to them to have as many social workers fully appraised of the new way of working towards permanence for their looked after children. The concurrency team found the solution in flexibly providing two different models for their local authorities. In one model information sessions could be held on the premises of the concurrency team and local authority workers would come to them; in the other model the team needed to go out to local authority premises.

The importance of information sessions for the local authority social workers in particular was illustrated in the experience of one project. The documents prepared for court had described the local authority plan as "adoption" for one case referred to the concurrency team. But it was clear to the concurrency team manager that these were not in line with the expectations of concurrent planning, which appeared to have been fundamentally misunderstood. The point was taken up with a senior manager:

> *Although this is the most likely outcome, I think the judge will wonder why the local authority are asking for a concurrent planning placement at all. Judges are aware that concurrent planning involves the concurrent planning project not only providing a placement which could develop into an adoptive placement in the future, but also an assessment service of birth parents and the extended family . . . Whether the mother co-operates with such an assessment is not really the point, the point is she will have been given that opportunity. [The social worker] might wish to expand upon this adding that the concurrent planning project could do such an assessment of the child and (its) mother's capacity to meet [the child's] needs within . . . the*

next three months if need be . . . It would be helpful for the care plan to explain that in concurrent planning the child would move from the temporary foster carer to a concurrent planning carer while an assessment of the mother and other family members was undertaken. This is what happens in all concurrent planning cases, the idea being that the child is in a secure base while the court makes its decision. This plan will meet the child's needs as s/he will then have the opportunity to develop a secure attachment with the carers at an earlier age than if there was a move to mainstream adoption should the court eventually reach such a decision.

It is clear that the necessity of "spelling out" the principles underlying concurrent planning would have been less likely to be needed if the social workers in this department had been able to attend information sessions with the concurrency team.

The overall experience of the teams suggests that this groundwork is time-consuming, but that if the right practitioners are able to attend it provides a useful body of support and understanding when the cases are referred. The team leaders picked out, in particular, the importance of local authority and CAFCASS managers being fully involved from the start of project. The role of the local authority legal departments is also important; solicitors in private practice tended to be briefed individually, and the merits of the concurrency approach would be discussed with them on a case-by-case basis.

All the teams worked hard to offer appropriate information to other professional bodies. Presentations were made to guardians and children's Panel solicitors, and information packs prepared for these key groups. One team subsequently considered they should have talked to these influential professionals earlier than they did. One team alone was responsible for 15 training events, was approached by eight local authorities or independent adoption agencies for advice on concurrent planning, and presented material at nine conferences of co-professionals in the space of three years.

It is important to record that all three projects experienced delays in the preparation of essential paperwork by local authorities: concurrency carers felt particularly strongly that they were often ill-served by their child's social worker. This sometimes led to delays that were totally unacceptable. One team leader linked this poor performance with a commonly found lack of understanding about the attachment needs of small children.

v) Finding the support programmes for birth parents

The research evidence is clear that when families are engaged fully with support services the prospect of successfully parenting their child increases (Jones, 1998). Once the birth parents and families have been referred, the new concurrency team will be expected to identify the resources locally that could be used to support the work with the birth parents. Schene (2001) notes that concurrent planning 'intensifies, rather than relieves, the agency's responsibility to provide effective (rehabilitation) services – and intensifies the debate around what is reasonable versus what is available'. This advice is in the context in the USA of the mandatory responsibility to show that an agency has made "reasonable efforts" to reunify a family. While there is no such responsibility in UK law, it would not be wise to admit birth parents to a concurrency programme when their central problems could simply not be addressed by any readily available facility or in the timescales recommended by the courts.

As a starting point it is worth quoting the Director of one project who commented:

> *Rehabilitation is actively pursued, but very difficult. One problem is to be clear about what needs to change and how this can be brought about. Parents often do well in the contact sessions, but the actual problems needing resolution are not solved there.*

He drew attention to a device invented by one of his workers: a "jigsaw" that showed birth parents how the contact sessions were only a part of the whole assessment that was being undertaken. It was emphasised to them that the report going to the court at the final hearing was the complete picture, not just about the parents' attendance and "performance" in the contact sessions.

The birth parents will have been selected to participate in the concurrency projects because the professionals will have identified some reason to hope that their central problems can be addressed in the time-scales that will be set by the courts. As Katz *et al* (1994a) have emphasised:

> *The central problem must be identified, distinct from the many problems that may exist within the family . . . our only hope of reunification is correctly to see and treat that which caused the placement to be necessary. Directing services at secondary issues is misleading to the family and ineffective in the long run. We should ask what factor must change in order for this child to return home.* (p 10)

It did seem that the identification of the central problem could not always be followed by providing access to an appropriate service. It is not for one moment being suggested that the project workers in the present three concurrency teams were sidetracked into providing for problems that were not central to the issue of the children's return. But access to the key rehabilitative facilities could be difficult. In the planning stages for one project, an experienced team leader identified the following resources that, locally, would need to be available for the proposed birth family work:

- psychiatric assessment facilities for young children and parents;
- therapeutic resources (e.g. family therapy, parent-infant psycho-therapy);
- day centres, family aides to provide support, supervision and training for birth parents;
- resources for extended supervised contact;
- health advice and monitoring via health visitors, general practitioners, child development teams and paediatric community consultants where appropriate.

To this list might be added the increasing need for drug and alcohol programmes for birth parents, and intensive programmes of anger management for individuals. Some of these programmes were easier to locate than others, but even when found there might be waiting lists of applicants (see Chapter 7). A new team needs not only to get hold of (or build up) a list of the local facilities, but also to include the pro-fessionals running these schemes in their initial distribution of information about concurrent planning and, whenever possible, in the information sessions.

As we have reported in Chapter 7, two of the teams experienced some difficulty in finding suitable programmes of help for their birth parents in the locality. One project manager reported to the advisory group that they were having difficulty accessing services for anger management, counselling or psychotherapy. This project also reported the grave lack of appropriate services for the birth fathers. Locally, there were numerous women's centres, but no comparable services for men. When specialist programmes can be found it is sometimes difficult for birth parents to understand or agree the need to attend: one couple complained that their child was much younger than the ones being talked of in the parenting programme; another couple said they thought it was enough to attend the contact sessions: 'We've had three other children, we know about how to bring them up.' Somehow it had escaped them that since the other three had been taken into care there might be something to learn. It was clear that the three projects provided some support for acquiring or improving parenting skills in the contact sessions. Although some parents joined "parenting classes", it was unclear what the content of these were. Many established parenting programmes seem to require that the parent "practises" new techniques with their child in the home setting, which was obviously not an option for the concurrency birth parents as none of them had children living with them. The concurrency team will need to investigate carefully the content of such parenting programmes. Pugh *et al* (1995) noted that socially disadvantaged parents are unlikely to attend parenting classes voluntarily: often there are transport difficulties, little supportive childcare if they do have other children still with them, and a "curriculum" that does not address their needs. These barriers to attendance are particularly likely if there are time limits on their acquisition of new child-rearing skills.

Teams may have to address the political realities in their neighbourhood. Making comprehensive and intensive services readily available to failing birth parents seems unlikely at present. Their chances of demonstrating that they can acquire the necessary skills to look after their child would seem to be low. In such circumstances, the "rapid transfer to adoption" offered by the concurrent planning model will have strong appeal for childcare professionals, not necessarily for the right reasons, but to address straightforward realities.

Early on in one project, some providers of specialist services had expressed concern that the concurrency birth parents would be given priority over other applicants for their programmes. This is an important issue. There is an argument for providing priority places for these parents who are being expected to reform their behaviour or addictive habits within tight timescales. Where there are waiting lists (e.g. for addiction or domestic violence programmes) birth parents might otherwise only be offered a place on a scheme after the final hearing is planned or has taken place. This clearly is a problem that can only be sorted out at the local level, but it is one that needs early as well as ongoing discussion with the providers in order to avoid the accusations of "queue jumping". One team leader pointed out that when the use of the local programmes was working successfully, it was the result of proactive planning, so that parents could be given the opportunity to attend early on in the overall assessment.

One essential element in the provision of specialist support or training is in defining the extent to which a parent has "improved", and whether the improvement reaches the threshold of good enough parenting that will satisfy the courts. In discussions held between one concurrency team and the local authority social work managers, it was decided that, if there was agreement on the threshold criteria, this would provide a sound basis for assessing the parents' capacity to change sufficiently to parent their child. The specialist services for birth parents will need to be assessed by the new concurrency team for their ability to provide verifiable information on the parents' progress.

The workload of the concurrent planning teams

At the same time as choosing the necessary skills to have represented on the team, there needs to be full acknowledgement of the workload. Local authority field workers and some mainstream adoption teams commented early in the life of the concurrency projects that the number of cases these specialist teams carried seemed barely to justify the costs. We suspect that this will often appear as an issue until a concurrency model is fully accepted. It is therefore worth considering ways in which co-professionals can be advised about the range of services that might be provided by a concurrency team. But it should be emphasised that not all concurrency teams will want to work in the same way, nor find that one approach suits all local needs.

Typically a concurrent planning team might offer the following services, but the first two tasks were not always agreed with local authorities in the present study:

i) assessment of birth parents, either independently or in collaboration with the local authority;
ii) urgent exploration of the possibility of other birth family members taking the child;
iii) organising, supervising and recording the outcomes of contact arrangements;
iv) the recruitment, assessment and support for the carers;
v) the provision of reports at all directions and full hearings;
vi) finding suitable services for the birth parents, and enabling and encouraging them to attend; thereafter it was the responsibility of the parents to attend;[4]
vii) support to carers and birth families between final hearing and adoption hearing;
viii) provision of adoption counselling and documentation;
ix) adoption support services to the birth parents and the concurrency carers.

We have observed, however, that a great deal of work is done contributing to the decision that a child or family is *not* suited to concurrency. At times it has been the work of a moment to confirm that a concurrency team does not have a carer available who would be able to take the child or children that the local authority wishes to refer. At other times, the final decision that the case is not suitable may take many letters, meetings and exchange of information to establish. Although the number of referrals from social services departments was high, and the proportion of cases chosen for concurrency appeared to have settled at only about 10 per cent of referrals, substantial work was undertaken by the concurrency teams

---

[4] For example, in one project a worker herself took the two birth parents to where the parenting classes were being held and introduced them to the staff.

on another 10–20 per cent. This was a not insignificant part of the work of the three concurrent planning teams. The service level agreement renewed by local authorities in one area after three years took account of this contribution.

Finally, team leaders commented to the researchers on the demands this way of working makes on the concurrency workers. Some of the uncertainty and anxieties borne by the carers and by the birth families has to be shared by the concurrency teams.

Training and support for concurrency carers

i) *The training for carers* is a crucial part of a concurrency team's work. The reactions of the concurrency carers have been reported in Chapter 6, from which it was clear that the very large majority appreciated the information and support from the teams. Some of the issues that might be of particular merit in developing a new scheme concerned the contribution of people with expertise in medical matters or child development, but bearing in mind that the concurrency carers are laypeople. Contributions from other adoptive parents were clearly appreciated. A strong message seemed to be: 'tell us the worst, and we can then deal with it'. By and large concurrency carers reported themselves well satisfied with the preparation groups and the information on concurrent planning. There were some major concerns, however. Several concurrency carers reported that they felt left out of the flow of information about what was happening or should be happening at any one moment in the period up to the final hearings.

ii) *Information packs*. There were some useful suggestions from the concurrency carers about information "packs" for new recruits. Perhaps the most important component is the information necessary to a full understanding of the legal processes in concurrency and in adoption. These issues will have been covered in the preparation groups, and concurrency carers will have felt sufficiently well informed at the time to consent to becoming carers in the first place. But we are aware that many carers felt they were not well enough informed when they had moved further on in the overall concurrent planning process. This lack of understanding about exactly what was happening or due to happen appeared quite common and added to the uncertainties surrounding the child placed with them. There was some variation between teams in whether this information was always available to concurrency carers from the start of their involvement. A new concurrency team will wish to give some time and thought to preparing information packs.

Concurrency carers in the present study made useful suggestions about the information and clarification that would be needed:

- what the components would be of each of the stages of concurrent planning;
- how long each stage might last (fully acknowledging variability);
- with whom the responsibility lay to move the case on to the next stage (e.g. local authority social services, carer, carer's solicitor, combinations of these, etc.);
- a glossary of terms and acronyms used in child and family law and in the courts, and in fostering and adoption (in order to de-mystify the court and care jargon).
- entitlement to fostering allowances, and subsequent access to adoption allowances. The financial issues are of great significance to carers, particularly for single carers, but the household income may be reduced sharply when one carer is asked to give up work to care for the child. In the present study carers often mentioned that they had found these things out "in passing" or from other carers;
- being able to claim for their petrol costs or fares when, for example, bringing the concurrency child to contact;
- entitlement to grants for baby equipment, etc. and how to claim;
- the purposes of the contact sessions, and the contribution expected from the carers;
- a short reading list or photocopied articles on particular issues (e.g. health, behaviour, attachment);
- names and addresses of key organisations, including courts, children's panel solicitors, local authority, etc.

This is an urgent issue, and one it should be easy to deal with. If designed as a loose-leaf folder, for example, as one carer suggested, the local concurrency material could be inserted alongside the national material. With permission of the concurrency carer who designed one list, we append one such to this chapter. Such information could easily be shared between concurrency teams, and a variant produced for birth parents and their families. For example, the information about the purposes of the contact sessions would be different in the concurrency carers' pack compared with the birth parents' pack. The "jigsaw" device used in one team could usefully be included in a pack for birth parents.

Supporting birth parents

It appeared from the present research that birth parents were often "at sea" with the processes associated with a concurrent planning case. The researchers asked the birth parents whether they had received any information about concurrent planning before their child was placed in the scheme. Most said they had been given leaflets about the projects, and did understand what was being proposed. Some appeared to have only a hazy understanding of what was going on at the time of the first hearing. However, this was unlikely to be because they had *not* been told, or provided with some literature, and more likely to be because they had not read it, had not understood it, had subsequently lost it or had other major worries in their lives that prevented them from being able to take in this information. Some said that they had heard of the concurrency team and concurrent planning for the first time in court, and did not really understand the likely benefits; such an introduction came from their solicitor not from one of the team. Some of the advantages to them and the likely format of the work they will be asked to do in the following months are best described by the concurrency team. This gives the team a chance to explain the full range of expectations and the nature of the support they will give the birth parents.

There would seem to be substantial advantages in providing the birth parents with information packs that are similar to those supplied to concurrency carers.

From the concurrency team's perspective, there is a relatively brief window of opportunity in which birth parents need to prove they can change their parenting practices and their lifestyles; the challenge for the teams is to facilitate these changes, while persuading the parents of the urgency of the task. This can appear as a Sisyphean task, and one that receives little thanks.

The contact sessions

The tasks of providing facilities for the contact sessions, supervising the contact and reporting on the progress made by the birth parents are central to a concurrency team's work. In Chapter 8 a description is given of the way this work was organised in one of the evaluated projects, drawn up by an experienced family support worker. This description highlighted the importance of openness in the supervising of the sessions. Birth parents were told from the start that their behaviour and achievements in those sessions would contribute to the court reports, and this, with regular feedback, ensured that they could not be surprised by the final assessments. This family support worker drew attention to the importance of the same person supervising each session, and it was reported by the carers (in another project) that where this did not happen they were particularly unhappy. The consistency of arrangements, week after week, is as important to the concurrency carers as it is to the birth families. While the times and days of the contact may have been the same, some birth families and carers had sometimes to attend different venues, and accept the supervision of different staff. Our view is that the contact sessions were far more stressful than might appear on the surface, and to get these apparently small details right is important. Birth parents and carers told us that they felt they should not complain for fear of appearing "difficult". It goes without saying that, for the very young children in the three projects, it was also important that the setting and the people in charge should be the same every week. This appears to be an issue that senior managers would want to address in the early planning of new projects.

Preparing to support the carers if the child is returned to birth parents/family

Even though the numbers of children being returned to their birth parents or family has so far been small, it is important for new concurrency teams to give thought to what it would mean in terms of what work will need to be done. The circumstances of each case are likely to be different and a flexible, sensitive approach to supporting the carers will be vital. A child may be returned to birth parents after they have made steady progress throughout the concurrency placement, and during this time the carers may have been able to prepare themselves for the outcome. However, one must bear in mind that the details of the birth parents' progress will not be shared with the concurrency carers. The latter are likely to pick up the signals if, for example, the contact sessions are increased in number or length, but cannot know exactly what the concurrency team's assessment of the parents is going to be. An alternative pattern is that the outcome may be less predictable, for example, a child returning to a member of the birth family, with whom there has not been much contact. This may follow a shorter period of assessment, and even with advice about the changing plan, the carers may have much less time to adjust. The concurrency team's work will include helping carers cope with feelings of grief and loss and, in all probability, anger. The anger may be directed at a number of targets, including the concurrency workers, which may handicap their offers of help. Discussion may focus on the possible wishes of carers to "try again", either via the concurrency route or perhaps transferring to a traditional adoption team. It will be important that concurrency team members are available to help facilitate the carers' decision-making and give such information and support as are required. Workers may feel that this is obvious and best practice in social work, but most social workers do not have to organise the rehabilitation of children from a prospective adopter to a birth family. It is an unusual scenario and may call for particularly sensitive handling.

Court procedures

The *Prime Minister's Review of Adoption* (Performance & Innovation Unit, 2000) identified the courts as sharing responsibility for the delays found in most care proceedings. In the current study the courts set up systems that were intended to address this issue. Early in the life of each project the importance of setting up appropriate court procedures for concurrency cases became apparent, and the support of the local judiciary in each area ensured that the courts made efforts to hasten the concurrent planning cases through the necessary stages. The protocols for concurrency cases were agreed with local authorities, but for one project's children at least these were reportedly not always followed. This had led to some delays and difficulties around the hearings of half the cases. The protocol drawn up by the Inner London and City Family Proceedings Court has been included in Appendix H to indicate a possible plan of working together.

In the Coram Family Project the pressure of work in the Inner London and City Family Proceedings Court was, by 2002, leading to delays in final hearings. Consequently it was felt appropriate for local authorities to apply for Freeing Orders at the same time as the Care Orders. There was recognition that this would lead to a sharp rise in the amount of work on any one case at any one time for the local authority social workers. However, although the workload would rise while the new targets were being set up, there should eventually be no more work on any given case: it would simply be scheduled differently. The advantages in court time saved and more timely decisions for the adoptive families are obvious. Unfortunately, logic does not always win the day; local authorities were responsible for substantial delays that were impossible for the concurrency team to overcome.

Schene (2001), while providing practical advice on setting up concurrent planning, also focuses on the need for early co-ordination between the courts and the childcare agencies. She emphasises the importance of the courts sharing the philosophy behind concurrent planning as well as planning for the practical implications. In the early stages of the Manchester Adoption Society's concurrency work the support of the local judiciary was important.

The professional advisers to the projects were clear that the concurrency workers should be seen as expert witnesses with regard to their assessments of the birth parents' capacity to care for their children. Placement with the project would thus count as an expert placement. This was established in the Goodman Project, and was laid down in the court protocol for the Inner London Family Proceedings Court (see Appendix H). The importance of getting this agreed from the start cannot be exaggerated.

In the present study the concurrency team leaders found that delays were avoided if the need for expert witnesses was rigorously assessed and established early on in each case. Hunt (2000) has suggested that the timetabling of such assessments should not be settled in the first days of casework, but that by the end of the first month it should have become clear what expert reports will be needed for the final hearing. She also observed, in following 131 child protection cases, that decisions were delayed in 40 per cent of these by lack of court time or delays in getting expert reports, and on average this added nearly four months to the length of proceedings.

Final hearing and subsequent events

About a month before final hearing, a directions hearing is held (the Pre-Hearing Review) specifically to plan the smooth completion of the final hearing. At this hearing the parties will indicate their positions, and any disputes will become apparent. The final hearing may only be about the Care Order application, but it is becoming increasingly common to make an application for the Freeing Order at the same hearing. In the current research, 12 of the 24 concurrency cases were granted Freeing Orders at final hearing. If this is the case, the concurrency adopters will be entitled to file their adoption application as soon as they wish after this hearing. If the Freeing Order is not made at the final hearing, then the concurrency carers will need to be put in touch with children's panel solicitors who take the case forward. New concurrency teams need to be aware from the start of each case that the concurrency carers are likely to need this service, and will need to have a list of suitable practices available or have helped the concurrency carers to select a practice in their own area. As we have noted, this could be included in the information pack. We observed that some families were not given the information that they would need to brief a children's panel solicitor at this stage. In some cases there was mutual misunderstanding: the concurrency carer families thought that the next steps were to be taken by the concurrency team, while the team worker had assumed that the family knew they needed to find a suitable solicitor. It is clear that carers continue to need strong professional support to put in their applications, and this was not always forthcoming in the present study, leaving some carers puzzled and upset.

The concurrency carers continue to need the support of their concurrency team worker throughout the following stages. The child continues to be supervised by the local authority responsible for the Care Order, but this authority is also responsible for preparing the Schedule 2 report. In the present study several families waited unacceptably long for this to be completed; sometimes the deadlines set by the courts were not being met. The families had difficulty pressing their case with the local authority, and needed considerable support from their concurrency team worker. In turn, the team workers in these cases were frustrated by their inability to demand that the work be completed, even though they could see that there were adverse consequences to the delays.

Tracking the progress of cases

Each concurrency team had developed its own ways of tracking the progress of their cases. Bearing in mind that the concurrency work reported in this study was, by and large, started before the recent National Adoption Standards were published, this was not unexpected. Reporting to their advisory committees also involved supplying information on recruitment of carers, and referrals of children who did not join the concurrency programmes. New concurrency teams, however, will be expected to achieve the national targets for completing the adoption, and to provide information in a standardised format. Two of the projects in the present study exceeded the timescales specified in the national targets by many months.

By the end of the evaluation research two of the teams had given further consideration to how to record the progress of their concurrency cases within a structure that was not dissimilar from, but certainly was not exactly the same, as that being used for national adoption cases. It was not clear that these systems would enable management or steering groups to assess whether the specialist team was efficient or effective. This requires careful attention when a project is set up. In Chapter 5 we have reported the system that appears to be most useful, and have recorded the progress of the concurrency cases in the research study using this model. Concurrency projects that are setting up a new service might consider the advantage of using the same system to track the progress of their cases. This will enable them to establish whether any "bottlenecks" develop that contribute to delays in reaching permanent placements. A separate system would be needed to record the numbers of moves made by the child before a permanent family is found, but this is also an important statistic for a team know about.

Summary

- The main practice lessons that can be learnt from the experiences of the first three concurrent planning projects in England are described and discussed. Each project existed in a slightly different context from the others, and new concurrency teams will develop systems to suit their local circumstances. In particular, the characteristics of the child population for whom concurrent planning would be best suited need to be established in discussion with referring agencies.
- The introduction of concurrent planning represents a step change for most adoption agencies and local authorities. To be effective requires not only that the concurrency team review their own approach to permanence and reunification, but that they enable other professionals to do the same. Each team will need to allow substantial time for setting up, and disseminating the aims, expectations and new practice associated with concurrent planning to all the professionals who contribute to the child care plans.
- Preparatory work needs to include developing comprehensive information packs for concurrency carers and birth parents, so that they can understand each of the stages through which the case goes, as well as being able to foresee the upcoming stages.
- Further thought needs to be given to ways of tracking the concurrent planning cases through to permanence, to provide a uniform body of information to managers and government.
- A further useful source of information and advice about implementing a concurrent planning programme can be found in Schene (2001).

• • •

Facilitating the concurrent planning process for the carers

One of the concurrency carers put forward some suggestions for the ways in which the procedures could become more accessible for the carers. They are recorded here with permission of the author.

Prior to placement

- One-off discussion with independent counsellor to outline some of the feelings and emotions that might come up during the process;
- Looking further into the world of a birth parent;
- Exploring the perception that the process is very much weighted in the birth parent's favour and how to deal with (and accept) these feelings as part of the process;
- Understanding the issue of rights versus responsibilities for the carer.

At the time of placement

- A welcome pack from the concurrency team to include:
  - information sheet on the child (if he/she has been in care before the concurrency placement is being made) and the concurrency team or the local authority;
  - things the carer must do during the first week;
  - people the carer must expect visits from during the first few weeks – describing their role and the sorts of information they will require;
  - names and telephone numbers of social workers involved in the case;
  - definitions of the roles of the concurrency team workers and the local authority social workers;
  - legal representatives in the case and their roles;
  - any recommended reading;
  - a list of helpful tips from concurrency carers who have completed their concurrent planning procedures.
- A breakdown and schedule of fostering allowances and other financial support; addresses and telephone numbers of key local authority departments that are responsible for payments;
- Approximate schedule of likely different official stages throughout

placement (review meetings, directions hearings, final hearing), with brief explanation of the purpose of each stage;
- Offer of counselling by same counsellor as before if needed.

After the final hearing
- Debriefing regarding the final hearing;
- Agreed timetable with all parties involved in goodbye contacts;
- Information on timetable of fostering allowances;
- Framework and structure of life story work;
- Advice on information to be made available to carers on birth parents;
- Ongoing role of concurrency team or agency;
- Possible debriefing session for carer with concurrency team involved in case.

And in the event there is no Freeing Order, there should be an explanation of the following points:
- The grounds for any appeal by birth parent;
- How to put in the adoption application;
- The continuing responsibilities of the local authority;
- The remaining rights of the birth parents;
- The possible grounds for the birth parent to contest an Adoption Order.

11 Conclusions from the evaluation study of concurrent planning

Introduction

In the previous chapters we have reported the experiences of the concurrent planning teams, the concurrency carers and the birth families in the three projects in England that were running between 1998 and 2002. In contrast to the work of these projects, descriptions have also been provided of the work of the two mainstream adoption teams whose clients served as comparison groups – Manchester Adoption Society's Adoption Team and Trafford's Adoption and Permanency Team. We therefore were able to present the views and experiences of the adoptive parents and the birth parents whose children went through the traditional routes to permanent families.

In Chapter 1 we discussed how the rising concern about drift in failing to formulate permanency plans for children in care, and delay in implementing such plans when they did exist, formed the background to the decision by the Director of MAS to introduce concurrent planning from the USA to England. Experienced social workers were already becoming increasingly concerned about the number of moves between households that even quite young children experienced, and the likely – though ill-researched – conclusion that this independently contributed to behaviour problems among looked after children. About two years later concurrent planning teams were set up by Coram Family (a voluntary adoption agency) and Brighton & Hove Social Services. Each of these new projects requested that the Thomas Coram Research Unit evaluation team look also at the progress of their subjects.

Part of the context to the introduction of concurrent planning to the UK in 1996/97 was the (then) recent rise in the number of babies under 12 months for whom care plans included adoption. This rise was in sharp contrast to the steady reduction in the number of babies being adopted over the previous 30 years. The total number of Adoption Orders had risen to a peak of 25,000 in 1968 at a time when there was some acceptance of sexual relationships before marriage, but less acceptance of single motherhood. During the 1960s a substantial proportion of these adopted children were babies born "out of wedlock" (Ivaldi, 1998). A decade later the proportion of baby adoptions had dropped sharply (*ibid*, p 1). During the 1980s the emphasis in social work was increasingly on the needs of older children for adoptive placements. By the mid 1990s, however, the proportion of baby adoptions rose again. Among children adopted in England in 1994/6, 52 per cent had entered local authority care aged under one year (*ibid*, p 11), and 25 per cent had been placed aged under one year. By 1998/99 the proportion of adopted children entering care aged under one year had risen to 66 per cent (Ivaldi, 2000) and 9 per cent had been adopted under one year (*ibid*, Table 4.2). The general trend from 1994 onwards was a reduction of the age of entering care, of placement for adoption and of Adoption Orders.

This does not mean, however, that there are no older children in need of permanent (including adoptive) families. The reduction in the average age of adoption may be leaving a larger proportion than before of older children whose experiences before coming into care make them a particularly needy group with special care requirements. As Dance (1997) has expressed it: 'These older children, with memories and histories of their own, enter adoptive placements with a complex array of psycho-social needs' (p 2). In the UK a higher proportion of children in care are placed for adoption (over 5 per cent in 2001, Department of Health Bulletin 2001/25 (2002b)) than any other developed country, with the exception of the USA (Selwyn and Sturgess, 2001). Any deficiencies in the systems that are used to find adoptive placements thus affect a relatively large number of looked after children. For the same reasons, any improvements in these procedures should be available for as many cases as possible.

The aims of the evaluation

Success, as Thoburn (2002) has noted, is open to several definitions in permanent family placement. The present study was set up to test whether the concurrent planning procedures would lead to more rapid achievement of permanence for the child, and reduce the number of moves the children experienced before a permanent placement. It was also intended to test whether there were measurable or qualitative gains for the children, the birth parents and the adoptive or foster-adopt (concurrency) carers from following one or other route to permanent placements.

Carers, birth parents and adoptive parents were interviewed at the start and end of the follow-up period (12–15 months) to collect information about their experiences and reactions to the processes through which they and the children were going. They also supplied information at both time points on the developmental status of the children. This included age-appropriate measures of behaviour and attachment.

The results of the evaluation

Chapter 4 gave details of the referrals to the concurrency projects that identified the very young age of the children, both when taken into care and when first placed with concurrency carers. When we compared the ages at which the children were referred to the three placement groups, it was shown that the concurrency cases were significantly younger than the children in the two mainstream comparison groups. But when the ages at the start of the last care episode were compared, it was clear that the MAS Adoption Team sample had been much younger when they first came to social workers' attention. Delay in moving positively to permanency planning had led to them being older when they entered the research comparison group, and were finally placed for adoption.

The backgrounds of the birth parents rated on the Poor Prognostic Indicators suggested no significant differences between the concurrency families and the birth families in the mainstream adoption groups. In contrast, the concurrency birth parents were rated significantly more positively by the project workers on the Strengths in Families checklist than the birth parents in the two mainstream groups. This suggested that at least some positive aspects in the children's families were being identified by the concurrency project workers that were almost entirely absent from the families in the two mainstream groups. However, one experienced team leader believed that this difference might be an artefact of the stage in the history of the case at which the Differential Prognosis checklists were completed. In his view the birth parents in the two mainstream groups had moved so far beyond being expected to take their children home that positive ratings on the Strengths in Families would have been almost perverse. He considered it likely that when these children were first taken into care at least some proportion of their parents might well have been rated more positively.

In Chapter 5 we presented the results for the concurrent planning cases and the two mainstream comparison groups (Trafford and MAS Adoption Teams cases) in terms of the length of time taken to achieve permanence and the number of moves experienced by the children. On both these indicators the concurrency children had significant advantages. However, because the mainstream comparison sample was significantly older than the concurrency cases, the length of time before permanence for the latter was compared also with the national figures for looked after children under one year in England in the period of the current evaluation study. Here again the concurrent planning cases could be shown to have moved to permanence in a significantly shorter time.

Turning to the measures of the children's progress in their new placements during the follow-up period, it was found that the large majority were judged by the carers and new parents so positively when they were newly placed that there was little room for statistically significant improvement over the following 12–15 months. However, theoretically, that still left the children open to being judged *less* well adjusted by the end of the follow-up period, but this did not happen. Nearly all these relatively young children were rated by the new parents and carers who were interviewed as well adjusted and closely attached to household members at the start and end of the evaluation period. There are two possible reasons for these results on behaviour and development. First, the new parents who chose not to see the researchers at follow-up might have been experiencing more difficulties with their children than the ones who were interviewed: indeed, there was some small anecdotal evidence to suggest this was the case. We thus selectively had data on the "best adjusted" children. Second, because they were so young when they came into care, the children in the concurrent planning projects had experienced little or no previous abuse or neglect, and apart from the reactions of several concurrency children to their birth mothers having continued their addictions during pregnancy, there were no obvious triggers to disturbed behaviour or development. This would not have been true, however, for the two mainstream groups in which the children came from backgrounds so disturbed that return to the birth family was not an option. The evaluation did not continue long enough to determine how successful any of the placements were going to be in the long term either by an assessment of the quality of the children's subsequent development or adjustment to family life, or by adoption disruption. However, infant adoptions have been found in many studies to carry a high probability of success in terms of parental satisfaction and the children's subsequent social and cognitive progress (Castle *et al*, 2000), so one may conclude that the outlook for the concurrent planning cases in the present sample is promising.

On the other hand, it would not be appropriate to disregard the difficulties that were reported by the concurrency teams, the carers and the birth parents. The projects were new, and the carers often reported, not always happily, their sensations of being "guinea pigs". Practitioners and parents were feeling their way. Concurrent planning is no automatic panacea for the problems of drift and delay. Because the progress of a case is dependent on the collaboration of several organisations, it was still possible for delays to creep in. The courts, the local authorities, the children's guardians, legal services and the concurrency teams all play a part in determining the speed with which a case progresses, and it was clear that in some cases unacceptable delays had developed. Because the children were so young it is unlikely that they experienced any ill effects from these delays; the burden was borne almost entirely by the concurrency carers. We did detect also that for birth parents and for the carers there was a need for better information in the form of detailed reference packs that they could consult when in doubt as to what was happening or due to happen. We consider this important.

In Chapters 6 and 7 we presented the material from the interviews with parents and carers on their experiences of the mainstream or concurrent planning procedures. This qualitative material showed that the concurrent planning approach was clearly stressful for most of the adults, though in different ways for the birth parents and the concurrency carers. However, nearly all the adults also recognised the value of the approach for the welfare of the child. Concurrency carers reported their anxiety and stress about the uncertainty of the placement: would the child return to her birth family or not? For some carers there was additional stress from unnecessary delays and inefficiency, usually from the local authorities. Some of the same stress was apparent from the birth parent interviews, but there was also evidence that this group appreciated the fresh approach to their often long-term problems and the particular support of the concurrency teams. For some this had enabled them to make voluntary, but well-informed decisions to relinquish their children. The close and frequent contact, supervised by the concurrency workers, had also facilitated this and enabled some birth parents to be confident that their children would be in safe hands for the future.

It is clear that concurrent planning with parents of very young children does, in one sense, force the issues of good-enough parenting into the open. While the parents are encouraged to address their own parenting capabilities, they have only limited time in which to do this – their commitment to change is on the line. We have noted in many interviews with birth parents, however, that they are unclear exactly what they are expected to do; one parent saying bitterly that she had done everything that was expected and still she had not got her child back. Presumably she had not done everything that was expected of her, but her confusion and resentment suggests that what she needed to do was poorly communicated. Another way of presenting this same difficulty would be to claim that she had failed to understand what was being said. Many professionals would in any case dismiss such a response as typical of some of their client group: they don't listen to what is said, and always feel hard done by. But perhaps that is exactly one of the problems that such a parent has; in which case it needs to be addressed with as much urgency as finding new housing. If such a difficulty can be overcome, then this could be of value for years to come, and in much wider fields than simply social services; bringing up a child involves communicating and collaborating with a range of professional organisations. Communication is difficult, when the client does not want to hear the message, but if concurrency is to live up to the original ideals then communication has to be improved. We draw attention to the non-verbal ways of helping with the key messages, such as the "jigsaw" approach to explaining the range of tasks facing a birth family in concurrent planning. The concurrency teams have emphasised the importance of telling birth parents that doing nothing is, in effect, doing something. One team leader said: 'We have to tell them that if they bury their heads in the sand, as many disadvantaged people are allowed to do, they are severely affecting their chances of getting their child back.'

Part of that message has to be about defining clearly what "good-enough" parenting is. The fact that the carers' family is nearly always better off, better educated, and better housed can add to the sense of hopelessness, and at times, of injustice, felt by the birth parents.[1] Many have said to us, in effect, that they do not stand a chance of getting their child back as they do not have a car, or a house with a garden like the adopters. The latter is, of course, guesswork, but not far short of reality, and the "garden" and the "car" are standing in for many other material benefits that birth parents rightly believe that the carers possess, while they do not. What they do not necessarily have a clear picture of is that the carers also possess other advantages as parents: they are good problem-solvers, they do not hit one another or their children, they are well organised, keep appointments, feed their children appropriately and regularly, control and correct them in age-appropriate ways, get them to school every day, or put them to bed at appropriate times. It has seemed to us, at times, talking to the birth parents that they are diverted from thinking about these differences between their lifestyle and that of the carers by the material differences in their circumstances. It is unusual to find parenting programmes that address these issues in terms of how they can be achieved regardless of material circumstances.[2] It is possible that Sure Start programmes may manage this.

There is no doubt that the high level of contact between concurrency carers and the birth parents can, at times, help the latter to see that there

---

[1] It is important to stress that the birth parents "guessed" this for themselves, and were, of course, never told anything about the material circumstances of the concurrency carers; but by and large it was true.

[2] It should not be thought that we regard material poverty as unimportant. The fact that such a high proportion of the UK child population lives in poor households affects their health, educational chances, leisure and play, and exposure to adverse influences outside their families.

are values and attitudes that they share. Unfortunately, hostility and total lack of empathy are also frequent reactions.

Despite these difficulties with some birth parents, many others, though not successful in getting their child returned, felt that they had been listened to and respected by the concurrency teams. The problems faced by professionals working with disadvantaged families, and some of the solutions, are well summarised by Hill (2000): providing clear information in writing, having positive attitudes both individually and in the agency, and being honest with the parents. These characteristics are embedded in the organisation of concurrent planning.

At a structural level, it was clear that the cases entering the concurrent planning projects were a highly selected group. The selection was influenced, as we have reported in Chapter 4, by the professional judgment of the local authority practitioners and the concurrency teams. Inevitably, it was also influenced by the availability of suitable carers. The senior consultant to the three concurrency projects has stated to the researchers:

> *The selection of children and families to come into the projects has been a complex and at times confusing process. Unfortunately, neither the law nor the Government guidance provides descriptions of which birth families will inevitably fail or be able to change sufficiently quickly to meet their children's needs. Instead, assessments of the capacity of birth families to change sufficiently within a relatively short timescale have to be related to the legal criteria in both care and adoption proceedings as well as to psychosocial theory.*

Not surprisingly there can be considerable variation within and between different local authorities and courts.

On one particular issue the Differential Diagnosis checklists do not provide information that can be crucial to the decision to accept a case for concurrent planning. The concurrency workers, with social services colleagues, needed to assess the motivation of birth parent/family members both to change and to work with professionals. Nevertheless, as we have noted, a failure to work with social services in the past seemed not to predict with any accuracy the capacity of birth parents to work well with the concurrency project workers. Consideration has also to be given to what the court may already have said about the need for further work with the parents. In the course of the present study there have been cases where the court has said that there were sufficient grounds to proceed immediately to adoption without using a concurrent planning approach; and others cases where the court has insisted on the need for further work despite a local authority view that nothing further could be done.

The evidence from other studies of concurrent planning

Published information on the outcomes of concurrent planning is surprisingly thin, given the importance of the aims and the advantages that appear from the few studies that have been done. We have quoted (Chapter 1) the improved timescales for achieving permanence in the early years of the Lutheran Social Services (LSS) work (see also below). In 1998 in Minnesota, USA, nine counties introduced concurrent planning with dedicated funding from the Department of Human Services. An evaluation of children placed with foster carers in 1998 and 1999 was continued through 2000.[3] In summary, the outcomes were deemed sufficient to argue for an extension of the programme: there had been a significant reduction in the time children spent in foster care, and a small reduction in the number of moves children experienced. Stakeholders expressed satisfaction, but did have some concerns about the availability of services and "timelines". It appeared that in the short term costs did not reduce, but it was expected that overall longer-term outcomes would be better, and this might lead to lower expenditure for these children in later years.

There are a considerable number of references to concurrent planning on the internet. These nearly always report programmes in the USA, but few give any statistics about the successful achievement of their stated aims. Since the Adoption and Safe Families Act 1997 in the USA, the concept of concurrent planning is encouraged, though not mandated. Schene (2001) reports case studies in three states. In the Lutheran Social Services sample of 39 cases served between July 1986 and February 1988, 30 (76 per cent) had achieved permanent families: 28 going to their

[3] Report to the 2001 Minnesota Legislature, January 2001. Minnesota Department of Human Services, Family and Children's Services Division.

concurrency carers (21 through relinquished rights, and 7 through having parental rights terminated). Two children (5 per cent) returned home. During this period the average time taken to achieve permanency was 13.2 months, and 32 (82 per cent) of the children had only one placement. A later study reported on 92 children over the first ten years of the LSS team's work. For these children the length of time from intake into the programme to permanency was 10 months, 85 (92 per cent) had only one placement and 13 children (14 per cent) returned to their birth families.[4]

In California the San Mateo County Human Services' Youth and Family Service Division launched a concurrent planning and foster-adoption programme in 1980. Figures for 1990–1996 reported that children were in the programme for a median length of five months, compared with 17 months for California State. There is no information on whether the children in the programme differed in any demographic or personal characteristics from other out-of-home children. In 1997 the California legislature enacted a new law requiring concurrent planning for all out-of-home (looked after) children; no figures are yet available for the state as a whole.

A more detailed study was made of the outcomes for children in two counties in Colorado in which concurrent planning was mandatory between 1995 and 1998 (Schene, 1998). A total of 235 children were followed for 18 months: 130 children in the expedited permanency programme, and 105 comparison children. The proportion in permanent homes at the end of 18 months was significantly higher in the concurrent planning group. No further information about the quality of the children's circumstances or their adjustment and development is publicly available.

These results look promising in terms of the speed of resolving the placements of the children, although there is almost no information on the medium or long-term development of the children. Adoption does not, nor can it, always carry outcomes for the children that are trouble-free. Fergusson *et al* (1995), tracking adopted children in a New Zealand

---

[4] At the time of publication the LSS is following up 105 placements between 1987 and 1995.

birth cohort, found that the environmental advantages of the group were not always reflected in their psychosocial adjustment in adolescence. In particular, conduct problems, juvenile offending and substance abuse were all present to a greater extent than among the children reared in two-parent birth families, although less than among the adolescents born into and staying with one-parent families. One of the key questions about the advantages of concurrent planning is whether the simple addition of a speedy resolution of the looked after child's case has implications for later adjustment. For this reason there is an outstanding need for careful monitoring of the outcomes within the UK childcare jurisdiction. If the present three projects continue or new projects are started, such longer-term prospective monitoring of the children and their families should be built in to all post-adoption contact. Separately, but importantly, consideration needs to be given to the best way of tracking the progress of cases through the legal stages, and how most usefully to compare the results with those emerging from the application of the tracking tool in the National Adoption Standards for England.

The changing national trends for looked after and adopted children

Some considerable changes have occurred nationally in recent years in the looked after child population. The numbers of looked after children in England had been falling steadily in the early 1990s, but since 1995 have risen, at first slowly, but since 1997 at an annual average rate of over 4 per cent to a total of 58,900 in March 2001. Since 1997 the numbers of children looked after who moved on to be adopted have also risen; since 1998/99 by 40 per cent to 3,067 in 2000/2001. The proportion of children looked after who are adopted has risen from four per cent in 1996 to just over five per cent in 2001 (Department of Health, 2002b). Figure 11.1 (derived with permission from Bulletin 2001/25) illustrates these changes. The rise in the number of adoptions in recent years in England is almost entirely accounted for by children in the one to four year age group. In the most recent year for which figures were available at the time of writing, two-thirds of the adopted children were under five years (Department of Health, 2001c). The explanations for

Figure 11.1

Looked after children who were placed for adoption or adopted, 1998/9 to 2000/01, England (Arrows represent the movement of children during the years)

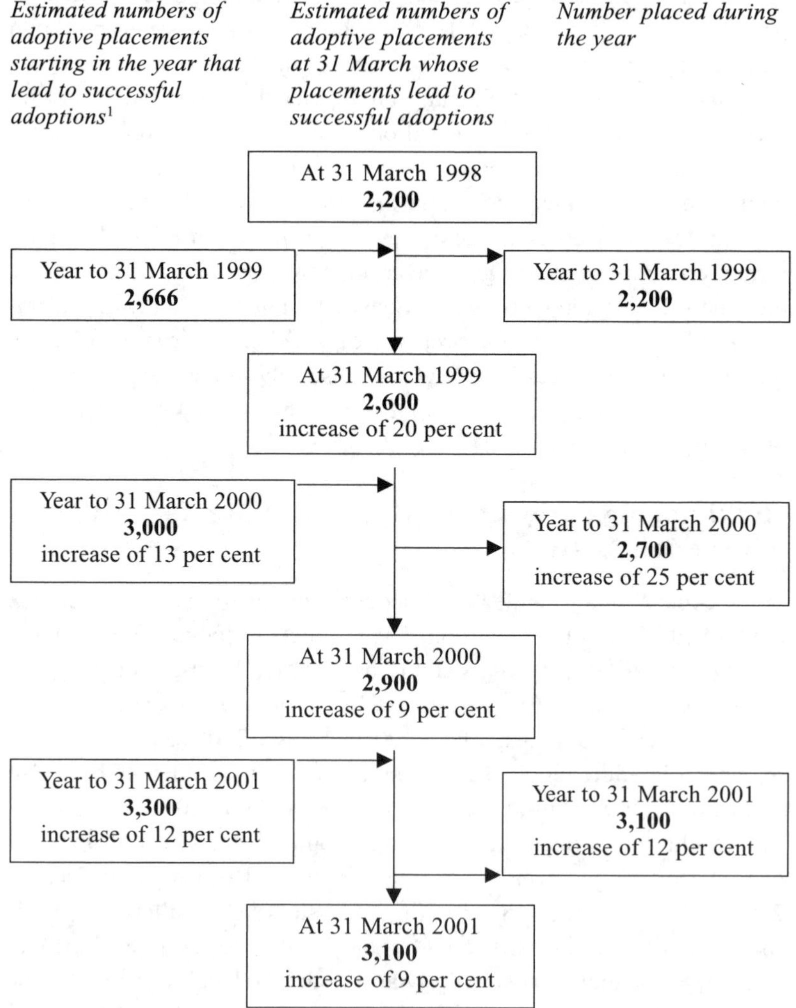

[1] These figures have been adjusted to allow for the fact that approximately 92 per cent of the adoptive placements end in adoption. It should also be noted that not all adoptive placements are recorded as such, so the numbers of children placed at 31 March are likely to be underestimates.

this change are not yet clear. It may be that fewer people are coming forward to adopt the older children. But it is also the case that more of the younger children nowadays have Care Orders, and decisions are being taken earlier to make adoption the care plan (Thoburn, 2002).

Recent changes in UK government looked after children policy

During the period following the Manchester Adoption Society's decision to introduce the concurrent planning approach to their work, the Government introduced a substantial number of initiatives aimed at speeding up the decision-making for looked after children in England and Wales. Guidelines and advice to local authorities have been contained in a succession of documents since 1998 (LAC 98/20; Quality Protects – introduced with substantial supportive funding in 1998, and the new National Adoption Standards for England (Department of Health, 2001b)). The Framework for Assessment of Children and Families (Department of Health *et al*, 2000; Gray, 2001) strongly supports the concurrent pursuit of options for looked after children, and the continuous monitoring of the effectiveness of services offered to families. Monitoring implies that agencies and local authorities will better be able to decide on a timely course of action that can ensure permanency for the child.

Government policy also increasingly emphasises the importance of timely adoption (Department of Health, 1998; Department of Health, 2001b), and most recently that more looked after children should be placed for adoption. The changes in the numbers of adopted children and the fall in the average age at adoption noted above may have their origins in these new initiatives. Tough new Public Service Agreements were set in place in 2001 that will require local authorities in England further to increase their adoption placements to 40 per cent of looked after children by 2004/5. This would have the effect of raising the numbers from 2,700 in 2000 to nearly 3,800 by 2005: the total rose by 12 per cent to 3,067 in 2000/1. Figure 11.1 illustrates the progress towards these higher numbers over the last four years.

The numbers of children in care appears to be increasing (Department of Health, 2002b). Many more children are now born to drug-addicted parents who are frequently judged unfit to care for them. The success rate for addicted parents was not promising in the current study: no birth parent completed a detoxification programme in the timescales set by the courts. Indeed, few attended more than one or two sessions. The overall increase in addicted parents may therefore be contributing to the rise in the numbers of looked after children. Katz (1996) reported such an effect in the USA, and the consequent importance of ensuring speedy and effective decisions about alternative permanent placements (with family or non-family) for the children.

"What works?"

The results of the present evaluation study of concurrent planning are particularly important in the context of the current debate about "What works" (Davies, 2001). On the face of it, the present study supports the claim that concurrent planning definitely "works" for young children from carefully selected families. There are costs (in terms of stress to birth parents and to carers) but maybe these are secondary when set against the primary interests of the children. However, we should sound some warnings: as we have noted, selecting the birth families (and the children) required considerable judgment; keeping up the pressure on local authority social services to complete their reports on time was not always easy. Once this method of working is extended to new types of families and children (for example, older, with the risk of more damaged and disadvantaged backgrounds) concurrency teams may find the challenges become greater.

Perhaps one of the least expected challenges in the present study was the lack of understanding of the aims of concurrent planning among local authority social workers. We discovered widely differing opinions about whether concurrent planning was best targeted at (new-born) babies and toddlers or at older children, or whether it had a useful or ethically responsible place at all in achieving permanence for looked after children. It clearly did not help in some authorities that the concurrent planning team needed the co-operation of traditionally separate local authority teams that deal with family placement, birth families and contact arrangements. Sometimes this led to social workers pronouncing concurrent planning too complex a concept to handle. There was some confusion also about what the term meant, and we found social workers and children's guardians using it to describe quite different programmes. There is a good argument for ensuring that some knowledge of this approach to achieving permanence for young children is now incorporated into social work training.

This had clearly not been the case in Brighton & Hove, at least by the time the evaluation was started. In some areas there was a feeling that the babies could be looked after effectively by local authorities, but in Brighton & Hove there was a common perception outside, as well as within, the concurrency team that concurrent planning had a preventive role and that concurrency was appropriately being used with new-born babies. In this local authority social workers outside the concurrency team seemed especially aware of the protracted legal proceedings that could surround finding permanence for small children, and that concurrent placements cut this short while still offering the birth parents a chance to prove their capabilities.

Selwyn and Sturgess (2001) have stated that concurrent planning 'rests on a set of questionable assumptions'. First, whether the children can be identified early enough; second, whether sufficient numbers of concurrency carers can be found; and third, whether relatives can be found and assessed early enough in the processes leading to permanency. The current evaluation research suggests there are few grounds for anxiety on any of these scores. As the concurrency projects became better known in their localities, and local authority social workers grew more confident, referrals increased and were more likely to fit the criteria for inclusion. In all three projects a steady flow of concurrency carers was recruited using several sources; members of the Goodman Adoption and Fostering Panel have commented: 'We continue to be impressed by the calibre of families applying to become (carers) and their commitment to the philosophy and principles of concurrent planning' (MAS, Annual Report 2001–2002.)[5]

Early assessment of relatives was also common. Indeed, as the birth family begins to understand that a placement in the wider family is one possible solution to the birth parents not being able to take the child back, the concurrency teams have found relatives asking to be assessed.

---

[5] Available from MAS, 47 Bury New Road, Manchester M25 9JY.

At the end of the day, the evidence from the present short-term evaluation will need to be confirmed by longer-term assessments of the children's development and the success of their concurrent planning placements. In particular, only a long-term follow-up will answer the outstanding medical questions that can inevitably haunt the placements of such young children. We noted with interest that, since the end of the evaluation reported here, Brighton & Hove intend to track the children placed by their team, but consider this should be done for all the concurrency cases.

The place of concurrent planning in finding a permanent family

Concurrent planning obviously should not be judged as the only way, or necessarily the "best" way, to reduce the length of time children are looked after before permanence is achieved for them. Nor need it be the only way to reduce multiple moves for looked after children. In the USA, legislation introduced in 1997 has set new and tighter timescales in the courts and for the time by which a final decision on permanent placement must be made. In Norway, the law defines that no more than two years of foster care can pass before a permanent placement is determined by the courts. Without these specific constraints or guidelines, it is still possible for looked after children to encounter delay in the childcare system in the UK although the evidence presented from this study suggests strongly that concurrent planning will significantly reduce this.

The evidence from the present study and the limited evidence from the USA suggest that concurrent planning may well provide a significantly effective tool in the search for better ways of arranging permanence for looked after children. The present evaluation study shows that the first three concurrent planning projects in the UK present a model of working to achieve permanence for looked after children that has much to offer. There were the inevitable difficulties of embarking on a new way of working and these showed in the slow recruitment of cases and carers, and some misunderstandings with local authority social work teams about the nature of the concurrency work. However, the careful selection of cases, the high quality of assessment, and the encouragement and support of very disadvantaged birth parents indicate the advantages of this way of getting permanent placements for the children. Above all, the children would appear to have gained significant advantages from this approach. They experienced fewer moves and substantially less time in impermanent care. In the small sample in this study only two children (8 per cent) had to move again after their placement with the concurrency carers, and they returned to their birth family with whom they had had high levels of contact throughout the previous months. As Newburn (2001) has pointed out, however, to be effective evaluation has to be used by someone or some organisation. Emphasising, as it does, the importance to the child's development of attachment to a permanent family, concurrent planning must be a very important addition to UK childcare provision and deserves to be used far more widely.

The study reported here had a very short timescale: families were seen only 12–15 months after the child had been placed with them. The concurrency children were very young and largely joined families with no other children, and were not placed with siblings. It will be important to establish in later years what the longer-term consequences will have been of using this approach to achieving permanence. Equally, a larger sample (of subsequent cases) would enable the evaluation to answer more questions about the overall satisfaction of the adoptive parents, the further experiences and feelings of the birth parents, and the subsequent development of the children. In particular, the effects of the post-adoption contact arrangements that could not be investigated in the present study would be worthy of special attention. It will also be important to see how concurrent planning could help the older child. As Harwin and Owen (2002) have noted recently, there is an urgent need to increase the numbers of adopters who are prepared to take sibling groups, and older children (many of whom may have special needs). As concurrent planning projects are able to demonstrate their value as well as the "risks", and as post-adoption support becomes better established, this task may become easier.

It is right to end this report with the views of the practitioners who make the key decisions about looked after children, and of the birth parents and carers who participated. As we have reported, not all of them were happy all the time, but the overall message from those who were interviewed was very positive.

One former Assistant Director of Social Services has said: 'We mustn't focus on plans, but on outcomes for the children'.[6] A senior local authority social work manager said to the researchers:

> *If concurrent planning and the assessment process is working well, there should not be any risk for the child. The child is in a "win/win" situation, either going back to their parents after work has been done, or having a secure and loving home with people they have lived with already.' Another senior manager agreed: 'When you look at [concurrent planning] from the child's point of view you are [putting] the child on a very secure, planned path which lots of other placements do not afford.*

The setting in which further concurrent planning projects will work also looks promising. The new Adoption and Children Act 2002 seems to have shifted the ground to give the child's welfare precedence over other considerations (Marsh and Thoburn, 2002).

Although we only saw a minority of birth parents, several expressed their appreciation of the concurrent planning approach: 'I would have loved to have gone there with my first baby. Then I wouldn't be in this pickle.' And the carers also endorsed the programmes.

> *If the child returned to the natural parents that was a risk for us. But the positive aspects of that were explained to us. OK, while we might be bereaved, disappointed, upset, we would also, hopefully, feel we had taken part in a positive process and that if the child did go back to the parents, that was the best thing. I think we both knew that really [concurrency] was the better route. Perhaps not for us, but for the child, yes.*

Writing in 1998, Weinberg and Katz warned: 'Whenever a new idea is gaining popularity there is a risk that it will become so over-simplified and oversold that its original merit is lost' (p 10). So far, in the UK setting,

[6] Jim Crook, formerly Assistant Director of Social Services, York; Quality Protects Development Team, 1999.

the merits have not been diminished. On the basis that policy-makers need to know "what works", it is possible to say with confidence that concurrent planning worked well for the children in this study.

Summary

- The concurrent planning projects developed their work against a background of increasing encouragement from the Government to move more children into adoptive placements.
- The concurrent planning cases moved faster to permanence and involved the children in fewer moves between carers.
- Overall, the children in the concurrent planning placements and the adoptive placements did not show any evidence of harm on developmental and relationship measures.
- Comparative studies from the USA are hard to track down, but such as do exist suggest that the UK experience is exceptionally positive.
- On the basis that policy-makers need to know "what works", it is possible to say with confidence that concurrent planning worked well for the children in this study.

Appendix A
Methodology

Details of the sample are given in Chapter 2 and details of measures are given in Appendix B. Below we describe the procedures used to acquire data on each child's case.

Data collection

Data were collected from case notes and from interviews with concurrency carers, foster carers (in Trafford), adoptive parents and birth parents. In recognition of the fact that numbers of cases would be small, an early decision was taken to incorporate several opportunities to collect qualitative as well as quantitative material on the placements. For example, parental satisfaction with the placements, with the children's progress, and with the services they had received from any source were seen as important elements in the evaluation study (Tizard, 1977; Groothues *et al*, 1998/99).

During the preparation groups held by MAS, Coram Family and the Brighton & Hove adoption team, the prospective adopters and concurrency carers were told about concurrent planning (see also Chapter 3 for a description of the work of the three concurrency teams). The research was explained to the respective groups by the concurrency team leaders, or (at the Goodman Project) by the Director of MAS. At MAS and the Goodman Project prospective adopters were all asked to choose whether they would agree to join the research evaluation after they had been through Panel. It was noted by the teams when families had agreed, and the researchers were told. Leaflets explaining the study were prepared for adoptive families, prospective adopters, concurrency carers and birth parents in the five different settings: MAS and Trafford Adoption Teams' groups, Goodman Project, Coram Family Project, and Brighton & Hove. These leaflets explained the study and the arrangements for confidentiality of data, and the right to withdraw at any stage in the research process.

When a prospective adopter or a concurrency carer had been through Panel, the project teams contacted the researchers and passed on the family name and address. The researchers then wrote to ask for an interview: all those who had originally agreed to participate were recruited into the evaluation. When the researchers visited for the first time, they explained the nature of the study and written informed consent was obtained.

As we have noted in Chapter 2, permission was granted by Trafford Social

Services for researchers to interview foster carers with responsibility for the children who were subject to care proceedings and where adoption was the recommended care plan; all the foster carers agreed to be interviewed. Once these children were placed with adoptive families, the new parents were contacted for the follow-up interview, and the foster carers were not seen again. The new adoptive parents were written to and permission was sought for an interview and for questionnaires to be completed by them and the teachers (where appropriate). Written informed consent was obtained either when a visit was made to the new parents or by post when questionnaires were completed though a family interview was refused.

The interviews

Interviews with adoptive families and concurrency carer families

Pre-placement

Written informed consent was obtained from all those who agreed to be part of the evaluation. A semi-structured interview was used in the pre-placement interview to explore the reasons for choosing either the concurrent planning option or the traditional adoption route. Further questions covered feelings and experiences about the preparation and selection procedures, any delays encountered in moving to placement and expectations of meeting the child and the birth parents. In the concurrency carer families questions also explored capacity to face and deal with loss and disappointment.

Post-placement

Upon notification of a placement, researchers wrote to the adoptive parents or the concurrency carers requesting an interview approximately six weeks time after placement. It was explained that this would give the child time to settle in to the new family, and the new "parents" time to get to know the child. The second interview with the adoptive families and the concurrency carers focused on the circumstances surrounding the placement, meetings with the birth parents or other family members, and the health and development of the newly placed child. The impact of the placement on the parents and any other members of the family was investigated, and parents questioned on satisfaction with the placement. They were asked to complete the behaviour and emotional adjustment and attachment questionnaires (see below, "Measures") on the newly placed children, adding any further comments of their own. Interview questions also covered these issues. Concurrency carers were also asked to describe their experience of and feelings about the initial arrangements for contact with the birth family. Other issues were explored as they arose, e.g. health issues such as handling drug-withdrawal in a baby or specific medical anxieties. When it was appropriate, permission was sought to contact the nursery or school that the newly placed child was attending. Parents were asked to complete the General Health Questionnaire (see Appendix B, "Measures").

Follow-up interview

The third visit to the MAS adoptive parents and the concurrency carers was made after 12–15 months. At this point, the parents were asked to complete the same questionnaires that they had completed at the start of their care of the index child. They were also asked to comment on their experience of adoption or concurrent planning over the previous year (15 months), and their satisfaction with the outcome and the procedures surrounding the placement and the services they had received. For some MAS adopters it was not possible to fit the third, follow-up interview into the research timetable. When the Coram Family concurrency team joined the evaluation research, the same pattern of two early interviews and one follow-up interview was planned with the concurrency families.

The incorporation of the Brighton & Hove project at a later stage of the research had two effects on the data collection. For families who were at an early stage of the concurrency programme, the first interviews were held, but there was insufficient time to hold follow-up interviews within the timescale set by the research. For others who were further along the route to the final hearing at the point of agreeing to participate in the research, it was too late to conduct the pre- and post-placement interviews in the same timetable that had been achieved with the other two concurrency groups. In these Brighton & Hove cases, data were collected retrospectively on why the parents had chosen concurrent planning, and they were encouraged to recall as much as possible of the early experience of placement and contact. For many parents these had been vivid experiences and we are confident that there was little data lost, although it must be accepted that subsequent events and experiences (such as the final hearing or adoption hearing) may have coloured their narratives. They were not asked retrospectively to complete standardised measures relating to the children at the time of placement.

Interviews with Trafford foster carers and adopters

The researchers were told by the leader of the Trafford Adoption and Permanency Team when a referral had been made from the field social work teams. A visit was then made to the foster carers to get information on the children's health, development and, when appropriate, educational progress (see Appendix B, "Measures"). Permission had been obtained from the local authority to get the school questionnaires filled in by teachers where appropriate (see Appendix B, "Measures"). The preliminary pre-placement interview was, of course, not appropriate in full for these foster carers, but they were asked for information surrounding the child's placement and any specific problems that were being found. Information on contact arrangements for the children with their birth families was obtained. When the Adoption and Permanence Team placed children with prospective adopters, a letter was sent 12 months after the first contact with the child's foster carers, asking for a follow-up interview. Where the child was still with the Trafford foster carers, the 12-month interview was held with them. In both cases the parental carer was asked to complete repeat questionnaires for the child.

Interviews with birth parents

The researchers contacted birth parents through their local authority social worker, adoption worker or through the concurrency team worker, who passed on a letter explaining what the purposes of the research were. It was suggested that the interview would give parents an opportunity to put their point of view, and confidentiality was emphasised. The letter also included information about the small payment at the completion of an interview.

A semi-structured interview was held with the birth parents that covered their understanding of the current position for their child; the information they had been given about concurrent planning, and whether they felt they had understood what was being proposed for their child or family; how much they felt they had been involved in the decision-making; and the sources of their personal support during the concurrency period. Finally, they were asked about contact and their satisfaction with the arrangements. The large majority of these interviews were held in the project buildings, but researchers held some interviews in their homes. This material was coded and the results are given in Chapter 6. The birth parents' views on contact in the concurrency projects are included in Chapter 8. The interviews were, with permission, audio-taped and a small payment was made to birth parents, partly as an encouragement for them to participate, but in recognition of their help. The interview with birth parents of children placed through MAS or Trafford SSD was an adapted version of that described above, excluding the questions referring to concurrency but covering all other areas relating to decision-making, placement and contact with the child and adopters.

Everyone who was interviewed was asked if they would give permission for their comments to be quoted in the final publication, when the researchers thought it would be helpful. Parents were also written to at the end of the project asking them to confirm their agreement to this.

Measures used for the children

Initially, it was expected that the children would be drawn from across the age groups from birth to eight years – the ages for which concurrent planning had originally been designed. It was only as the research progressed that it became increasingly clear that there would be no children over the age of three years, and that many selected to go through concurrent planning would be admitted to the scheme when only a few weeks old. If this predominance of very young babies had been foreseen, questionnaires specific to the development of babies in the first year of life would have been used, based on the premise that children placed with adoptive parents at very young ages, or from birth, differ hardly at all in their behaviour and achievement of developmental milestones from the general population (Brodzinsky, 1993, quoted in Triseliotis, 2002).

The measures (given in detail in Appendix B) were selected to track development: behaviour, social skills and competencies. The selected measures are not developmental screening measures because they do not include clearly defined pass/fail rules. The aim of a screening test is to detect abnormality. In infancy and childhood the range of what is normal is very wide, and the predictive value of developmental tests is relatively poor in the field of behaviour. None of the selected measures would be appropriate for predicting later behaviour or development. While behaviour at three, four and five is strongly predictive of later behaviour, the early behaviour of babies is not predictive of later behaviour.

As mentioned in Chapter 2, the measures for children were derived from among those included in the Looking After Children Assessment and Action Records (Department of Health, 1995).[1] These assessment and action records cover seven developmental dimensions: in each dimension there are checklists for the social worker to complete. The purpose of the checklists is to identify the child's current situation and determine whether or not there is a problem. The checklists have not been validated for use as rating systems for identifying the capabilities or behaviour of the children in different age bands. The checklists used in the present survey were for the following age bands:

i) Aged under 12 months; one and two years; three and four years: emotional and behavioural development.
ii) Aged over four years – at home, and at school: emotional and behavioural development.
iii) Aged under 12 months; one and two years; three and four years: attachment.
iv) Aged one and two years; three and four years: self-care skills.

---

[1] These were developed and designed by the Dartington Social Research Unit in association with colleagues from the Universities of Bath, Bristol and Swansea, the National Children's Bureau and other agencies in the child care field.

Emotional and behavioural development

For the babies under 12 months this ten-item checklist covers sleeping and eating, self-injury, irritable and demanding behaviour, with three items on attachment and responsiveness. For the children aged one and two years, the ten items are increased to 15 with the addition of questions on fear, restlessness and social responsiveness. For the three and four-year-olds the items include questions on pro-social behaviour, unhappiness, and disturbance of conduct or concentration.

For children over four years, the Strengths and Difficulties Questionnaire (Goodman, 1997) was used to identify behaviour problems (hyperactivity, emotional problems, difficulties with peers, and conduct problems) and a global pro-social score. For each sub-scale the score can range from 0 to 10 provided all five items have been completed. From the first four subscales a Total Difficulties score is derived that has a range of 0 to 40. The Total Difficulties Score and the separate Pro-social score can be used to define "caseness"; the cut-off points have been chosen so that roughly 80 per cent of a community sample would show "normal" behaviour, 10 per cent would be borderline and 10 per cent would be abnormal. In a high risk sample, as in the present study, likely "cases" are identified by a borderline or abnormal score on one of the sub-scales.

With permission from the parental carer, a copy of this questionnaire was also sent to the nursery or school for children over four years, with a covering letter explaining their inclusion in an (unspecified) research project. The parents frequently took the questionnaire to the child's teacher themselves, and returned it to the researchers.

Attachment

One of the important issues in the successful transfer of children from their birth families to the fostering and adoptive families is their capacity to develop appropriate attachments to their new family members (Rutter, 1995; Howe, 1998).[2] Information about attachment between the children and those who had day-to-day care of them and any other children in the household was recorded on a simple questionnaire completed by the parental carer (see

[2] One of the original intentions in the present study was to assess attachment capability in the carers and the birth parents. The Adult Attachment Interview (AAI) (George, Kaplan and Main, 1985) was to be used to derive adults ratings of adoptive and foster-adopt parents. These would then be compared with ratings for the children from the Story Stem interview developed by Hodges and Steele which explores aspects of attachment in children over four years. Since there were so few children in this category, and none in the concurrent planning groups, neither of these measures were used.

Appendix B). This set of questions was taken from the Looking After Children record booklets. The questions are the same for all age groups, viz: How well does the child get on with the people he or she lives with? Answers can be recorded as very well; quite well; not well and badly.

Self-care skills

Simple activities were recorded for each age group: for one and two-year-olds items included putting on coat and shoes and feeding self; for the three and four-year-olds the items included going to the lavatory alone, dressing and using a knife and fork, and helping to tidy play things away. The checklist was completed by the parental carer.

Statistical procedures

The analyses were carried out using SPSS-PC. Because the sample size was small, the association between categorical variables was tested by using Fisher's exact test. Differences between groups on the continuous measures were compared using Mann-Whitney U-tests using exact p values because the scales were non-normal.

Appendix B
The measures

1. Strengths & Difficulties Questionnaire Parents/ for children aged 4–16

For each item please mark the box for *Not true, Somewhat true* or *Certainly true*.

Please give your answers on the basis of the child's behaviour in this last month

Child's name .... boy [ ] girl [ ]

Child's date of birth ....

	Not true	*Somewhat true*	*Certainly true*
Considerate of other people's feelings	[ ]	[ ]	[ ]
Restless, overactive, cannot stay still for long	[ ]	[ ]	[ ]
Often complains of headaches, stomach-aches or sickness	[ ]	[ ]	[ ]
Shares readily with other children (treats, pencils, toys)	[ ]	[ ]	[ ]
Often has temper tantrums	[ ]	[ ]	[ ]
Rather solitary, tends to play alone	[ ]	[ ]	[ ]
Generally obedient, usually does what adults ask	[ ]	[ ]	[ ]
Many worries, often seems worried	[ ]	[ ]	[ ]
Helpful if someone is hurt, upset or feeling ill	[ ]	[ ]	[ ]
Constantly fidgeting or squirming	[ ]	[ ]	[ ]

	Not true	*Somewhat true*	*Certainly true*
Has at least one good friend	[ ]	[ ]	[ ]
Often fights with other children	[ ]	[ ]	[ ]
Often unhappy, down-hearted or tearful	[ ]	[ ]	[ ]
Generally liked by other children	[ ]	[ ]	[ ]
Easily distracted, concentration wanders	[ ]	[ ]	[ ]
Nervous or clingy in new situations easily loses confidence	[ ]	[ ]	[ ]
Kind to younger children	[ ]	[ ]	[ ]
Often cheats or lies	[ ]	[ ]	[ ]
Picked on or bullied by other children	[ ]	[ ]	[ ]
Often volunteers to help others (parents, children, teachers)	[ ]	[ ]	[ ]
Thinks things out before acting	[ ]	[ ]	[ ]
Steals from home, school or elsewhere	[ ]	[ ]	[ ]
Gets on better with adults than children	[ ]	[ ]	[ ]
Many fears, easily scared	[ ]	[ ]	[ ]
Sees tasks through to the end, good concentration span	[ ]	[ ]	[ ]

Do you have any other comments or concerns?

Thank you
Children & Families Study, Thomas Coram Research Unit, London

2. Self care skills for children aged 1–2 years

Carer's interview

Child's name . . . .

Social skills and development – 1–2-year-olds
Which of the following can your child do?
(please tick the box which best describes your child)

	Fully mastered	*Learning how to do it*	*Not doing it yet*	*Don't know*
1. Controls bowels	[ ]	[ ]	[ ]	[ ]
2. Controls bladder during the day	[ ]	[ ]	[ ]	[ ]
3. Puts on her/his own coat	[ ]	[ ]	[ ]	[ ]
4. Puts on her/his own shoes or boots	[ ]	[ ]	[ ]	[ ]
5. Drinks from a cup	[ ]	[ ]	[ ]	[ ]
6. Feeds self with a spoon	[ ]	[ ]	[ ]	[ ]

Total self care score [ ]

3. Self care skills for children aged 3–4 years

Carer's interview

Child's name . . . .

Social skills and development – 1–2-year-olds
Which of the following can your child do?
(please tick the box which best describes your child)

	Fully mastered	*Learning how to do it*	*Not doing it yet*	*Don't know*
1. Use the toilet alone	[ ]	[ ]	[ ]	[ ]
2. Wash & dry hands	[ ]	[ ]	[ ]	[ ]
3. Blow nose	[ ]	[ ]	[ ]	[ ]

	Fully mastered	*Learning how to do it*	*Not doing it yet*	*Don't know*
4. Dress/undress self	[ ]	[ ]	[ ]	[ ]
5. Use knife and fork	[ ]	[ ]	[ ]	[ ]
6. Recognise own possessions	[ ]	[ ]	[ ]	[ ]
7. Help tidy away playthings	[ ]	[ ]	[ ]	[ ]
Total score	[ ]			

4. Ratings of emotional and behavioural development

Babies under one year old

Concurrency carers or foster parent's interview: Babies under one year

How has your baby been behaving over the last three months (or as long as you have known him or her) – please tick the box which best describes him or her.

	Definitely like the baby	*Quite like the baby*	*A bit like the baby*	*Not at all like the baby*
Some babies:				
1. Look at their carer(s) when they need reassurance	[ ]	[ ]	[ ]	[ ]
2. Readily smile and respond to their carer(s)	[ ]	[ ]	[ ]	[ ]
3. Like their carer(s) to show them physical affection	[ ]	[ ]	[ ]	[ ]
4. Get demanding and impatient with carer(s)	[ ]	[ ]	[ ]	[ ]
5. Constantly want picking up and soothing	[ ]	[ ]	[ ]	[ ]

	Definitely like the baby	*Quite like the baby*	*A bit like the baby*	*Not at all like the baby*
6. Are extremely fretful or irritable	[ ]	[ ]	[ ]	[ ]
7. Cry all the time	[ ]	[ ]	[ ]	[ ]
8. Have a poor appetite or extremely variable eating pattern	[ ]	[ ]	[ ]	[ ]
9. Have difficulty in sleeping or a disturbed sleep pattern	[ ]	[ ]	[ ]	[ ]
10. Deliberately injure themselves (e.g. by rocking or head-banging)	[ ]	[ ]	[ ]	[ ]

Are you really worried by any of these things? If so, please specify which

....

....

....

....

5. Emotional and behavioural development

Children aged 1–2 years

Please mark the answer which best describes how your toddler has been behaving over the last two to three months, not just today.

	Definitely like the child	*Quite like the child*	*A bit like the child*	*Not at all like the child*
Some children:				
1. Look at and go to their carer(s) when they need reassurance	[ ]	[ ]	[ ]	[ ]

	Definitely like the child	*Quite like the child*	*A bit like the child*	*Not at all like the child*
2. Readily smile and respond to their carer(s)	[ ]	[ ]	[ ]	[ ]
3. Like their carer(s) to show them physical affection	[ ]	[ ]	[ ]	[ ]
4. Get demanding and impatient with carer(s)	[ ]	[ ]	[ ]	[ ]
5. Are socially withdrawn or excessively shy	[ ]	[ ]	[ ]	[ ]
6. Share out treats with others	[ ]	[ ]	[ ]	[ ]
7. Let others join in things they are doing	[ ]	[ ]	[ ]	[ ]
8. Constantly want picking up and soothing	[ ]	[ ]	[ ]	[ ]
9. Are extremely fretful or irritable	[ ]	[ ]	[ ]	[ ]
10. Are very restless and fidgety	[ ]	[ ]	[ ]	[ ]
11. Cry persistently	[ ]	[ ]	[ ]	[ ]
12. Have a poor appetite or extremely variable eating pattern	[ ]	[ ]	[ ]	[ ]
13. Have difficulty in sleeping or a disturbed sleep pattern	[ ]	[ ]	[ ]	[ ]
14. Are frightened of particular things or situations (e.g. strangers, loud noises or animals)	[ ]	[ ]	[ ]	[ ]
15. Deliberately injure themselves (e.g. by rocking or head-banging)	[ ]	[ ]	[ ]	[ ]

Are you really worried by any of these things? If so, please specify which

. . . .

. . . .

. . . .

. . . .

6. Family attachments

Family relationships

How closely attached is the child to the following people?

		Very closely	*Quite closely*	*Not closely*	*Poor relation -ship*	*n/a d/k*
Mother (birth, foster, adoptive)		[ ]	[ ]	[ ]	[ ]	[ ]
Father (birth, foster, adoptive)		[ ]	[ ]	[ ]	[ ]	[ ]
Other children in the same house	1.	[ ]	[ ]	[ ]	[ ]	[ ]
	2.	[ ]	[ ]	[ ]	[ ]	[ ]
	3.	[ ]	[ ]	[ ]	[ ]	[ ]

Completed by . . . .
(please name your relationship with the child, e.g. mother, adoptive mother, foster mother)

Date of completing this form . . . . / . . . . / . . . .

Appendix C
Differential diagnosis in concurrent planning

1. Strengths in Families Checklist

Parent–child relations	Parent shows empathy with child Parent is observably responsive to child Parent puts the child's needs ahead of her own Child is happy in the parent's presence Parent has raised child for significant time In the past parent has met child's needs Parents accepts some responsibility for current problems
Parent support systems	Parent has good relationships with other adults who do not have similar problems Parent has meaningful support that can be used immediately (religious, work-based) Extended family provide support
Past support systems	Evidence that family can support or has supported members appropriately Relatives offered help with current placement Relatives have followed through with help in the past There are significant non-family who have helped in the past Significant non-family have followed through with help in the past
Family history	Family's culture emphasises mutual help Parents had consistent parenting Parents had childhood needs met
Parents' self-care	Parent's own health good Parents use appropriate medical care Parent's hygiene and appearance good Parents have stable housing history Parent has solid job history Parent has school achievement certificates Parent has employable skills

Child's Development	Child shows age-appropriate cognitive abilities Child able to do age-appropriate tasks Child shows evidence of conscience development Child has appropriate social skills No major behaviour problems

2. Poor Prognostic Indicators for birth families

Catastrophic prior abuse • Parent killed or seriously harmed another child and no significant change has occurred • Parent has repeatedly harmed this child • Child experienced physical or sexual abuse in infancy
Dangerous lifestyle • Parent's only financial support from drugs, prostitution, street life • Parent addicted to debilitating drugs/alcohol • Domestic violence between partners • Recent history of serious criminal activity • Mother abused drugs or alcohol during pregnancy
Significant child protection history • Parental rights to another child terminated, no change • Three plus CPS interventions for separate events • Child has suffered more than one form of abuse • Other children placed away from family for 6+ months • This child abandoned with others; or parent does not visit when child looked after • Preventive services have failed • Parent under age 16 with no support systems • Parent has asked to relinquish more than once
Significant personal history • Parent diagnosed with severe mental illness that has not responded to previous health care • Parent has chronic mental illness that responds slowly or not at all to health care • Parent has learning difficulties, has shown self-care deficits and has no support system for parenting • Parent grew up in foster or residential care; or in family with inter-generational abuse

Appendix D
Information for birth families from the concurrent planning teams

1. The Goodman Team

A message for parents

Most parents reading this leaflet will not have their child/ren living with them at present.

The Court is likely to be making decisions about your child's future and you probably have mixed emotions. You may be feeling anxious because you don't know what's happening or you may be feeling a little relieved because things have been getting on top of you.

Whatever your feelings, if your local authority social worker has spoken to you about the Goodman Team as a way of planning for your child's future you are likely to have many questions you want answering.

We hope this leaflet will answer some of your queries and concerns, but we also hope you will agree to talk to a Team worker who can tell you more about what we can offer.

What is the Goodman Team?

The Goodman Team offers a new way of working with children and families.

The Team's aim is to reduce the number of moves and changes children often have whilst living away from their birth parents, so children have the best possible care while their long term future is decided.

The Goodman Team offers young children a different experience. Our first priority is to work out whether it will be possible for the child to return to live with their birth parents, or with other birth relatives. While these two possibilities are being explored, the Team offers placement with specially prepared families who are approved both as foster carers and as potential adopters. These families are committed to helping us reunite birth families and children if this is possible.

However, if the Court decides that the child cannot return home, these special carers are ready to offer the child the security of adoption without facing further moves and changes. Quite often children are placed in a temporary foster home whilst decisions are being made. This can go on for long periods and sometimes children may be moved to different foster homes. For young children this can be very confusing and upsetting as they do not understand what is happening to them. When children are moved around their behaviour can become more difficult and challenging, and they become harder to care for.

What about birth parents?

You are very important to your child and nothing will change the fact that you are the child's birth parent whatever happens in the future.

The Team is here to offer you the best chance to be reunited with your child, if that is what you want. Things may have gone wrong but now you have an opportunity to put them right. Goodman staff are here to help you, and we will be honest with you, not only about what *you* may need to do, but also about what you can expect from *us* to make sure your child's future is settled as soon as possible.

What could happen to my child?

If your child is placed by the Team she or he will either return to you or to a relative or will be adopted by their Goodman carer.

How is this decided?

There will be different people who will be involved in writing reports and giving evidence to the Court: your social worker, the Guardian ad Litem [now called Children's Guardian], Goodman staff and other professionals. The Court will also want to hear your views and your solicitor is there to help you with this.

Because some children cannot return to their birth parents, Goodman staff also talk to other relatives right at the start to see what possibilities there are for the child to live with other family members.

After hearing the evidence about all possible options the Court will decide on the child's future.

What does the Goodman Team offer my family?

The Goodman Team can often undertake work which the Court ask for more quickly that social workers in busier social services departments. The Team workers are available to work with you and your child and will offer you support during and after the assessment process. You will have one, sometimes two, Team workers specially for you.

A separate worker will work with the Goodman carers to support and advise them. Your child will also be visited by the local authority social worker.

What happens in an assessment?

When the Court asks us to make an assessment it means Goodman staff meeting you, your child (if they are old enough) and with other members of your family to look at what needs to change or improve in order for your child to return home. We will listen carefully to what you say. We can help best if you tell us about your difficulties, but we also want to help you think about what goes well in your family. The purpose is to get a really clear understanding of what needs to change for you to be able to meet your child's needs and to find out if you need any special help in order to do this.

It is important that we write down whatever you agree to do so there is a clear plan. We will be honest with you throughout the assessment process, and we will write down what we offer to do as well as what is expected of you.

What about my child?

The Team offers your child a placement with Goodman carers who can provide your child with security and a sense of belonging, whilst you work to make permanent plans for your child.

You will be introduced to the Goodman carers and they will ask your advice about your child's likes, dislikes and daily routine.

They will bring your child to the Goodman offices to see you at agreed times. There are rooms available with play equipments so you and your child can be together in pleasant surroundings. This contact time also gives opportunities for you and the Goodman carers to keep each other informed about how your child is doing.

Is this just a way of having my child adopted, whatever I do?

No. This is a new way of trying to make your child feel secure while we are working with you to see if she/he can return home or not.

Do I lose contact if my child is adopted?

Not necessarily. We try to negotiate the most appropriate adoption contact arrangements for each individual child and encourage openness. As a minimum we try to arrange for birth families to receive news and photos of their child every year. Because birth relatives and Goodman carers get to know one another well, we have found that if an adoption order is made, contact is much more open than in "traditional" adoptions, and in come circumstance birth families and adopters continue to meet.

The Team also offers post-adoption support from Manchester Adoption Society. This means the workers continue to be available for all concerned after and adoption order is made.

Please discuss the Goodman Team with your solicitor and take legal advice. Team staff are always available to explain what is involved to your solicitor or any other adviser or advocate you may have.

Birth families who have been involved with the Goodman team have found it helpful. Here are a couple of comments they have made:

> *Birth mother:* There have never been any sudden surprises. I've always known what's happening and everythings's been explained and written down for me so it's really clear.
>
> *Birth father:* When we come to the project offices we are treated with respect.

Our offices are not part of a Social Services Department. They are quiet and private with comfortable rooms to meet with us and rooms with play equipment where you can spend time with your child.

2. Coram Family Concurrent Planning Project: Information for parents

How this project can help parents whose children are at present living away from them because of care proceedings in the Courts

Most parents reading this leaflet will not have their child living with them at present. The Court will be making decisions about your child's future and you may be feeling angry or sad or confused. You are probably worried about what is going to happen to your child in care.

This leaflet contains information about a new way of involving you as a parent in planning for your child's future. The Coram Family Concurrent Planning Project is a new way of working with families. It is a partnership between Islington and Camden Social Services and Coram Family. Its aim is to reduce the number of moves and changes children often experience while living away from their birth parents, so the child has the best possible care while his or her long-term future is decided. This way of working is already being used in Manchester at the Goodman Project.

The Project is a way of helping parents and their children in situations where there are care proceedings before the courts and long-term plans for the children need to be made. Staying in a temporary foster home is often not good for young children especially if they have to move several times while waiting for decisions to be made. This is bound to make the children more difficult to care for whether they return to their parents when the Court makes a decision or are later placed for adoption.

The Coram Project offers young children a different experience. Our first priority is to try to make it possible for the child to return to live with you. The next choice is for the child to be cared for by another relative. While these two possibilities are being explored, the Project offers your child placement with a specially prepared family who are approved both as foster parents and as potential adopters. These families are committed to helping us reunite birth parents with their children if this is possible. However, if the Court decides that the child cannot return home to you or another member of your family, these special carers are ready to offer the child the security of adoption without facing another move.

The service for you as parents

The Court will decide what assessments you need to have and when reports need to be completed by, so that there are no unnecessary delays. The Court will also say how often you should see your child. We will offer you:

- Your own social worker who will be available to support you through the assessments the Court will ask you to have;
- A written agreement setting out what you are expected to do and what help is available;
- Help with any practical arrangements;
- Opportunities for contact with your child;
- Opportunities to talk things through with your own social worker who will have time to see you regularly.

What could happen to my child?

The Court will decide whether your child can return to you or another member of your family on the basis of the evidence from you, and from reports, and evidence from social workers, the Project staff, the Guardian *ad Litem* [now Children's Guardian], and any other professionals who have been asked to do an assessment or give an opinion.

If the Court decides that your child cannot return to you or another member of your extended family then the best plan will be for your child to have the security of adoption by the people who are already familiar to you and your child. This would avoid an upsetting move for your child. You would already know the carers and we hope you would feel confident that they could give your child the love and security that he or she needs. We hope that you would also feel that the carers respect and understand you and will be able to tell the child later on that you loved him or her but that you had some problems which made it difficult for you to look after them.

The Carers will be specially selected and trained. It will be their job to help support you by keeping the relationship going with your child. You will be able to meet them and get to know them when they bring your child to contact. They will be able to tell you what is happening to your child and what progress he or she is making.

You may find it helpful to discuss this leaflet with your solicitor to help you decide whether or not to accept a referral to the Coram Family Concurrent Planning Project.

We would be very pleased to meet you and answer your questions about our work. Please feel free to call and make an appointment.

3. Brighton & Hove: Information for birth families

Most parents reading this will not have their children living with them. The Court will be making decisions about your child's future and it is likely that you are feeling angry, confused, sad or a mixture of these emotions.

What is the Concurrency Team?
The concurrency team is a special team within the Children and Families Division at Brighton & Hove Social Services. It aims to work with families whose children are not living with them at the moment, but it is hoped that with the right help and support they can look after their children again.

The aim of the concurrency team is to work in a new way to reduce the number of moves experienced by children while the court is deciding their future. It is recognised that moves for children whilst their future is being decided is very unsettling and can make them confused and emotionally upset. This will make caring for them in the future very difficult.

The project places children with special carers so the children do not have to move unnecessarily. The carers, known as foster-adopters, work closely with the concurrency team to bring about rehabilitation with the birth family as the first option, however, they are also committed to adopting the child if this is not possible.

Why is this different?
What usually happens when children cannot be cared for by their parents is that they go to live with foster carers whilst work is being undertaken with the parents and a decision is being reached about their future in the court. This can take a long time and the children may have to move to different foster placements. This can cause a lot of difficulties for the children and can mean that they will experience traumas in the future.

The focus at all times is permanency for your child so that they are not living with uncertainty for extended periods of time. Ideally we would want your child to be returned to your care, however, if this is not possible we would assess members of of your family who may be able to care for your child. If this is not possible your child would remain with the foster-adopter and be adopted by them.

Why is this better for the birth parents?
It means you will know the carers for your child and will be able to share information with them. They will equally be able to tell you how your child is doing. You will meet with them regularly as they will bring your child to contact and take part in reviews.

Contact between you and the your child will take place regularly. Initially contact will be supervised but as you progress, the need for this may diminish. Contact will initially be set by the Court agreement, but can be increased or decreased if it is in the best interests of your child. This will be discussed with you at every stage and decisions will be based on your behaviour rather than just what you tell us.

You will work alongside the social worker to identify why you were not able to care for your child. The next stage will be that help will be given to you so you can work to overcome difficulties and problems identified. This process would be clear from the outset with very specific tasks for you and the social worker to complete. Many parents find this helpful because in enables them to focus on the needs of their child and how they need to change for them.

The work that you will have identified with the social worker will be given time limits. This again enables you to focus on your child's timescales and their need for security.

Worries expressed by birth parents

It may worry you that concurrent planning is just a short cut to adoption for your child. This is not the purpose of concurrent planning and the initial aim is for your child to be returned to your care, but if this is not possible then the permanent placement for the child needs to be secured as soon as possible. The work that is completed with you is very intensive and focused and aims to give you every opportunity to care for your child.

We believe that children have a right to know about their birth family and if you were unable to care for your child, we would endeavour to maintain contact between you and your child. This may be in a variety of ways, either face-to-face or by letter. The social worker would discuss this with you in much more detail if the need arose.

After the court has made its decision you will conitnue to have access to support, whether this is to care for your child or as a result of the decision that you can no longer care for your child.

What happens now?

You should discuss concurrent planning with your legal advisors and your family. We will then arrange to meet with you to discuss the work in more detail and answer any questions you may have.

Your child's social worker's name is . . . .

Telephone number: . . . .

Appendix E

Information for professionals from the concurrent planning teams

1. The Goodman Team[1]

Permanency planning for children and families

The Goodman Team offers fostering, adoption and rehabilitation for those younger children and families most in need of rapid and effective decision-making to achieve a permanent plan for the future.

The Goodman Team offers an independent service to local authority social services departments and the Courts.

The origins of concurrent planning
The concept of concurrent planning originated in Seattle, USA in 1981. Lutheran Social Services of Washington and Idaho inaugurated a pilot project bringing together professional knowledge and experience about effective casework, outreach services and system-related change with the aim of preventing foster care drift.

The Goodman Team – Background
In this country, Manchester Adoption Society and Bury and Salford Social Services Department researched the applicability of concurrent planning to childcare planning and consulted widely with the judiciary, lawyers, Guardians ad Litem and social work practitioners before launching the Goodman Project in March 1998. The project included an independent research component to evaluate the outcomes of the concurrent planning approach to child placement.

After its initial three years as a pilot project, Manchester Adoption Society is continuing to offer concurrent planning placements. The Goodman Project will become the Goodman Team, and will take referrals from other local authorities in the Greater Manchester area broadening out the scope of the Team; however, the remit of the work will remain the same.

---

[1] This version of the leaflet was prepared after the evaluation period was concluded, when the Goodman Team was able to take cases from a number of local authorities, not just Bury and Salford.

Why is the "Concurrent Permanency Planning" in the Goodman Team different from other forms of foster care and adoption?
The Goodman Team is a programme designed to prevent the harmful effects of prolonged uncertainty about the future on both children and families involved in the "care" system. It aims to work towards family reunification while, at the same time, developing an alternative permanent plan.

Traditionally, substitute families have been recruited and approved to either foster or adopt, *but not both*. When young children enter the care system, however, some are at serious risk of not returning to their birth family and eventually need adoption.

Separating fostering and adoption builds in at least one move for the child from temporary foster home to the adoptive home. Often children experience not one but several moves and spend long periods in fostering situations designed only to be temporary.

BAAF research "Surveying Adoption"

- 44 per cent of children entering the care system aged 0–12 months had four or more placements before joining adopters.
- The mean overall duration of care was 3 years 1 month in all the children surveyed in LA care.
- On average, best interest decisions had been made within 1 year 4 months after the child started to be looked after. It took another 7 months before placement with adopters was achieved.
- By comparison, children placed in the Goodman Team on average from placement to adoption order has been made has been 8–12 months with best interest decisions being made between 3–6 months.

Such moves and uncertainty regarding the future can be very unsettling for young children who need a sense of stability and belonging if they are to thrive and not be further damaged by their experiences in care placements. The Goodman Team seeks to identify the children most at risk of drifting in so-called temporary care and works intensively with their birth families to enable effective decision-making about the child's future to be reached as swiftly as possible. Crucially, while working with the birth family, Goodman workers also support the placement of the child with specially approved and prepared "Goodman carers" who help to work towards the child's return to the birth family but who are also committed to adopting the child themselves if this proves impossible.

The Goodman Carers play a vital role by being able to bring about effective visiting arrangements between parents and child during the period of fostering and trying to develop helpful relationships with birth relatives, so that right from the start they can co-operate as much as possible regarding planning for the child's upbringing, whichever family the child eventually achieves permanence with. This approach also aims to facilitate openness in the adoptions resulting from Goodman placements.

Making a referral to the team
Ring initially and speak to one of the team members.

Team referral criteria are:

- Children under 6 where the child is subject to care proceedings which will last for several months and potentially will delay achieving permanence.
- The family history/background would indicate adoption is one strong option but there are issues to be resolved and work to be done with the immediate or extended family which might lead to rehabilitation.
- AND we have an appropriate Goodman carer available for the child/ children in question.

The Goodman Team offers

- An open, honest and positive approach which keeps the focus of planning on the best interests of the child and the child's timescale.
- An independent assessment, jointly instructed by the parties in care proceedings regarding the potential for the birth family to parent the child.
- Contact using the team's contact rooms up to three sessions per week.
- Trained and well supported Goodman foster carers who are willing to take the risk of caring for a child whose future is legally uncertain and who are committed to help the child return to the birth family should that be the plan.
- If a return to the birth family is not possible, continuity of care via adoption by the Goodman carers.

The Goodman Team package also includes

- Payment of allowances to the foster carer.
- Reimbursement for birth families travel expenses to contact and assessment sessions.
- If adoption becomes the plan, the completion of Form Es and Schedule 2 reports.

- A long-term post-adoption service to birth families, adopters and adoptees, should the child remain with the permanency planning carers.

Comments from individuals who have been involved in permanency planning for children over the past three years:
- Guardian *ad Litem*: 'I could not fault any part of the work, it was excellent.'
- Local authority legal adviser: 'The depth of assessment reports was commendable as was the excellent relationship established between the Goodman workers and the (birth) mother.'
- Birth mother: 'There have never been any sudden surprises. I've always known what happening and everything has been explained and written down for me so it's really clear.'
- Birth father: 'When we come to the Project Offices we're treated with respect.'

2. The Coram Family Concurrent Planning Project

Information for other agencies and members of the Judiciary, Children's Panel Solicitors, Guardians *ad Litem* and other professionals.

November 1999

Aim

The Project aims to provide an assessment and placement service for children aged 0–24 months, who are subject to care proceedings initiated either by Camden or Islington Social Services Department. During 2000–2001 we hope to place 8 children, and 10–12 children in subsequent years.

Children will be selected on the basis that they are expected to remain in care for several months before the final hearing, and that whilst it looks likely in the light of all the circumstances that the child may require adoption, nevertheless there remains a prospect that rehabilitation to the birth family could be achieved.

Children will be referred to the Coram project by the local authority if, at the Court Hearing which initiates care proceedings or at a subsequent Directions Hearing, the Court directs that it is a suitable case for concurrent planning. The Court will give directions as to what assessments need to be carried out and set out a timeframe for the work, including a further interim hearing and the date for the final hearing.

Children will come from families who have serious difficulties in parenting, e.g. where there are long-term problems of substance abuse, or of mental illness, or where previous children have been removed from the family through the Courts, or where one of the parents is a Schedule 1 offender and currently remains resident in the family home. Specialist assessments may be conducted by adult and/or child and adolescent psychiatrists, by drug dependency clinics and by other specialist resources, in addition to the assessment of parenting skills. Treatment may include programmes for drug dependency, management of aggression and a range of other therapeutic interventions. Treatment should be provided within timescales relevant to the children's needs.

Placements
The revolutionary nature of the project is that it will offer "either/or" placements. Carers will be recruited, trained and supported to care for the children on a fostering basis whilst their birth parents' capabilities are being assessed. They will bring the children to regular contact meetings and work to ensure that the children maintain and develop a healthy attachment for their parents. If the outcome of the assessment is for rehabilitation, the carers will support the children through a period of transition. However, if the children are deemed to be in need of adoption, it is expected that the carers will apply to adopt, thus avoiding breaks in attachment and further delays whilst adopters are sought.

3. Brighton & Hove Department of Social Care and Health

Concurrency Team: Information for professionals
The concurrency team offers fostering, adoption and rehabilitation work for those children aged 0–5 years who are most in need of rapid and effective decision-making to achieve a permanent plan for their future.

We aim to serve children and families of all racial, cultural and religious backgrounds.

The Concurrency Team was established in August 1999 with Quality Protects funding to promote good childcare practice by working towards a permanence plan for children at the earliest opportunity. The staff team are all experienced social workers with considerable experience in child protection and child placement. The work involves complex child protection cases, which are placed before the court prior to the child being moved to a foster-adoptive placement.

The concurrency model is based on a model developed in Seattle by Linda Katz, where they have been using concurrent planning for 15 years, and the Goodman Project run by Manchester Adoption Society which has been working in this way since March 1998.

The Linda Katz model has three main stages of the work; they are interpreted as:

- engaging with the birth parents to identify the key areas of concern;
- working with parents to address these concerns; and
- supporting them to sustain the identified changes.

Each of these stages will last approximately three months and the timescales will be clearly laid down in written agreements. It will be made clear from the outset that if birth parents cannot meet very specific targets then the plan will be for their child to be placed permanently with either extended family members or adopted by their foster-adopters. **The aim of concurrent planning is to prevent damage to the child as a result of delay, placement moves and uncertainty**.

Contact

Foster-adopters are expected to bring the child to contact sessions with the birth families, attend LAC reviews and case conferences where appropriate.

The birth families will therefore have a relationship with the potential adopters of their child. The experience of Seattle has found that this has aided the process of both the birth parents' acceptance of the adoption and the foster-adopters' support of the children's rehabilitation back home. We are very careful to keep the addresses and family names of the foster-adopters confidential.

The child is placed under foster care regulations. Should the work towards rehabilitation prove to be unsuccessful, a meeting of the Permanence Panel following the final hearing of the care proceedings will endorse the change of the placement from foster to adoptive status.

Process

The team has established a rolling programme of recruiting foster-adopters with three preparation groups a year, so that we can meet the placement needs of the children who are referred to us. We currently have a small group of carers awaiting a child placement and a number of placements at various stages of the concurrent planning process.

The key worker roles are divided between the team members so that the foster-adopters and the child do not have the same worker. The third social worker co-works the birth family assessments with the child's social worker. A Community Family Worker supervises the contact sessions, which take place in the team's contact room.

Pre-birth assessment work

The team offers a time-limited, intensive piece of work, which will be undertaken with all the appropriate members of the birth family to ascertain whether the child could return to the birth parents or other members of the extended family.

Eligibility criteria

We work with children aged 0–5 years who have a poor prognosis of being returned home. There is a separate referral leaflet which details clear eligibility criteria.

Team names, address and telephone number.

Appendix F
Information for the concurrent planning carers

1. The Goodman Team

Concurrent planning for children and families
Some families who are considering adoption will be interested in this initiative designed to introduce a new concept into the field of adoption and fostering.

Traditionally families have been prepared and assessed to either foster or adopt and these two ways of caring for children have been viewed quite separately. There is a small group of children where there are serious concerns about their parent's ability to care for them and where it is possible that adoption may be in their best interest. However, prior to final decisions being made and whilst assessments of their parents are being undertaken, these children will be placed in foster care. Sadly many spend long periods in "temporary" foster care and may experience many moves. If the court then decides adoption is appropriate they face a further move to their adoptive family. However, we know that young children need a sense of stability and belonging if they are to thrive. We also know that uncertainty and moves to new placements can be disruptive and damaging. So why do we have a system which seems to encourage moves and prolong uncertainty?

We have seen many cases where children have been affected by this process. Here is just one example:

> *Suzie and Billy were two and three years old when they first needed to be looked after by foster carers. They spent one night in an "emergency" foster home, and then moved to a "short-stay" foster home while the crisis in their birth family was investigated. After a fortnight, however, they had to move again to another "short-term" home, as the second foster home had other commitments. Nearly two years later Suzie and Billy were still waiting for their future to be decided and were still living in "short-term" care. Although they stayed in their third foster home, they had to go to different foster homes whenever their foster carers went on holiday. Suzie and Billy were toddlers when they first came into care but they had already started school by the time they were placed for adoption.*

The majority of children coming into short-term care return to their birth families within a few days or weeks. However, for a small but significant number of children, social workers realise at an early age that a return home may not be possible. This was the situation in Suzie and Billy's case and these are the children this new way of working is designed to help.

The Goodman Team

Concurrent planning was developed in America and was carefully studied by the Manchester Adoption Society. It is now being put into practice for the first time here in the UK via the Goodman Team. We are recruiting, preparing and supporting families who are prepared to foster a young child and to work with us to establish whether or not a safe return to their birth family can be achieved, within the child's timescale. If not, the "Goodman carers" are then committed to adopting the child themselves.

The Goodman Team offers the Goodman families

- Thorough preparation;
- High levels of support;
- The chance to be part of an exciting new development in child care.

Which children are placed via the Team?

- New born to age six who are subject to care proceedings;
- Need looking after, either alone or with sisters and brothers;
- May show the effects of abusive experiences;
- May have medical or behavioural problems sometimes as a result of parents' drug or alcohol abuse during pregnancy;
- May have gaps in their known life history.

What are the benefits of becoming Goodman Carers?

You will:

- Be an integral part of a team approach to enable the child's birth parents to reach responsible decisions about their child's future
- Know that you are providing stability to a child;
- Receive thorough preparation and ongoing training;
- Receive help and advice from professionals and other carers in similar situations to your own;
- Receive a high level of accessible support from experienced workers, including your worker's home telephone number for urgent use before, during and after placement;

- Receive fostering allowance and have necessary equipment provided;
- Be looking after a child who may, if appropriate, become your legally adopted child.

2. The Brighton & Hove Concurrency Team

Brighton & Hove Concurrency: An innovative project for children who need a permanent home.

Could you foster a child with a view to adoption?
Children are adopted by a wide range of people: couples, single people, gay or lesbian people or those over forty, and people from a wide range of cultural and religious backgrounds.

Please phone: .... for details

What is concurrent planning for children?
Concurrent planning for children (0–5 years) aims to achieve permanent families for the most vulnerable young children in local authority care. The child is placed directly with foster-adopters, whilst the Court makes a decision about their future. The child either returns home to their birth parents, or is adopted by the foster-adopters. The difference between the concurrent route and the regular route to adoption are diagrammatically represented [see p 304].

Why is concurrent planning good for children?
- Children move to live with potential adopters at the earliest opportunity, which means fewer moves for children in care;
- Children are able to form a closer relationship with a family sooner;
- Foster-adopters have special training and skills that enable them to make a commitment to children where there is uncertainty about their future;
- Responsibility for all decision-making regarding children is held within one team;
- Concurrent planning for children can result in fewer contested adoptions.

Regular route to adoption

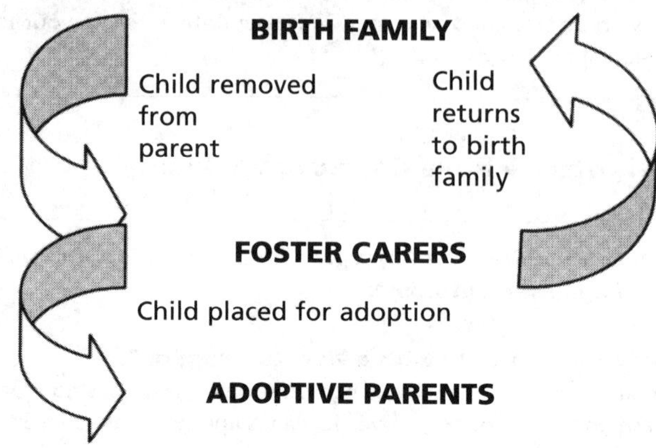

Concurrent planning route to adoption

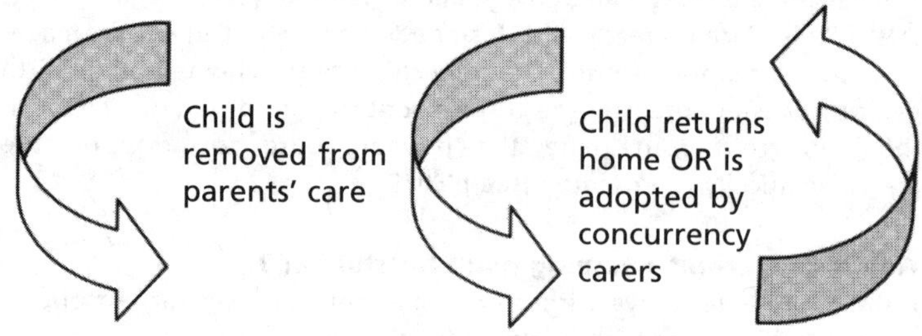

Appendix G

Assessment Agreement between birth parents and the Goodman Project

Name of child Date of birth
Mother's name Date of birth
Father's name Date of birth

Mother's address and telephone number:
Father's address and telephone number:

Parental responsibility: yes/no
Legal status of child:
Date of initial Order obtained:

Is child on Child Protection Register? yes/no
If so, date of registration category?
Date of Review Conference

Concerns

a) Summary of concerns leading to child or children being removed from parents' care
b) Does the parent agree about these concerns?
c) If not, what are the parents' views about why their child was removed from their care?

Strengths in Family

a) Parents' views
b) Child's views (if of an age to give them)
c) Project workers' views
d) Views of other professionals

What changes need to be made?

a) What does the parent or parents think needs to change to convince the Court they can parent their child?
b) What do the Project workers think needs to change for the child to return to her/his parents?

c) What do other people who are involved (e.g. child's social worker, health visitor, significant family members) think needs to change (Please list each person and their views).

Who needs to do what?

NAME	TASK	WHEN	WHEN/HOW TO REVIEW

When will this agreement be reviewed?
Who will be involved in this?
Where will this be done?

DATES OF ASSESSMENT SESSIONS

DATES AND TIMES OF CONTACT VISITS

OTHER ISSUES (please note any issues that have not been covered, including any disagreements)

THIS AGREEMENT WAS MADE BETWEEN AND AGREED BY THE FOLLOWING PEOPLE:

Name	Signature	Date

Appendix H
Court protocols used in concurrent planning cases in Inner London and City Family Proceedings Court

Coram Concurrent Planning Project
Inner London and City Family Proceedings Court

1. Draft First Directions

1.1 The matter to be listed before .... District Judge (Magistrates' Court) on .... (estimated length of hearing one hour) by which hearing the parties to have discussed further directions and time-tabling of the case (together with any application for psychological or any other assessment, etc) which will be considered by the court at the hearing.

2.2 The court notes that the local authority, the mother, and the Guardian (when appointed) will be considering the possibility of instructing the Coram Concurrent Planning Project to assess the viability of rehabilitation with the mother while concurrently planning a permanent placement if rehabilitation is not possible.

1.3 Liberty to all parties to discuss the case with workers from the Coram Project.

1.4 Leave to the local authority to disclose all case papers to the Coram Project.

5.5 The local authority to provide information from the Coram Project in writing, as to whether a referral to the Project is or may be appropriate, to be filed with the court by ....

5.6 Local authority to file interim care plans by ....

5.7 Leave to the solicitor of the child to provide Inner and North London GALRO Panel Manager with details of these directions and date of next hearing in support of request for earlier appointment of Guardian. NB court would fax these to panel for information to assist in appointing GAL.

Coram Concurrent Planning Project

2. Possible Subsequent Directions (Joint)

2.1 The parties shall instruct the Coram Project in the terms of a joint letter of instruction in order for the Coram Project to assess the viability of rehabilitation, at the same time concurrently planning for permanent placement with intended foster carers if rehabilitation is not possible. The letter of instruction shall be drafted by the Local Authority for approval of .... for counter signature by solicitors of the mother and the Guardian ad Litem and the Local Authority to file the letter with the court by ....

2.2 This matter to be listed for hearing of the application to renew the interim care order on

1 ....

2 ....

3 ....

The attendance of all parties is excused on the above occasions provided written consent of each party to the renewal of the Interim Care Order is filed with the court by 4pm on the day preceding the renewal date or the continuing consent signed by all parties has not been withdrawn by any of the parties, notice in writing having been given to the court of such withdrawal not later than 4pm on the day preceding the hearing.

2.3 This matter to be listed for a directions hearing before .... on ....

2.4 The Local Authority shall file an interim report together with a report from the Coram Project by ....

2.5 It is recorded that the court approves the placement of .... with permanent planning carers identified by the Coram Project.

2.6 The matter be listed for a directions hearing 2 weeks before the date set for the final hearing, the directions appointment to be listed before .... District Judge (Magistrates' Court) on ....

Court protocol for social services lawyers and children and families social workers in care cases involving concurrent planning project[1]

The following protocol is intended for use whenever Islington or Camden Social Services and Legal Departments are intending to issue care proceedings in which the care plan will, or is likely to, involve a foster/adoptive placement arranged via the Coram Family Concurrent Planning Project.

In such cases the following steps should always be taken:

1. As soon as it is identified that a case will be a Concurrent Planning Project case, the conducting solicitor should immediately inform the Justices' Clerk or her Deputy, at the Inner London City Family

[1] Prepared by the Legal Department, Islington, July 2000.

Proceedings Court by telephone that such a case is about to be issued through the Court Office. The case will, if possible, then be listed before . . . .

2. The Court should still be alerted even where a case may come within the Concurrent Planning Project, but has not yet been confirmed as a Concurrent Planning Project case, in order to enable the above listing to be made.
3. The Justices' Clerk will identify a Court Clerk to whom the case will be allocated, and who will provide continuity of dealing with that particular court file.
4. The Court will appoint a solicitor from the Children's Panel within 24 hours of receipt of the application, once notified of a Concurrent Planning Project case. The Court will alert the Inner London GALRO Panel that the case is a Concurrent Planning Project case when making the request for a Guardian ad Litem to be appointed. The GALRO Panel will then appoint a Guardian ad Litem as a matter of priority.
5. The Local Authority should make explicit in the Form C13 (Supplement for an Application for a Care or Supervision Order) that specific directions relevant to a concurrent planning directions should be appended to the C13, indicating which of those directions will be sought at the hearing.
6. The Interim Care Plan should set out the details of any intended Concurrent Planning Project placement, as indicated in the precedent care plan document.
7. The Local Authority's social work statement in support of the initial application should exhibit all the publicity leaflets about the Concurrent Planning Project produced by Coram Family. There are separate leaflets providing relevant information to parents, foster-adopters and professionals. All of these should be exhibited, to ensure that all parties are provided with relevant information about the Project at the earliest possible stage in the proceedings.
8. A review directions hearing will always be listed midway through the case.
9. It may be proposed that experts be instructed, in addition to the parenting assessment/s to be carried out by the Concurrent Planning Project (in conjunction with any appropriate Family Centre) as part of the Concurrent Planning programme. The party or parties wishing to instruct an expert should be able to provide the Court with clear reasons why an expert opinion in respect of any parenting issues is required over and above the professional opinion provided by the Concurrent Planning Project/Family Centre assessment.
10. Wherever possible, experts should be instructed by way of a letter of instruction agreed by all parties.

Appendix I
Comparisons of the concurrent planning parents and those from the two adoption teams

Table 1

Strengths in Families: Parent–child relationship, by the three placement groups

Score on Parent–child relationship	*MAS Adoption Team*		*Placement by: Concurrency projects*		*Trafford A&P Teams*	
	N	*%*	*N*	*%*	*N*	*%*
Less than 3	16	89	9	39	16	76
3–6	2	11	14	61	5	24
Total children	**18**	**100**	**23**	**100**	**21**	**100**

[N = 62; not known = 6] χ^2 = 12.14, 2df, p = <.003 [Fisher's Exact test]

Table 2

Strengths in Families: Support systems within the birth parents' families, by the three placement groups

Score on Support Systems within Birth Parents' Families	*MAS Adoption Team*		*Placement by: Concurrency projects*		*Trafford A&P Teams*	
	N	*%*	*N*	*%*	*N*	*%*
0	12	67	11	55	21	100
1–3	6	33	9	45	0	0
Total children	**18**	**100**	**20**	**100**	**21**	**100**

[N = 59; not known = 9] χ^2 = 13.71, 2df, p = <.002 [Fisher's Exact test]

Table 3

Strengths in Families: Past support systems in the birth family, by the three placement groups

Score on Past Support Systems in the Birth Family	*MAS Adoption Team*		*Placement by: Concurrency projects*		*Trafford A&P Teams*	
	N	*%*	*N*	*%*	*N*	*%*
0	15	83	9	45	15	71
1–5	3	17	11	55	6	29
Total children	**18**	**100**	**20**	**100**	**21**	**100**

[N = 59; not known = 9] χ^2 = 6.32, 2df, p = <.04 [Fisher's Exact test]

Table 4

Strengths in Families: Parents' upbringing and family culture: by three placement groups

Score on Parents' Upbringing and Family Culture	*MAS Adoption Team*		*Placement by: Concurrency projects*		*Trafford A&P Teams*	
	N	*%*	*N*	*%*	*N*	*%*
0	15	83	9	47	18	86
1–3	3	17	10	53	3	14
Total children	**18**	**100**	**19**	**100**	**21**	**100**

[N = 58; not known = 10] χ^2 = 8.09, 2df, p = <.02 [Fisher's Exact test]

Table 5

Strengths in Families: Parent's self-care and maturity: by the three placement groups

Score on Parents' Self-Care Abilities	*MAS Adoption Team*		*Placement by: Concurrency projects*		*Trafford A&P Teams*	
	N	*%*	*N*	*%*	*N*	*%*
>3	9	50	9	42	12	57
3–7	9	50	10	58	19	43
Total children	**18**	**100**	**19**	**100**	**21**	**100**

[N = 56; not known = 12] not significant.

Table 6

Strengths in Families: Child's development, by the three placement groups

Score on Child's Appropriate Development	*MAS Adoption Team*		*Placement by: Concurrency projects*		*Trafford A&P Teams*	
	N	*%*	*N*	*%*	*N*	*%*
<5	7	39	10	83	10	48
5	11	61	2	17	11	52
Total children	**18**	**100**	**12**	**100**	**21**	**100**

[N = 51; not applicable = 12; not known = 5] χ^2 = 6.08, 2df, p = <.05 [Fisher's Exact test]

References

Adcock, M (1980) *Social Work Dilemmas: Terminating parental contact*, London: BAAF.

Adcock, M (1991) 'Significant harm: implications for the exercise of statutory responsibilities', in Adcock, M, White, R and Hollows, A (eds) *Significant Harm*, Croydon: Significant Publications, pp 11–28.

Adcock, M and White, R (eds) (1994) *Good Enough Parenting: A framework for assessment*, London: BAAF.

Ainsworth, M D S, Blehar, M C, Waters, E and Wall, S (1978) *Patterns of Attachment: A psychological study of the strange situation*, Hillsdale, New Jersey: Erlbaum Associates.

Alcalay, R, Tyebjee, T, Taplin, S and O'Loughlin, L (2001) *Adoption, Fostering and Concurrent Planning: A study of awareness, attitudes, motivations, barriers and implications for communication*, San Francisco, Community Task Force on Homes for Children. Also available on: www.bakids.org/content/packardreport

Aldgate, J, Pratt, R and Duggan, M (1989) 'Using care away from home to prevent family breakdown', *Adoption & Fostering*, 13:2, pp 32–7.

BAAF (1996) *Planning for Permanence*, London: BAAF.

Bagley, C (1993) *International and Transracial Adoptions*, Aldershot: Avebury.

Bailey, S, Thoburn, J and Wakeham, H (2002) 'Using the "Looking After Children" dimensions to collect aggregate data on well-being', *Child and Family Social Work*, 7: pp 189–201.

Barber, J G, Delfabbro, P H and Cooper, L L (2001) 'The predictors of unsuccessful transition to foster care', *Journal of Child Psychology and Psychiatry*, 42:6, pp 785–790.

Beckett, C (2000) 'Waiting for court decisions', *Adoption & Fostering*, 24:2, pp 55–62.

Bentovim, A (1991) 'Significant harm in context', in Adcock, M, White, R and Hollows, A, (eds) *Significant Harm*, Croydon: Significant Publications, pp 29–60.

Bishop, S, Murphy, M, Jellinek, M, Quinn, Sister, D and Pointrast, Judge F (1992) 'Protecting seriously mistreated children: time delays in a court sample', *Journal of Child Abuse and Neglect*, 16, pp 465–74.

Bowlby, J (1953) *Child Care and the Growth of Love*, London: Penguin Books.

Bowlby, J (1965) *Child Care and the Growth of Love*, Second Edition, London: Penguin.

Bowlby, J (1969) *Attachment and Loss: Volume 1 Attachment*, New York: Basic Books.

Brodzinsky, D M (1993) 'Long-term outcomes in adoption', *The Future of Children*, 33, pp 153–66.

Browne, D and Maloney, M (2002) ' "Contact irregular": a qualitative analysis of the impact of visiting patterns of natural parents on foster placements', *Child and Family Social Work*, 7, pp 35–45.

Bullock, R, Little, M and Millham, S (1993) *Going Home: The return of children separated from their families*, Dartington Publishing Co.

Campbell, S B (1995) 'Behaviour problems in preschool children: a review of recent research', *Journal of Child Psychology & Psychiatry*, 36:1, pp 113–49.

Castle, J, Beckett, C, Groothues, C and the ERA Team (2000) 'Infant adoptions in England: policy and practice at placement', *Adoption & Fostering*, 24:4, pp 45–6.

The Children Act, London: The Stationery Office.

Children Act Advisory Committee (1994) *Annual Report 1993/4*, London: Lord Chancellor's Department.

Children Act Advisory Committee (1997) *Final Report*, London: Children Act Advisory Committee.

Cichetti, D, Toth, S L and Hennessy, K (1989) 'Research on the consequences of child maltreatment and its application to educational settings', *Topics in Early Childhood Special Education*, 9, pp 33–5.

Cohen, J (1988) *Statistical Power Analysis for the Behavioral Sciences*, New York: Academic Press.

Cohn, A H (1987) 'Is treatment too late: what ten years of evaluative research tells us', *Child Abuse and Neglect*, 2, pp 433–42.

Corby, B (1987) *Working with Child Abuse*, Oxford: Oxford University Press.

Dance, C (1997) *Focus on Adoption: A snapshot of adoption patterns*, London: BAAF.

Dance, C, Rushton, A and Quinton, D (2002) 'Emotional abuse in early childhood: relationships with progress in subsequent family placement', *Journal of Child Psychology & Psychiatry*, 43:3, pp 395–407.

Davies, C (2001) 'Developing interests in child care outcomes measurement: a central government perspective', *Children & Society*, 12, pp 155–60.

Department of Health (1995) *Looking After Children: Assessment and Action Records*, London: The Stationery Office.

Department of Health (1998) Local Authority Circular (98)20, *Achieving the Right Balance*, London: Department of Health.

Department of Health (1999) *Adoption Now: Messages from Research*, Chichester: John Wiley & Sons.

Department of Health (1999a) *Meeting the Challenges of Changes in Adoption: Inspection of voluntary adoption agencies*, London: Department of Health.

Department of Health (1999b) *New Approach to Social Services Performance*, London: Department of Health.

Department of Health (2000) *Adopting Changes: Survey of inspection of local authorities adoption services*, London: Department of Health.

Department of Health (2001a) *National Adoption Standards for England*, London: Department of Health.

Department of Health (2001b) *Improving Practice: Tracking children*, London: Department of Health, Adoption & Permanence Task Force.

Department of Health (2001c) *Children Adopted from Care in England: 2000/2001*, Department of Health.

Department of Health (2002a) *The Children Act Report, 2001*, London: Department of Health.

Department of Health (2002b) *Statistical Bulletin 2001/25 Children Adopted from Care in England: 2000/2001*, London: Department of Health.

Department of Health, Department of Education & Employment, and Home Office (2000) *Framework for Assessment of Children in Need and their Families*, London: The Stationery Office.

Deutsch, D K, Swanson, J M, Bruell, J H, Cantwell, D P, Weinberg, F and Baren, M (1982) 'Over-representation of adoptees in children with Attention Deficit Disorder', *Behavior Genetics*, 12, pp 231–38.

Fahlberg, V (1994) *A Child's Journey Through Placement*, London: BAAF.

Fanshel, D (1982) *On the Road to Permanency: An expanded data base for service to children in foster care*, New York: Child Welfare League of America.

Feldman, L H (1991) *Assessing Effectiveness of Family Preservation Services in New Jersey Within an Ecological Context*, Trenton, NJ: Department of Human Services, NJ Division of Youth Services, pp 1–40.

Fergusson, D M, Lynskey, M and Horwood, L J (1995) 'The adolescent outcomes of adoption: a 16-year longitudinal study', *Journal of Child Psychology & Psychiatry*, 36:4, pp 597–615.

Fergusson, D M and Horwood, L J (1999) 'Prospective childhood predictors of deviant peer affiliations in adolescence', *Journal of Child Psychology & Psychiatry*, 40:4, pp 581–92.

Fergusson, D M and Horwood, L J (2000) 'Exposure to inter-parental violence in childhood and psychosocial adjustment in young adulthood', *Child Abuse & Neglect*, 22, pp 339–57.

Freeman, P and Hunt, J (1998) *Parental Perspectives in Care Proceedings*, London: The Stationery Office.

Garnett, L (1992) *Leaving Care and After*, London: National Children's Bureau.

George, C (1996) 'A representational perspective of child abuse and prevention: internal working models of attachment and caregiving', *Child Abuse & Neglect*, 20:5, pp 411–24.

George, C and Kaplan, N and Main, M (1985) *Adult Attachment Interview Protocol*, (3rd edn) Unpublished manuscript, University of California at Berkeley.

Goldberg, D (1978) *Manual of the General Health Questionnaire*, Windsor, UK: NFER Nelson.

Goldberg, D *et al* (1997) 'The validity of two versions of the GHQ in the WHO study of mental illness in general health care', *Psychological Medicine*, 27, p 191.

Goldberg, S (2000) *Attachment and Development*, London: Arnold.

Goodman, R (1997) 'The Strengths and Difficulties Questionnaire: a research note', *Journal of Child Psychology & Psychiatry*, 38, pp 581–86.

Goodman, R (1999) 'The extended version of the Strengths and Difficulties Questionnaire as a guide to child psychiatric caseness and consequent burden', *Journal of Child Psychology & Psychiatry*, 40, pp 791–99.

Goodyer, I M, Kolvin, I and Gatzanis, S (1987) 'Recent undesirable life events and psychiatric disorder in childhood and adolescence', *British Journal of Psychiatry*, 147, pp 517–23.

Gough, D (1993) *Child Abuse Interventions*, Glasgow & London: Public Health Research Unit, University of Glasgow and HMSO.

Gray, J (2001) 'The Framework for the Assessment of Children in Need and their Families', *Child Psychology & Psychiatry Review*, 6:1, pp 4–10.

Groothues, C, Beckett, C and O'Connor, T (1998/99) 'The outcome of adoption from Romania: predictors of parental satisfaction', *Adoption & Fostering*, 22:4, pp 30–40.

Hartup, W W (1989) 'Social relationships and their developmental significance', *American Psychologist*, 44, pp 120–26.

Harwin, J and Owen, M (2002) 'A study of care plans and their implementation and their relevance for Re W & B (Children: care plan) and Re W (Child: care plan)' in Lord Justice Thorpe and C Cowton (eds) *Delight and Dole: The Child Act 10 years on*, Bristol: Jordans.

Heneghan, A M, Horwitz, S M and Leventhal, J M (1996) 'Evaluating intensive family preservation programs: a methodological review', *Pediatrics*, 97:4, pp 535–542.

Hill, M (2000) 'Partnership reviewed: words of caution, words of encouragement', *Adoption & Fostering*, 24:3, pp 56–68.

Hodges, J and Tizard, B (1989) 'Social and family relationships of ex-institutional adolescents', *Journal of Child Psychology & Psychiatry*, 30, pp 403–38.

Holloway, J (1997a) 'Outcome placements for adoption or long-term fostering', *Archives of Disease in Childhood*, 76, pp 227–30.

Holloway, J (1997b) 'Foster and adoptive mothers' assessment of permanent family placements', *Archives of Disease in Childhood*, 76, pp 231–35.

Hollows, A (2001) 'The challenge to social work', *Child Psychology & Psychiatry Review*, 6:1, pp 11–15.

Howe, D (1996) 'Adopters' relationships with their adopted children from adolescence to early adulthood', *Adoption & Fostering*, 20, pp 35–43.

Howe, D (1997) 'Parent-reported problems in 211 adopted children: some risk and protective factors', *Journal of child Psychology and Psychiatry*, 37, pp 401–12

Howe, D (1998) *Patterns of Adoption*, Oxford: Blackwell Science.

Howe, D (2001) 'Age at placement, adoption experience and adult adopted people's contact with their adoptive and birth mothers: an attachment perspective', *Attachment and Human Development*, 3:2, pp 222–37.

Howe, D, Brandon, M, Hinings, D and Schofield, G (1999) 'Disorganised, controlling and unresolved patterns', *Attachment Theory, Child Maltreatment and Family Support*, London: Macmillan Press, pp 122–66.

Howe, D and Fearnley, S (1999) 'Disorders of attachment and attachment therapy', *Adoption & Fostering*, 23:2, pp 19–30.

Howells, J G (1974) *Remember Maria*, London: Butterworths.

Hunt, J (1997) 'Child protection, the courts and the Children Act', *Children's Services News*, London: Department of Health.

Hunt, J (2000) 'Making and implementing timely legal decisions for children: research on a court sample', in Buchanan, A and Hudson, B L (eds) *Promoting Children's Emotional Wellbeing*, Oxford: Oxford University Press, pp 193–208.

Ivaldi, G (1998) *Children Adopted from Care: An examination of agency adoptions in England – 1996*, London: BAAF.

Ivaldi, G (2000) *Surveying Adoption: A comprehensive analysis of local authority adoptions 1998–1999 England*, London: BAAF.

Jackson, S (1989) 'Education of children in care', in Kahan, B (ed.) *Child Care Research, Policy and Practice*, London: Hodder & Stoughton.

Jackson, S (1994) 'Educating children in residential and foster care', *Oxford Review of Education*, 20:3, pp 267–79.

Jackson, S and Thomas, N (2000) *What Works in Creating Stability for Looked After Children?* (2nd edn), Ilford: Barnardo's.

Jaffe, P G, Wolfe, D A and Wilson, S K (1990) *Children of Battered Women*, Newbury Park, CA.: Sage Publications.

Johnston, J (2001) 'Evaluating national initiatives : the case of "on track" ', *Children & Society*, 15, pp 33–6.

Jones, D P H (1987) 'The untreatable family', *Child Abuse & Neglect*, 11, pp 409–20.

Jones, D P H (1998) 'The effectiveness of intervention', (pp. 91-120) in Adcock, M and White, R (eds) *Significant Harm* (2nd edn), Croydon: Significant Publications, pp 61–84.

Jones, D P H (2002) *Intervening with Children and Families – Evaluating the likelihood of future harm to the child*, ICC Conference: "Achieving Permanence", Birmingham.

Jones, D P H, Bentovim, A, Cameron, H, Vizard, E and Wolkind, S (1991) 'Significant harm in context: the child psychiatrist's contribution', in Adcock, M, White, R and Hollows, A (eds) *Significant Harm*, Croydon: Significant Publications, pp 115–24.

Katz, L (1990) 'Effective permanency planning for children in foster care', *Social Work*, 35:3, pp 220–26.

Katz, L (1996) 'Permanency action through concurrent planning', *Adoption & Fostering*, 20, pp 8–13.

Katz, L and Robinson, C (1991) 'Foster care drift: a risk assessment matrix', *Child Welfare*, LXX:3, pp 347–58.

Katz, L, Colacurcio, L, Cordes, K (1994) *Preparing Permanency Planning Foster Parents*, Seattle, WA: Lutheran Social Services.

Katz, L, Spoonemore, N and Robinson, C (1994a) *Concurrent Planning: From permanency planning to permanency action*, Seattle, WA: Lutheran Social Services.

Katz, L, Spoonemore, N and Robinson, C (1994b) *Courtwise: Making optimal use of the legal process to ensure early permanence for children*, Seattle, WA: Lutheran Social Services.

Kempe, R S and Kempe, C H (1978) 'The untreatable family', pp 128–31, in *Child Abuse*, London: Fontana Open Books.

Lambert, L, Essen, J and Head, J (1977) 'Variations in behaviour ratings of children who have been in care', *Journal of Child Psychology & Psychiatry*, 18, pp 335–46.

Lewis, J U D (2001) 'Made to measure? evaluating community initiatives for children: Introduction', *Children & Society*, 15, pp 1–4.

Logan, J (1999) 'Exchanging information post adoption: views of adoptive parents and birth parents', *Adoption & Fostering*, 23:3, pp 27–37.

Logan, J and Smith, C (1999) 'Adoption and direct post-adoption contact', *Adoption & Fostering*, 23:4, pp 58–9.

Lowe, N, Murch, M, Borkowski, M, Weaver, A, Beckford, V with Thomas, C (1999) *Supporting Adoption: Reframing the approach*, London: BAAF.

Lyons-Ruth, K (1996) 'Attachment relationships among children with aggressive behaviour problems: the role of disorganised early attachment patterns', *Journal of Consulting and Clinical Psychology*, 64, pp 64–73.

Main, M, Kaplan, N and Cassidy, J (1985) 'Security in infancy, childhood and adulthood: a move to the level of representation', in I. Bretherton and E. Waters (eds) *Growing Points of Attachment Theory and Research*, Monographs for the Society for Research in Child Development, 50(1–2) serial no. 209, pp 66–104.

Maluccio, A N, Ainsworth, F and Thoburn, J (2000) *Child Welfare Outcome Research in the United States, The United Kingdom and Australia*, Washington DC: CWLA Press, pp 1–6.

Marsh, P and Thoburn, J (2002) 'Policy digest: the adoption and permanence debate in England and Wales', *Child & Family Social Work*, 7:2, pp 131–32.

Masson, J, Harrison, C and Pavlovic, A (1997) *Working with Children and Lost Parents*, York: Joseph Rowntree Foundation.

Maughan, B and Pickles, A (1990) *Adopted and Illegitimate Children Growing Up*, Cambridge: Cambridge University Press.

Monck, E (1997) 'Evaluating therapeutic intervention with sexually abused children', *Child Abuse Review*, 6:3, pp 163–78.

Monck, E, Graham, P, Dobbs, R and Richman, N (1994) 'Adolescent girls II: background factors in anxiety and depressive states', *British Journal of Psychiatry*, 165, pp 770–80.

Morgan, P (1998) *Adoption and the Care of Children: The British and American experience*, London: IEA Health & Welfare Unit.

Murch, M and Mills, L (1987) *The Length of Care Proceedings*, Bristol: Socio-Legal Centre for Family Studies, University of Bristol.

Neil, B (2000) 'The reasons why young children are placed for adoption: findings from a recently placed sample and discussion of implications for subsequent development', *Child & Family Social Work*, 5:4, pp 303–16.

Newburn, T (2001) 'What do we mean by evaluation?', *Children & Society*, 15, pp 5–15.

Newton, R R, Litrownik, A J, Landsverk, J A (2000) 'Children and youth in foster care: disentangling the relationship between problem behaviors and number of placements', *Child Abuse & Neglect*, 24:10, pp 1363–1374.

Oyserman, D and Benbenishty, R (1992) 'Keeping in touch: ecological factors related to foster care visitation', *Child & Adolescent Social Work Journal*, 6, pp 541–54.

Parker, R, Ward, H, Jackson, S, Aldgate, J and Wedge, P (eds) (1991) *Assessing Outcomes in Child Care*, London: HMSO/The Stationery Office.

Patton, M Q (1981) *Creative Evaluation*, Sage: Newbury Park, CA.

Pecora, P, Whittaker, J K, Maluccio, A N and Barth, R P with Plotnik, R D (2000) *The Child Welfare Challenge*, New York: Aldine de Gruyter.

Performance & Innovation Unit (2000) *Prime Minister's Review of Adoption*, London: Cabinet Office.

Pike, V (1976) 'Permanent planning for foster children: the Oregon Project', *Children Today*, 5, pp 22–5.

Prison Reform Trust (1991) *The Identifit Prisoner*, London: Prison Reform Trust.

Pugh, G, De'Ath, E and Smith, C (1995) *Confident Parents, Confident Children*, London: National Children's Bureau.

Quinton, D, Rushton, A, Dance, C and Mayes, D (1997) 'Contact between children placed away from home and their birth parents: research issues and evidence', *Clinical Child Psychology & Psychiatry*, 2:3, pp 393–413.

Quinton, D, Rushton, A, Dance, C and Mayes, D (1998) *Joining New Families: A study of adoption and fostering in middle childhood*, Chichester: John Wiley & Sons.

Quinton, D and Murray, C (2002) 'Assessing emotional and behavioural development in children looked after away from home', in Ward, H and Rose, W (eds) *Approaches to Needs Assessment in Children's Services*, London: Jessica Kingsley Publishers, pp 277–308.

Raynor, L (1980) *The Adopted Child Comes of Age*, London: Allen & Unwin.

Rowe, J and Lambert, L (1973) *Children Who Wait*, London: ABAA.

Rushton, A, Treseder, J and Quinton, D (1988) *New Parents for Older Children*, London: BAAF.

Rushton, A, Treseder, J and Quinton, D (1995) 'An eight-year prospective study of older boys placed in permanent substitute families: a research note', *Journal of Child Psychology & Psychiatry*, 36, pp 687–96.

Rushton, A and Mayes, D (1997) 'Forming fresh attachments in childhood: a research update', *Child & Family Social Work*, 2, pp 121–27.

Rutter, M (1979) 'Maternal deprivation 1972–1978', *Child Development*, 50, pp 283–305.

Rutter, M (1995) 'Clinical implications of attachment concepts: retrospect and prospect', *Journal of Child Psychology & Psychiatry*, 36:4, pp 549–72.

Rutter, M (1972) *Maternal Deprivation Reassessed*, Harmondsworth, Middlesex: Penguin.

Rutter, M, Quinton, D and Hill, J (1990) 'Adult outcome of institution-reared children: males and females compared', in Robins, L and Rutter, M (eds) *Straight and Devious Pathways from Childhood to Adulthood*, Cambridge: Cambridge University Press, pp 135–57.

Rutter, M and the ERA Study Team (1998) 'Developmental catch-up and deficit following adoption after severe global early deprivation', *Journal of Child Psychology & Psychiatry*, 39:4, pp 465–76.

Rutter, M and O'Connor, T (1999) 'Implications of attachment theory for childcare policies', in Cassidy, J and Shaver, P R, *Handbook of Attachment*, New York: Guilford Press, pp 823–44.

Selwyn, J and Sturgess, W (2001) *International Overview of Adoption: Policy and practice*, University of Bristol.

Sharland, E S H, Croucher, M, Aldgate, J and Jones, D P H (1996) *Professional Intervention in Child Sexual Abuse*, London: HMSO/The Stationery Office.

Schene, P (1998) *Expedited Permanency Planning in Colorado: An evaluation*, Prepared for the Colorado Department of Human Services, November 1998 (unpublished).

Schene, P (2001) *Implementing Concurrent Planning*. Available from Edmund S. Muskie School of Public Service, 96 Falmouth Street, PO Box 9300, Portland, Maine 04101-9300, USA.

Stein, M and Carey, K (1986) *Leaving Care*, Oxford: Blackwell.

Terling, T (1999) 'The efficacy of family re-unification practices: re-entry rates and correlates of re-entry for abused and neglected children reunited with their families', *Child Abuse and Neglect*, 23, pp 1359–70.

Thoburn, J, Murdoch, A and O'Brien, A (1986) *Permanence in Child Care*, Oxford: Blackwell.

Thoburn, J (2002) *Adoption and Permanence for Children who Cannot Live Safely with Birth Parents or Relatives*, Norwich: University of East Anglia, Research in Practice Briefing Paper 5.

Thompson, R A (1999) 'Early attachment and later development', in Cassidy, J and Shaver, P R (eds), *Handbook of Attachment*, London: Guilford Press.

Thorpe, D (1987) 'Career patterns in child care – implications for the service', *British Journal of Social Work*, 18:2, pp 137–53.

Tizard, B (1977) *Adoption: A second chance*, London: Open Books.

Tizard, J and Tizard, B (1971) 'The social development of two-year-old children in residential nurseries', in Shaffer, J (ed.) *The Origins of Human Relations*, London: Academic Press, pp 147–160.

Triseliotis, J, Borland, M and Hill, M (1998) *Fostering Good Relations*, Edinburgh: The Scottish Office.

Triseliotis, J (1998/99) 'Is permanency through adoption in decline?' *Adoption & Fostering*, 22:4, pp 41–9.

Triseliotis, J (2002) 'Long term fostering or adoption? The evidence examined', *Child & Family Social Work*, 7, pp 23–33.

van Djiken, S (1988) *John Bowlby: His early life*, London: Free Association Books.

Wachs, T D (1992) *The Nature of Nurture*, Newbury Park, CA: Sage.

Wald, M, Carlsmith, J and Leiderman, P (1988) *Protecting Abused/Neglected Children: A comparison of home and foster placement*, Stanford, CA: Stanford University Press.

Wall, N (1999) 'Concurrent planning – a judicial perspective', *Child & Family Law Quarterly*, 11:2, pp 97–108.

Warnock, M (2000) *Mary Warnock: A memoir*, London: Duckworth.

Wattenburg, E (1997) *Redrawing the Family Circle: Concurrent planning – permanency for young children in high risk situations*, Center for Urban and Regional Affairs, 330 HHH Center, 301, 19th Ave, Minneapolis. See www.cura.umn.edn.

Weinberg, A and Katz, L (1998) 'Law and social work in partnership for permanency: the Adoption and Safe Families Act and the role of concurrent planning', *Children's Legal Rights Journal*, 18:4.

Weneke, U, Goldberg, D P, Yalcin, I and Ustun, B T (2000) 'The stability of the factor structure of the General Health Questionnaire', *Psychological Medicine*, 30, pp 823–29.

White, R (1991) 'Examining the threshold criteria', in Adcock, M and White, R (eds), *Significant Harm* (2nd edn), Croydon: Significant Publications, pp 3–10.

Wise, S (2001) 'A framework for responding to vulnerable children and their families', *Family Matters* (Australian Institute of Family Studies), 59, pp 17–21.

Zeanah, C H, Boris, N W and Scheeringa, M S (1997) 'Psychopathology in infancy', *Journal of Child Psychology & Psychiatry*, 38:1, pp 81–100.